To Die and Not Decay

To Die and Not Decay

Autobiography and the Pursuit
of Immortality in Early China

Matthew V. Wells

Asia Past & Present

Published by the Association for Asian Studies, Inc.

Asia Past & Present: New Research from AAS, Number 5

Asia Past & Present: New Research from AAS
Series Editor, Martha Ann Selby, University of Texas at Austin

"Asia Past & Present: New Research from AAS," published by the Association for Asian Studies, Inc. (AAS), features scholarly work from all areas of Asian studies. In addition to scholarly monographs, translations, essay collections, and other forms of scholarly research are welcome for consideration. AAS particularly aims to support work in emerging or under-represented fields.

Formed in 1941, the Association for Asian Studies (AAS)—the largest society of its kind, with more than 7,000 members worldwide—is a scholarly, non-political, non-profit professional association open to all persons interested in Asia.

For further information, please visit www.asian-studies.org.

Published by:
Association for Asian Studies, Inc.
1021 East Huron Street
Ann Arbor, Michigan 48104 USA
www.asian-studies.org

Library of Congress Cataloging-in-Publication Data

Wells, Matthew V., 1972–
To die and not decay : autobiography and the pursuit of immortality in early China / Matthew V. Wells.
p. cm. — (Asia past & present)
Includes bibliographical references and index.
ISBN 978-0-924304-58-3 (alk. paper)
1. Autobiography—Chinese authors. 2. Autobiography—Authorship. 3. Autobiography—Social aspects—China—History—To 1500. 4. China—Biography—History and criticism. 5. Biography as a literary form. 6. Ge, Hong, 284–364. Baopuzi. I. Title.
CT34.C6W45 2009
808'.06692—dc22
2009043301

Cover photographs: Baopu Daoyuan, dedicated to Ge Hong, above West Lake in Hangzhou, PRC. Front cover photo by author, 2007. Back cover photo courtesy of ImagineChina.

Contents

Acknowledgments

The term *monograph* seems more than a little disingenuous, as many hands have shaped this manuscript and, in turn, my development as both a scholar and a teacher. Friends and colleagues have generously given me their time, insight, and encouragement over the years. Eric Cunningham, Anthony Clark, and Jianjun He have always provided thoughtful conversation about this topic and have been endlessly supportive. I feel deeply indebted to my professors at the University of Oregon, Stephen Durrant, Maram Epstein, Michael Fishlen, Wendy Larson, Jeffrey Hanes, and John Lysaker. This book grew out of my doctoral dissertation, and their insights, guidance, and classes aided my writing in important ways. I wish especially to acknowledge Mark Unno for criticism, advice, unending encouragement, and continued interest in this book.

Several grants and scholarships supported all stages of my research. The University of Oregon's Center for Asian and Pacific Studies together with the Freeman Foundation provided multiple grants for professional development, research, and travel. Lori O'Hollaren at the Center for Asian and Pacific Studies was extremely helpful in the grant application process. A Fulbright-Hays Dissertation Fellowship provided financial support for a year of study at Xiamen University. The College of Arts and Sciences at Eastern Oregon University also provided me with funding for last minute research and materials.

The kindness and professionalism of Martha Selby, Jonathan Wilson, and Gudrun Patton of the Association for Asian Studies made the process of publication instructive and enjoyable. I also wish to thank the reviewers for the AAS *Asia Past and Present* series for insightful criticism and observations that furthered my understanding of this subject.

An earlier version of chapter 4 appeared in the journal *Early Medieval China* (2004). It has been revised and reprinted here with kind permission from Dr. Cynthia Chennault and *Early Medieval China*.

Finally, I must thank my wife Margaret, with whom all things are possible.

Glossary of Major Chinese Texts and English Translations

Romanized Title	English Translation
Baopuzi	The Master Embracing Simplicity
Baopuzi Neipian	Inner Chapters of the Master Embracing Simplicity
Baopuzi Waipian	Outer Chapters of the Master Embracing Simplicity
Baopuzi Waipian zixu	Authorial Postface to the Outer Chapters
Bei shi	History of the Northern Dynasties
Chunqiu	Spring and Autumn Annals
Daode jing Heshang gong	Daode jing with Heshang gong commentary
Dian lun	Authoritative Discourses
Dongguan Hanji	Han Records of the Eastern Lodge
Fayan	Model Sayings
"Gui qu lai ci"	Upon Returning
"Gui yuan tian ju"	Returning to Live in My Gardens and Fields
Gushi kao	Investigations of Ancient History
Han shu	History of the Former Han
Han shu chao	Notes on the History of the Former Han
Hou Han shu	History of the Later Han
Jin ji	Record of the Jin
Jin shu	History of the Jin
"Li sao"	Encountering Sorrow

"Lun wen"	Discourse on Literature
Lunheng	Arguments Weighed
Lunheng ziji pian	Chapter of Authorial Self-Record to Arguments Weighed
Lunyu	Analects (also Analects of Confucius)
Lüshi chunqiu	Annals of Lü Buwei
Mengzi	Mencius
Renwu zhi	Treatise on Human Abilities
Sanhuang wen	Text of the Three August Ones
Shang shu	Book of Documents (also simply Documents)
Shenxian zhuan	Traditions of Divine Transcendents
Shi ji	Grand Astrologer's Record (Record of the Grand Historian)
Shi jing	Classic of Poetry (also Classic of Odes)
Shishuo xinyu	A New Account of Tales of the World
Shitong	Generalities on History
Song shu	History of the Song
Soushen ji	Inquest into the Spirit Realm
Sui shu	History of the Sui
Taishigong zixu	Grand Astrologer's Authorial Postface
Wu zhi	Record of Wu
"Wuliu xiansheng zhuan"	Biography of Mr. Five Willows
Xijing zaji	Miscellaneous Record of the Western Capital
"Xuzhuan"	*Shitong* chapter: Authorial Postface
Yinyi zhuan	Traditions of Recluses
Zhou shu	Book of Zhou
Zhouyi	Zhou Changes
Zuozhuan	Zuo Commentary to the Spring and Autumn Annals

Introduction

"Life never works except in retrospect. And writing makes you look back. Because since you can't control life, at least you can control your version."

— Chuck Palahniuk, *Stranger Than Fiction*

Autobiographical writing speaks to the variety of human existence and to the universal impulse to render life as art. The present study builds on previous scholarship on Chinese autobiography by examining the autobiographical writing of Ge Hong 葛洪 (ca. 283–343) and comparing it to other early texts of the genre. Ge Hong was a minor official during the early Eastern Jin 東晉 dynasty (317–420) and is best known for his interest in Daoism, alchemy, and techniques of longevity. But religious and esoteric writing represents only a portion of Ge Hong's literary productivity, which reflects the broad range of his education and experience.

Most important for our purposes here, Ge Hong is the author of two "authorial postfaces" (*zixu* 自敍, sometimes also 自序) appended to his most celebrated work, *Baopuzi* 抱朴子, translated variously as *The Master Embracing Simplicity* or *The Master Embracing the Unhewn*.[1] Ge Hong probably wrote *Baopuzi* during his early retirement between 306 and 314 and intended it as an expression of his syncretic philosophical and religious thought, one that promoted the possibility of transcendent union with the Dao grounded in strict moral and ethical self-cultivation. Consequently he divided the text into two volumes, the *Neipian* 內篇, or *Inner Chapters,* and the *Waipian* 外篇, or *Outer Chapters*, and wrote a postface for each section. According to Ge Hong himself, the *Neipian* is concerned with Daoist (*dao* 道) topics of immortality, transcendence, elixirs, and strange phenomena while the *Waipian* is concerned with Confucian (*ru* 儒) topics such as the successes and failures of men. The *Neipian zixu* 內篇自敍, or "Authorial Postface to the *Inner Chapters*," which concludes the so-called Daoist portion of the text, contains little biographical detail and is a fairly abstract self-portrait. On the other hand, the *Waipian zixu* 外篇自敍, or "Authorial Postface to the *Outer Chapters*," which concludes the so-called Confucian section of *Baopuzi*, meets the most basic expectation of autobiography, namely, that it is a prose narrative of an individual life written by that person.

Moreover, in the postface to the *Waipian*, Ge Hong makes explicit reference to his predecessors, becoming the first Chinese author of an autobiographical work to see such writings as texts influential for his own self-narrative. But unlike his predecessors, Ge Hong displays an awareness of and comments specifically on the issue of self-representation. For this reason I view Ge Hong as offering the first substantial contribution to the "criticism of autobiography" in Chinese literature and regard his autobiographical work as an excellent point of departure for a study of early Chinese autobiography.

The division of Ge Hong's *Baopuzi* into inner and outer chapters and his attempt to weave disparate textual and religious traditions into a single school of thought are emblematic of his own biography and historical context. Ge Hong was born on or close to the year the Western Jin 西晉 dynasty founded by the Sima 司馬 clan overcame the southern kingdom of Wu 吳, unifying China for the first time in almost a century. He lived to see Sinofied Turks divide China again in 317 and establish the Zhao 趙 kingdom north of the Yangzi River. Born to a once thriving southern family, his father's death and intense civil unrest at the turn of the fourth century diminished the promise of his birth. The scope of his writing suggests that he received considerable education in canonical texts, but according to statements in the *Baopuzi Neipian* he also entered the tutelage of Zheng Yin 鄭隱, an adept who, in turn, had studied under Ge Hong's uncle, Ge Xuan 葛玄. Thus, in addition to a canonical education Ge Hong received esoteric instruction in a religious tradition in which his family played an important role.[2] Ge Hong remained within the orbit of public life and did not devote himself entirely to religious practice or withdraw willingly into reclusion. But after a brief but distinguished period of military service, he saw his aspirations quashed by the murder of his benefactor in 306 and spent nearly a decade in retirement in the far south. During this time he composed a significant body of writing and immersed himself in the religious traditions of his family, which emphasized canonical Daoist texts and *waidan* 外丹, techniques of longevity that share some features with European Renaissance alchemy.

Around 314, as some semblance of social order gradually returned to the region under Sima Rui 司馬睿 (276–322), who would reign as Emperor Yuan 元 beginning in 317, Ge Hong emerged from retirement and received honors for his prior military service. It is also likely that he filled official positions under the patronage of the powerful minister Wang Dao 王導 (276–339), a close ally of Sima Rui. Ge Hong's official biography and autobiographical writing suggest that he refused official positions during this period, but, as I will argue in chapter 3, we have several reasons to doubt these claims. We shall see that Ge Hong was probably employed in the writing of state-sanctioned history in the company of other, notable literati of the era. In 331 he retired to the south and avoided public life until his death; his official biography states that he left in search of the raw materials for concocting elixirs of transcendence, and there is no reason to doubt this assertion. He died while living in the southern reaches of the Jin state; religious tradition holds the date of his death—and subsequent transcendence—to be 363 while most modern scholars place the date of his death at 343.[3]

This book lies at the intersection of two very different but equally fascinating strands of scholarship, the history and narratology of early Chinese self-narrative and the study of Ge Hong and his surviving work. Consequently, different assumptions and methodologies have given it shape. On the one hand, this study draws on narrative and autobiographical theory as found in the work of James Olney, Philippe Lejeune, and others. Taken as a whole, this body of criticism focuses on the relationship between the author and the text, the self and the self-narrative, and inclines toward a postmodern analysis of literary tropes, narrative strategy, and nodes of subjectivity in which there is "neither *autos* nor *bios* before the text—the act of textuality forms the outline of the life and the self."[4] On the other hand, this book draws from the broad field of sinology to adopt a more conventional philological and historiographical approach. In investigating the literary and historical context of early Chinese autobiography, and Ge Hong's work in particular, I adopt a more modernist historiographical perspective that takes seriously the idea that Ge Hong was a "real person." I hope that the final result of this combination of approaches is a depiction of Ge Hong as a complex figure negotiating the various facets of his life and subjectivity, which were sometimes in conflict with one another. While we cannot isolate Ge Hong and reduce him to his historical factuality, his effort to craft an extensive literary image seems to give weight to a historical person who wished to reveal and propagate the details of his own life. He was also deeply concerned with controlling those details through self-narrative, which above all else is a text concerned with the power of self-definition. Ge Hong is thus neither a transparent, historical figure nor simply a series of intertextual entanglements.

Previous studies of Ge Hong's postface and early Chinese autobiographical writing have generally focused on late imperial or modern autobiographies, emphasizing the role of early texts in the genealogy and development of later forms of the genre. But discussion of early texts in such studies is necessarily brief and replete with modern assumptions with regard to the origin of autobiography as a genre as well as the quality of the individual self expressed within the text. Most scholars of modern autobiography link early autobiographical writing to the formal concerns of early historiography and biography. According to this view, pre-Ming biography used interchangeable individuals for illustrations of broader, historical principles. Hence the life of the individual was irrelevant, as the biography submerged any fidelity to the historical person in a wave of literary trope and allusion. In the case of autobiographical writing, the formal characteristics that organized biography also limited the intrusion of subjectivity into the narrative; the purpose of such texts was instead to organize the material of the subject's public life within the rubric of a particular stock type or cluster of titles and familial relations.[5] Reticence and impersonality became the norm as autobiographers adopted the stringent historiographical standards of biographical writing.[6] Structure and trope essentially acted to restrict self-expression. It is for this reason that scholars of late imperial and modern autobiography generally consider Tao Qian's 陶潛 (365–427) "Wuliu xiansheng zhuan" 五柳先生傳 (Biography of Mr. Five Willows) to represent the early paradigm of autobiography, the "self-conscious writing of oneself in a biography."[7] Tao adopted the formal style of biography, but in his sparing, abstract biography he rejected "mainstream" literati society and ideology and embraced the life of the hermit while shunning social convention.[8] Through his autobiographical work, Tao rejected a "historical, utilitarian" attitude toward biography as well as the "relation-centered" ideology that previously formed the basis of such texts and thereby expressed some of the individuality we seek as modern readers, even if he discloses little biographical information.[9]

It is true that in recent centuries Western autobiography has shared a close etymological and historiographical relationship with biography, but few studies of Chinese autobiography acknowledge that the Western canon of self-narrative began in a primordial soup of diverse genres and texts, including practically any text that took the author as the subject or, more broadly still, attempted to convey the author's lived experience. Many of these texts, written prior to the establishment of any etymological or historiographical link to biography, express little concern for the expression of a unique, individual, and historical self; they are instead oriented toward religious confession or apology, narrative forms in which gross biographical omissions and inaccuracies are the norm.[10] Thus rigorous attention to formal features or a requirement for ostensible historical factuality may only unnecessarily limit our field of study to modern demands on the genre. We may regard Tao Qian's unhistorical self-description as autobiography because of formal characteristics, but we seek, and find, historical individuals reduced to mere trope and text. Or we may hunt and peck within traditional literature for those texts that correspond more closely to modern notions of individual self-expression, yielding a broad genre predicated on the assumption that self-expression must reveal a historical individual expressing himself or herself beyond the limits of trope and structure. Such a view may cause us to reject texts possessing little ostensible biographical information or exclude out of hand a specious biography.[11] In either event, whether for etymological or epistemological reasons, we often view early Chinese self-narratives in modern, Western terms.

This study shall focus on early Chinese autobiography absent the teleological assumption that these early texts *led to* late imperial and modern Chinese autobiography. In so doing, I hope to divorce early Chinese autobiographical texts from the modern genre as it developed among May Fourth writers in the early twentieth century and examine them on their own narrative and theoretical terms. Furthermore, focusing on early autobiographical writing through the lens of premodern China allows us to reexamine the discourse and tropes of Western self-narrative, much as Martin Powers challenges the tropes of modern individuality in his recent study of visual perception and social order in early China.[12] In doing so, I hope not only to study Ge Hong's place in the history of Chinese subjectivity but to contribute one corner to the broader study of subjectivity and the continued evolution of self-consciousness.

Although Ge Hong has attracted a considerable amount of scholarly interest in recent decades, none of these previous studies has focused on the issues of subjectivity and self-narrative in a sustained, meaningful way. Without question, Ge Hong's religious and esoteric writings have received the most attention; James Ware may be said to have pioneered Ge Hong studies in the West with his translation of the inner chapters of *Baopuzi* in his *Alchemy, Medicine, and Religion in the China of A.D. 320: The Nei P'ien of Ko Hung*.[13] The most recent studies have translated and explored Ge Hong's *Shenxian zhuan* 神仙傳 (Traditions of Divine Transcendents) and discussed the relationship between the *Neipian* and the Great Clarity 太清 tradition of Daoist alchemy.[14] Ge Hong and his work also figure prominently in surveys of Daoism or Daoist-themed intellectual histories, with the *Neipian* providing evidence for techniques of transcendence in early China.[15] A few such surveys in Chinese have recontextualized Ge Hong's esoteric writing within a broader history of science and take his work to be a kind of protochemistry.[16] Only Jay Sailey's *The Master Who Embraces Simplicity: A Study of the Philosopher Ko Hung, A. D. 283–343*, a monumental translation and study of twenty-one chapters of the *Waipian*, addresses Ge Hong's *Waipian* and its position in Chinese intellectual history in detail.[17] Sailey's emphasis on the *Waipian* is unique in studies of Ge

Hong, but his massive survey of its contents only hints at the richness of the text waiting to be explored. With so strong an emphasis placed on Ge Hong's esoteric studies, it is no wonder that his autobiographical account has received so little analysis. Indeed, all of the works mentioned above share a relatively uncritical view of the biographical content of Ge Hong's authorial postface; while few briefly consider the obvious exaggerations or factual contradictions, they nevertheless reconstruct a "historical" person who corresponds to the person in the text.

My approach to Ge Hong's postface and *Baopuzi* emphasizes Ge Hong's stated desire to produce a single body or "school" of discourse 一家之言. This is hardly surprising given the long trend of interaction between textual traditions and philosophical schools (*rudao hubu* 儒道互补), especially after the fall of the Han dynasty.[18] *Ru* and *Dao* certainly functioned as imprecise categories within larger discourses, but they also held concrete meaning for Ge Hong, even as religious terms.[19] As a gesture toward a very different kind of immortality, that is, literary fame, Ge Hong's self-narrative begs a discussion of the relationship between the literary immortality of the literati class and the esoteric techniques of longevity and religious transcendence of Ge Hong's faith tradition. In this regard I have drawn on Lin Lixue's 林麗雪 *Baopuzi nei wai pian sixiang xi lun* 抱朴子內外篇思想析論 (An Analysis of the Thought of the Inner and Outer Chapters of the Master Embracing Simplicity) as a model for considering the text *as a whole*.[20] Because Ge Hong was deeply invested in multiple techniques of longevity, and he appears to have pursued all of them with considerable energy, we may regard him as an individual interested in different yet overlapping ways to immortality. I will argue that, for Ge Hong, these two modes of transcendence at different times supported or conflicted with one another but never seemed to require the rejection of one in favor of the other. In this regard the notion of longevity (*chang sheng bu si* 長生不死) or transcendence (*xian* 仙) in early China might be considered a broad, complex cultural ideal that may function simultaneously on many levels, however imperfectly.

While each of the chapters of this book address a different issue related to early Chinese autobiography and subjectivity, my overarching goal has been to address the topic through a small selection of early Chinese texts, focusing primarily on Ge Hong's writing, without losing sight of the larger field of criticism on autobiography in Europe and North America. The approach in this regard has been to use early Chinese authors and critics to challenge and refine a body of criticism that, for the most part, ignores texts in East Asian languages. What is interesting to me is how the historic transformation of European autobiography and its criticism, from Augustine of Hippo's

(354–430) prototypical *Confessions* to the present, has circled back to many fundamental questions posed by premodern Chinese authors for centuries. For this reason I begin with a discussion of a few of the core issues of early Western autobiography and its criticism and attempt to explain how they came to dominate our understanding of the Chinese tradition. I then read Ge Hong and his contemporaries to suggest how early Chinese authors may have understood and affirmed their subjective experience with a notion of autobiography that speaks to more recent scholarship on the subject. In this way I hope I to lay a little of the groundwork toward a more global theory (or a multiplicity of global theories) of autobiography.

Chapter 1 begins by discussing the relationship between traditional Western notions of subjective identity and previous attempts to define the genre of early Chinese autobiography. Any definition of autobiography rests on speculation over the nature of subjective experience and a cluster of practical demands on the individual author or authors of a particular period. For Augustine of Hippo, a new and radical theory of autonomous subjectivity expressed as a prose self-narration inaugurated the quintessential model of Western autobiography that continues to dominate modern, critical studies of the genre, whether the model be rejected or accepted. Indeed, scholars such as Suzanne Kirschner have argued that Augustine's narrative of loss and redemption lies at the root of modern theories of self in romanticism and later psychoanalysis as a mechanism for self-individuation.[21] The lingering influence of Augustine's model, coupled with reflexive views of Western individualism and its absence in East Asia, has prompted at least one modern critic to argue against the existence of an autobiographical tradition in Asia.[22]

More recent criticism of autobiography in Western languages stresses not only the arbitrary nature of the genre but also the fluid construction of the self who is the subject of the record, thereby challenging the assumption begun by Augustine that autobiography portrays the self "as it is," that we discover an ontologically distinct being through the writing of self-narrative. Writing an autobiography may be seen as a process of self-creation rather than a vehicle for self-discovery, as the self exists through—rather than prior to—the reflexive act of writing. In chapter 2, I describe how this formulation of autobiography resonates with early Chinese self-narrative in three important ways. First, it invites the possibility that one author may describe a multiplicity of "selves," each shaped by the formal demands of different genres such as verse or the authorial postface. Second, it asks us to understand the intellectual boundaries of early Chinese self-narrative in terms other than those borrowed from Western philosophy, critical theory, or religious experience. Third, it requires us to weigh what we know—or believe we know—of a historical person against his or her image as an author whose autobiography is an effort to identify with culturally significant archetypes rather than a transparent act of fidelity to the lived experience of an autonomous subject.

Chapter 3 uses this formulation of subjectivity to trace the models of character and action that constitute Ge Hong's autobiographical persona while attempting to explain them within both the context of Wei-Jin intellectual history and in terms of Ge Hong's immediate concerns for life and limb, position, and scholarship. My goal is to avoid reducing the autobiography to either set of interpretations by describing how Ge Hong may have understood and communicated his empirical experience and translated it into a narrative of lofty personal character with broad cultural content. The various adopted personae of Ge Hong's autobiographical narrative that I address here—southerner, philosopher, military commander, and recluse—are at least as fundamental as the sectarianism of textual and religious traditions such as Confucianism (*Ru*) and Daoism (*Dao*). Each of these personae reflects a concern with moral and ethical truth that supersedes any concern with accurate biographical detail in the conventional sense.

Ge Hong's pursuit of religious transcendence through *waidan* throughout his lifetime underscores each of the character typologies in his text. In this he adopted an attitude toward transcendence similar to those of many authors of verse such as Cao Zhi 曹植 (192–232), who frequently adopted the voice of a roaming immortal as a state of literary liberation. Although we cannot doubt Ge Hong's sincere desire for a religious transcendence that from one perspective appears to annihilate the self through union with the Dao, we cannot deny that this kind of transcendence was predicated on high standards of moral character and ethical conduct for the individual adept. Ge Hong associated such standards with Confucian moral principles and took their perfection as the foundation for his system of soteriology.[23] His pursuit of transcendence may signify his incomplete virtue in religious terms, but it justifies his participation in public life, which in turn becomes the space for enacting the literary tropes of virtuous character that ultimately conferred a different kind of transcendence and immortality on their author.

Chapter 4 addresses the intrinsic tension between autobiography and the tradition of historical writing in early China, for each claimed the power to arbitrate the durability of the individual, albeit in different and often conflicting terms. Ge Hong's postface to the *Waipian* is unique among its predecessors in that it takes the self as a legitimate subject and directly challenges the authority of the historian. He hoped to craft his legacy through self-narrative and write a text that would define and constrain how he would be "read" by future generations. We might say that, insofar as Ge Hong anticipates future readers, his autobiographical postface is a text principally concerned with power. He radically reinterpreted the act of authorial self-narration, placing autobiography and history in dialogue with one another in a struggle over the privilege to record the narrative of an individual life. Moreover, by counterpoising autobiographical prose with historiography, Ge Hong implies a stronger relationship between them than is found in the Western European tradition yet one that is deeper than the formal relationship posed by students of modern autobiography. The dominance of historical biography in eighteenth- and nineteenth-century European historiography gave rise to the view that all autobiographical writing constituted a single genre of "autobiography" but without the inherent tension between historiography and autobiography found in early China. In contrast, control over one's legacy in early China was an issue of great concern and may have become a creeping anxiety in Ge Hong's era, which witnessed an explosion of historical writing.

Because this book focuses on Ge Hong's autobiographical postface, it is primarily concerned with this subgenre of autobiographical prose, but hopefully will also be taken as a small contribution to the larger study of subjectivity in early China, which must ultimately consider a cross-section of autobiographical texts, including tomb epigraphs written by the deceased themselves, personal letters, poetry, and even self-portraiture. We may think of autobiography in any form on the most basic level as the stories people tell about themselves, with such narratives leading to rather than stemming from self-understanding. Autobiographers in nearly every genre draw on preexisting narrative types to give structure to the inchoate and largely meaningless mass of experience that constitutes a life. The difference between Ge Hong, as a representative of an early Chinese tradition, and a modern Western autobiography is not just that one is ancient and one is modern but that there are different typological schemes behind each one. While in the West these typologies may originate in the tradition of epic myths, tragedy, or religious confession, those of early China may originate in didactic history, political circumstance, or the lyric moment such as one finds in Qu Yuan's 屈原 (trad. 340?–278 BCE) "Li sao" 離騷 (Encountering Sorrow).

By seeking to explain how writers in early China "emplotted" their lives, or portions of their lives, as narrative, I hope to liberate early Chinese autobiographical texts from their more literal readings and develop a considered interpretation of the texts that takes into account the mode of subjectivity in a specific time, place, and genre. Autobiography must be understood as something that varies from place to place and time to time rather than as an "evolution" toward the modern genre as we understand it today. Modern autobiography is simply that, and while precedents may exist they can only be thought of as such in retrospect, much as Ge Hong cherry-picked certain precedents for his own work while disregarding others, creating a new and unprecedented self-narrative.

Autos and Autobiography

The Proscriptive Power of Genre

I t must be assumed that the constitution of the individual bears directly on the definition of autobiography as a genre, as the boundaries of individual identity determine the meaning of the "autos" in the text by asking who is the subject of the narrative. Moreover, because autobiographies may "provide us with an objective, indeed, a demonstrable image of the structure of individuality, varying from epoch to epoch," autobiographical writing allows us to further our understanding of the construction of individual identity in early China.[1] The study of early Chinese autobiographical writing both in English and in Chinese has been dominated by the modern expectation of autobiography as a personal narrative that discloses the experience of an autonomous individual. Even though our changing understanding of Western autobiography has come to undermine this fundamental, commonsense assumption during the last few decades, the persistence of this reading in the study of early Chinese autobiographical prose reflects the importance for modern scholars of early texts as a precedent for late imperial and twentieth-century Chinese autobiography. It is a view that takes early Chinese autobiographical texts to be the chrysalis stage of a modern genre regarded as the narrative of individual experience.[2]

For this reason, the secondary literature on early Chinese autobiographical writing typically limits the genre to a handful of texts that seem to conform to a modern sensibility of the relationship between memory and historicity, texts whose primary concern seems to be the fidelity between the life narrative and the author's lived experience. From this perspective, the early Chinese autobiographical tradition is often said to consist of the *Taishigong zixu* 太史公自序 (Grand Astrologer's Authorial Postface) of the Han dynasty historian Sima Qian 司馬遷 (?145–90 BCE); the "Chapter of Self Record" of the *Lunheng ziji pian* 論衡自記篇 (Arguments Weighed) of the Eastern Han essayist Wang Chong 王充 (27–97); the "Authorial Postface" to the *Dian lun zixu* 典論自序 (Authoritative Discourses) by Cao Pi 曹丕 (187–226); the "Authorial Postface" to the *Waipian zixu* of the Jin dynasty alchemist and scholar official Ge Hong; and the "Wuliu xiansheng zhuan" of the Liu-Song 劉宋 (420–78) author Tao Qian.[3] The first four texts listed here are authorial self-narratives, *zixu*, a short autobiographical postface attached to a longer work with which the author explains the creation of the masterwork in the context of his or her life.[4] Tao Qian's text is different than its predecessors in this regard, being the earliest known self-descriptive prose piece in Chinese literature to stand independent of another work. However all of these early autobiographical texts are typically seen from a modern perspective as self-descriptions or life narratives that are organized around the figure of an autonomous literary subject.

But prior to the early twentieth century, the texts of Sima Qian, Wang Chong, and Cao Pi were not regarded as "autobiography" as such, and some critics rejected their use as personal narratives. This group of texts, when it was considered at all, was regarded as belonging to the genre of the authorial postface, and critics debated the limits of their autobiographical dimensions. There are two existing formulations of the authorial postface as a genre in medieval Chinese literature. The earliest is that of Ge Hong, who was himself an author of an autobiographical postface appended to his masterwork *Baopuzi*, which was also his sobriquet, while the second is that of Liu Zhiji 劉知幾 (661–721), an early Tang dynasty historiographer. Ge Hong's delineation of the genre of the postface occurs through his citation of influential antecedents or by means of his adoption of some of their formal features, although he does not explicitly exclude other texts from the same genre; he thus highlights the accounts of Sima Qian, Wang Chong, and Cao Pi. What is interesting is the way in which this selection of texts—including also Ge Hong's—continues to influence the views of modern scholars of Chinese autobiography. The similarity may be based on Ge Hong's desire to establish clear precedents for his own narrative style, one that presented a vivid portrait of its subject, by carving out just such a tradition from a much more diverse group of texts that were, on the whole, more reticent and concerned with describing the production of the larger text to which they were appended. In contrast, Ge Hong's postface seems to meet many of the modern expectations for autobiographical narrative; it is a detailed narrative of the author's life that makes certain claims to be an accurate account of the subject. It is likely for this reason that he took as his antecedents only those predecessors whose work bears a strong resemblance to his own in terms of content and style, texts that also presented their subjects in more vivid detail. Such portrayals obviously resonate more strongly with the sensibilities of modern readers of autobiography, for they resemble the mode of self-confession, inaugurated with Augustine, to which modern readers have become accustomed.

While at first glance Ge Hong's autobiographical postface appears to craft an image of the subject as a modern, autonomous individual, we must consider the fact that most Chinese authors and critics were more concerned with enmeshing individuals within familial, political, or other social networks. The notion of autonomous subjectivity so familiar to modern readers was a concept of personal identity largely incongruous with early Chinese concepts of the self. As we shall see, even the social isolation of the recluse or hermit (*yinzhe* 隱者 or *yimin* 逸民), often cited as evidence for nascent forms of Chinese "individualism," was based on a definition of the self that was only significant through its recognition and affirmation by society. The value of the hermit did not lie in his ostensible—and frequently fictitious—isolation but in his strong and visible presence within society as a social and political critic.

It was precisely this notion of the individual—contingent and defined largely through social relationships—that was central to Liu Zhiji's formulation of the genre of the authorial postface in a chapter of his *Shitong* 史通 (Generalities on History) entitled "Xuzhuan" 敘傳 (The Authorial Postface). Indeed, Liu Zhiji is highly critical of those authors who he feels engage in self-description to the point of impropriety, defined as narrating their own accomplishments at the expense of familial or social bonds. In contrast, he lauds the work of several writers whose narratives are so reticent that they would fall far short of modern expectations for autobiography. Indeed, for modern scholars of early Chinese autobiographical writing, the most troubling aspect of Liu Zhiji's treatment of the subject may be his inclusion of certain texts in the genre of the authorial postface, in which the author is not the ostensible subject of the narrative, for it is from this genre that recent critics draw most of their early examples of autobiography.

A clear picture of the genre in its earliest forms, and Ge Hong's place in its development, cannot be drawn without first considering how a style of autobiographical prose that was not rooted in the idea of an autonomous subject developed in early China. Understanding the definition and limits of subjectivity during this period may clarify the reasons for the wide variation among different views of early Chinese autobiographical writing and the genre of the authorial postface. This chapter attempts to show that the apparent differences among Ge Hong, modern critics, and Liu Zhiji result from a misreading of the constitution of individual identity and literary subjectivity in medieval China. In this way I hope to demonstrate that Ge Hong's very careful process of self-creation and his selective demarcation of the authorial postface as a genre were a result of his needs as an author rather than the product of a radically antisocial stance or a climate of individualism during the Wei-Jin era. In order to understand exactly how modern critics misread early Chinese literary subjectivity, we need to begin with Augustine of Hippo, the "father" of Western autobiography, who continues to exert a profound influence on our understanding of the genre.

Augustine, Self-Narrative, and Subjectivity

Augustine's *Confessions* is a classic autobiographical work generally considered to be a key text in the development of autobiography and subjectivity in the West. Augustine's reflections on memory and the nature of the individual continue to influence modern and postmodern notions of literary subjectivity. Though roughly contemporary with Ge Hong's *Baopuzi*, *Confessions* has little practical comparative value, but Augustine's meditation on memory and its expression in art as a life narrative has had a lasting impact on critics of autobiography and their modern formulation of the genre both in China and in Europe and North America. One of the compelling features of Augustine's work is his invocation of a vivid and defining series of life experiences leading up to his conversion to Christianity around 386 CE. At this point in Augustine's story, the life narrative of the subject ends and Augustine launches into a lengthy meditation on time and memory. In terms of the organization of the text, Augustine's conversion marks the end of his documental life; all that remains is the individual soul before God. The structure of Augustine's autobiography—a vivid autobiographical description that culminates in a monumental life event—would become archetypal for the tradition in Europe and North America. Since an author must logically end an autobiography with an event other than his own death, he must find another form of narrative closure, which may be understood as a figurative death through which the life may be understood in its finality.[5] Augustine's autobiography thus imposed a pattern on his life that not only gave coherence to his experience but also provided the template followed by autobiographers and critics well into the twentieth century.[6]

Augustine's influence on later autobiography can also be seen in the tone of contrition and self-justification frequently evident in the genre. Augustine defines his life narrative as a confession, an act of penitence that is intimately bound up with memory, for one must first recall sins in order to seek forgiveness for them.

> My heart lies before you, O my God. Look deep within. See these memories of mine, for you are my hope. You cleanse me when unclean humors such as these possess me, by drawing my eyes to yourself and "saving my feet from the snare."[7]

Thus the heart of confession is the act of memory, which allows the confessor to "trace again in memory . . . past deviations and to offer . . . a sacrifice of joy."[8] The organization of *Confessions* reflects this idea by providing a laundry list of moral transgressions and deprecating self-description until the narration of his conversion.

While not all autobiography is contrition, until the close of the eighteenth century confession was considered one of three dominant modes of autobiographical writing in Europe and North America. In addition to confession, authors recalled their lives in the overlapping genres of memoir and apology. Life narrative in each of these three forms attempted to justify the life of the author through an appeal to a sympathetic reader or, in the case of religious confession, to an otherworldly judge. In the nineteenth century, the new genre of autobiography came to encompass these three categories after biography emerged as a formal mode of historiography and an association was made between historical writing and these autobiographical accounts. Prior to this time, the association between biography and autobiography was less clearly defined.[9] Memoir, a narrative of an event or era, the story of which is interwoven with the author's life, most closely resembled history in form and function. A confession, like that of Augustine, was designed to inspire imitation. The author's appeal for forgiveness on a moral, spiritual, and intellectual level was meant to inspire the reader's own self-reflection and repentance. The broad intention of apology was to vindicate one's own beliefs or actions, particularly in the face of public controversy or contemporary criticism.[10] The modern notion of autobiography emerged when these disparate autobiographical genres, already steeped in claims of historical accuracy, were wed to the nineteenth-century notion of analytical biography and the emerging "science" of modern historiography.

The differences among these early subgenres may not be immediately obvious. Augustine's text is an archetypical confession. The details of his early life before conversion have a powerful pedagogical element and are designed to inspire the reader's own soul-searching, but he does not ask the reader for forgiveness for these acts, which is the prerogative of God alone: "I need not tell all this to you, my God, but in your presence I tell it to my own kind, to those other men, however few, who may perhaps pick up this book. And I tell it so that I and all who read my words may realize the depths from which we are to cry to you."[11] Augustine intends his own life to serve as an example of self-reflection for the reader, which begins a process of individuation in religious terms but does not empower the reader to pass judgment. In contrast, although Jean-Jacques Rousseau (1712–78) titled his autobiography *The Confessions*, his stated intention to defend his actions by claiming that all men are his ethical equals tilts his text in the direction of apology. Rousseau was far more concerned with responding to gossip or rumor than becoming a paragon worthy of imitation. We might say that the Augustinian and eventual modern Western concern with issues of confession, accurate memory, and general accuracy are inseparable from their origins in Christian discourse. That is, Augustine defined autobiographical accuracy in terms of memory and factuality (history), which are essential because accurate historical confession is the condition or portal to divine transcendence (redemption). In modern (but not postmodern) autobiography, historical accuracy and factuality are retained as a salient feature but divine transcendence is largely eliminated in favor of different motivations.

For Augustine, the act of confession is the source for individuation, as the self emerges as an individual being only in relation to God, which is the only true reference point in Augustine's philosophy. His attempt to free the individual from material or corporeal ties may reflect his background in Manichaeism, which regarded the material world as evil and unworthy of God. These views may have been strengthened by his eventual rejection of Aristotle's theory of categories of substance.

> The meaning of [Aristotle's] book seemed clear enough to me. It defined substance, such as man, and its attributes. For instance, a man has a certain shape; this is quality. He has height, measured in feet, which is quantity. He has relation to other men; for example, he is another man's brother. You may say where he is and when he was born, or describe his position as standing or sitting. You may name his possessions by saying that he has shoes or carries arms. You may define what he does and what is done to him.[12]

According to Augustine, Aristotle's flaw lay in his emphasis on the substantive elements that constitute the human body and its context, a supposition that Augustine feared would lead to a mistaken view of God as a material being. In addition to rejecting the materiality of God, Augustine also emphasized the importance of the ethereal human soul over the material body as the fundamental level of individual identity: "And I know that my soul is the better part of me, because it animates the whole of my body. It gives it life, and this is something that no body can give to another body."[13] For Augustine, the body and its relationship to the material world are largely inconsequential for describing an individual. Instead, individual identity must be seen in terms of the immortal soul that draws meaning from beyond the material world. Augustine's lasting influence lies with the durability of his idea of subjective experience, that autobiography records the inward journey of the individual soul toward God.

Thus, in addition to a pedagogical purpose, the details of Augustine's early life also function—ironically—to turn the soul away from the body and toward God by engaging in a radical form of reflexivity. The turn to the first person is crucial to the understanding of God and thus the moral sources of the self.[14] Augustine equates true self-knowledge with the realization of God's grace, a process that begins with memory and self-description and ends with forgiveness and self-realization: "Whatever you feel through the senses of the flesh you only feel in part. It delights you, but it is only a part and you have no knowledge of the whole."[15] For Augustine, confession is an act of memory with revelation of the divine as a result, as the only real purpose of retracing the bitter past is to savor more fully the "sweetness" of his new faith.[16] The proof of God is found within, in the first-person experience of self-knowledge.[17]

It should come as no surprise, then, that defending the accuracy of memory is critical to Augustine's project, as an accurate memory of one's transgressions would seem necessary for a true and faithful confession. According to Augustine, memories are formed through the senses and reemerge in the mind, though sometimes in a chaotic fashion, so that memories must be "shepherded" and collected by the mind. This is the original *cogito* to which René Descartes referred, for the act of memory is entirely limited to the mind, and so the act of memory is intimately bound up with thought.[18] Although memories must be organized, Augustine never questions their accuracy, stating at one point, "O Lord my God, is this not the truth as I remember it?"[19] Memory is so accurate that events may be contemplated "over again as if they were actually present."[20] The narrative that results from an organized series of memories is made accurate through their collection, as the mind can weigh the relevance and position of the memories among each other. Augustine asserts, "When I use my memory, I ask it to produce whatever it is that I wish to remember."[21] Indeed, the process of organization may even produce memories that do not at first emerge, while other memories "present themselves easily and in the correct order just as I require them."[22]

For Augustine, knowledge of God—and therefore true knowledge of the nature of the soul—ultimately emerges in a space that is beyond the faculty of memory and therefore beyond the capacity for understanding. Although God can be found in the memory, knowledge of the divine is beyond the experiential process, being a "Truth" that is native to everyone's mind.[23] True self-knowledge lies in this unfathomable realm of faith, a place beyond memories, the experiences that form them, and the intellect that organizes them. Thus, although he may accurately recount his past, it is only faith itself that provides the ultimate realm of self-knowledge, taking the faithful from the world of experience and memory to knowledge of the individual soul and its relationship to the divine.[24] Although the religious purpose of Augustine's discourse was later abandoned, his assertion that the self is a product of the individual, introspective mind left its mark on later writers and critics of autobiography, who came to see the genre as the search for self-knowledge within a landscape of memories.

Interested Self-Presentation

Until recently, Western critics of autobiography saw the genre as constituted of historically accurate prose narratives, demonstrating the broader influence of both historiography and Augustinian discourse on the early study of autobiographical writing. More recent critics, from within the intellectual climate of postmodernism, argue that formal characteristics are secondary to more fundamental issues such the relationship between the author and the text or the significance of the act of reading. Several important issues emerge as soon as we acknowledge that there is an "I" behind most works of literature, but it is a subjectivity that is from one perspective the linguistic function of multiple perspectives, including that of the reader. Thus the definition of autobiography threatens to become so vast as to be meaningless or is altogether discarded through an overly simplistic reading of deconstruction.[25] In the first instance, reading all literature as autobiography gives rise to dubious attempts to see the "stamp of the author's self-image" even within texts that are highly resistant to this kind of reading; in the second, conventional notions of the author are destroyed by reducing contemporary deconstruction of autobiography to mere relativism.

For our purposes here, we will explore the way in which the scholarship of recent critics allows us to reexamine the genre of autobiography as those texts that propose a set of claims regarding the relationship between the author and the subject of the text that are unique or at least uniquely central for autobiography. One such notion of autobiography is Philippe Lejeune's concept of the "autobiographical pact" in which an "author proposes to the reader a discourse on the self."[26] Lejeune's definition is useful because it defines autobiography in the broadest terms as the act of self-narrative and the specific, accompanying claims to authorial self-expression rather than as a genre bound by a specific set of formal or stylistic characteristics. In Lejeune's view, any work of literature may be considered autobiography so long as its stated intention is to take the self as its subject. But Lejeune's autobiographical pact implies a strong distinction between an *autobiography* and a *life work*, both of which may provide the reader with a sense of the author. As James Olney writes:

> Man has always cast his autobiography and has done it in that form to which his private spirit impelled him, often, however, calling the product not an autobiography but a lifework. . . . [T]he final work, whether it be history or poetry, psychology or theology, political economy or natural science . . . will express and reflect its maker.[27]

In terms of Lejeune's notion of the autobiographical pact, autobiography must differ from a life work simply and only because it is a text in which the narrator, author, and subject are all claimed to be the same person.[28] Unlike a life work, autobiography takes the form of an "interested search" for the self, the author's attempt to shape his or her past, impose a pattern on life, and construct a coherent story. This story often works to justify or even to redeem the past, to make it part of a story that gives life purpose by taking it as a meaningful unity.[29]

Most modern critics of European autobiography follow the model established by Lejeune and Olney by arguing that the text represents the author's attempt to "recompose and interpret a life in its totality."[30] Roy Pascal echoes this view stating that, although autobiography is historical in terms of methodology, it represents an individual's "philosophical history," a text that seeks the "spiritual identity" of the author.[31] A text claiming to provide the spiritual identity of the author must necessarily differ from a historical biography, for the historian can only represent the mind of the subject through the intermediary of written sources and recorded actions. Pascal's notion seems to implicitly or explicitly defend an assumption that the question of identity resolves to some degree issues of accuracy and fidelity. In other words, an autobiography, regardless of its formal characteristics, is by nature an accurate account because the author and subject are the same while the author of autobiography is privileged to private insights that the biographer or historian is not. George Gusdorf, for example, while acknowledging that "every autobiography is a work of art," states that autobiographical texts reveal the author to us "in his inner privacy, not as he was, not as he is, but as he believes and wishes himself to be and have been."[32] In Gusdorf's view, autobiography should render a faithful portrait of the self above and beyond literary or artistic merits.

Significantly, Gusdorf resists the notion that a faithful record must be factually accurate in historical terms; an autobiographical account need not be factually precise so long as the portrait of the author is faithful to his or her "spiritual identity," as Pascal describes. This distinction between historical accuracy and the narrative of the inner subject seems to challenge Augustine's assertion that fidelity to lived experience is achieved through a past accurately remembered; nevertheless, Gusdorf clearly views the subject of autobiography in Augustinian terms as representing the inner, private individual. The troubling dilemma between inaccurate memories and life narrative may be resolved—and even considered acceptable—so long as the autobiography provides a faithful account of the subject as an individual consciousness.

Other critics have argued that such doubts over the accuracy of memory support the notion that autobiography creates rather than discovers the interior life of an individual. Changes to the author over time in terms of his or her context, personal perspective, range of experience, and so forth imply that he or she is not the same person who experienced the events that are recorded. Therefore, as James Goodwin states, "An autobiography represents the writer's effort, made at a certain stage of life, to portray the meaning of personal experience as it has developed over the course of a significant period of time."[33] In this sense autobiography differs from biography as a text that attempts to describe who the author has become through the story of how he or she got there.[34] The meaning of past events is thus shaped in various degrees by the requirements of the author's present narrative, which in turn must influence the contents of the life record itself. Even Augustine was willing to admit to omitting events in order to sharpen the didactic nature of his text, stating, "There is much besides this that escapes my memory and much too that I must omit, because I am in haste to pass on to other things, which I am more anxious to confess to you."[35] Moreover, by its very nature autobiography can never encompass the totality of all statements that could be applied to the subject, for the autobiographer can never in reality possess the perspective of a life in its entirety and so must conclude the story at some arbitrary point. This helps explain the appeal of Augustine's work as a model for later autobiography, for he proposes to the reader a "fictive death" or radical transformation of the self that stands in for the death of the subject. A fictive death allows authors to claim a kind of omniscience for their narratives, for it is only by standing beyond their prior lives that they possess the perspective that allows them to summarize accurately their life experiences.

The process by which memories are organized into a descriptive narrative thus implies some degree of disjunction between the "I" of the author and the "I" of the text, states of subjectivity that Lejeune describes as the "subject of enunciation" and the "subject of discourse." The claim of autobiography to take the self as its subject must be understood instead as the creation of an entirely new object of study or the reification of the self as both subject and object. For this reason, Olney argues that the subject of discourse—the "I" of the text—is always "a moment of the self as it is becoming, a metaphor of the self at the summary moment of composition" that alludes to but does not replace the author.[36] In this sense, autobiographical writing may be seen as a symbolic and therefore haphazard construction of the individual that exists by "subjecting the self to intelligibility" through dialogue with others, rendering the mass of life experience comprehensible to the reader by addressing common reference points of language and meaning.[37] In other words, autobiographies are conversations over the meaning of an individual life between agents using a shared language.

For Jürgen Habermas, it is for this reason that subjectivity may only exist along the "axis of interhuman communication."

> [T]he *performatively employed* concept of individuality . . . is invested in the claim to individuality that is put forth by a first person in dialogue with a second person. . . . [I]t is a matter of interested presentations of the self, with which a complex claim presented to second persons is justified . . . manifesting itself in a conscious way of life.[38]

Habermas might claim autobiography to be a process of self-creation rather than a vehicle for self-discovery, a process of self-creation that is necessarily social in its function. In similar terms, Stanley Cavell regards autobiography as a record of the self that exists through the enunciation of existence, a self that proves its human existence through writing but does not exist prior to the text.[39] This notion of autobiography challenges the assumption begun by Augustine that autobiography portrays the self "as it is," that we "discover" an ontologically distinct being through the writing of self-narrative. In these terms, the "accuracy" or "truth" of an autobiography cannot be measured against the truth of historical or biographical statements but only against the authenticity of the presentation of self, a presentation that is only meaningful in its intelligibility to others.[40]

While the views of Olney and Habermas may challenge the Augustinian tradition of textual fidelity as a one-to-one correspondence between the text and lived experience, the broad notion of autobiography as a text in which the author and the subject are the same remains central to any understanding of a genre that presupposes a self that is the subject of the narrative. But the recent challenges to memory and subjectivity outlined above describe a self that may assume no stability and cannot be described in terms of individual autonomy. Such a view of the self is useful because it allows for historically and culturally specific modes of subjectivity that may yield forms of autobiography at odds with modern notions of the genre as the record of an autonomous subject. Creating a metaphor of the self through a written dialogue with a defining community remains a process of self-identification, but one that occurs in consort with the demands of a community of readers. This notion of autobiography as a socially bounded act of self-creation rather than self-description creates space for a fuller consideration of early Chinese autobiographical texts, which have thus far been seen largely in Augustinian terms.

The Reconstruction of Early Chinese Autobiography

Prior to the modern period, early Chinese autobiographical texts were dispersed, like their Western counterparts, throughout a variety of literary styles and genres. These diverse works of literature do not seem to have been regarded together as a distinct genre of "autobiography," although several subgenres, such as the authorial postface, had already been subject to some critical attention, which we will examine in the next chapter. The process of casting these diverse texts into a single genre occurred in the early twentieth century when autobiographical prose became another means for intellectuals to draw sharp distinctions between modernity and tradition.[41] Individuality, which for Augustine was a radical new means of seeking the divine, was equally compelling for Chinese intellectuals who desired to assert an autonomous construction of an individual that was distinct from traditional culture. Notions of autobiographical writing, such as interested self-presentation, that define the self in less absolute terms would have been less useful in this regard, for it was autobiography in Augustinian terms that was an important tool for creating a subject that "takes itself seriously, asserts its autonomy against traditional society, and possesses an interiority" that could be represented in narrative form.[42] Part of this project included selecting texts from existing genres to form a "native" Chinese tradition of autobiography, or *zizhuan* 自傳, out of literature both canonical and vernacular.

For early-twentieth-century authors and intellectuals, molding so many different kinds of texts into the single genre of autobiography rested on the assumption that autobiography conforms to an Augustinian model as the life story of an autonomous subject written in a narrative style. Guo Dengfeng's 郭登峰 pioneering anthology *Lidai zixu zhuan wenchao* 歷代自敘傳文鈔 (An Anthology of Autobiographical Postfaces and Autobiography through the Ages), originally published in 1937, illustrates the influence of modern notions of individual autonomy on the recent development of the genre. In his introduction to the collection, Guo describes how autobiography had become one of the most fashionable genres of writing in literary circles, a result of China's importation of recent Western literary trends, which resulted in a veritable tidal wave of autobiographical writing.[43] Speaking of early writers of autobiographical texts such as Sima Qian and Ge Hong, he writes:

> The autobiographies that they wrote were not only works done with a high aesthetic value, but in them they also put forth their method of study, their life philosophies, and what aroused their spirits with regard to difficulties in the course of their scholarship and careers so as to teach others from their mistakes, attempting thus to serve as an example to future readers.[44]

It should be observed that the impulse for autobiographical writing Guo ascribes to early Chinese authors possesses a strong flavor of confession but differs from the Christian confessional tradition on several points. According to Guo, richly detailed narrative gives autobiography its function and purpose, transforming the experiences of the author into archetypes that may act as models that can help future readers understand their own circumstances. Absent is Augustine's appeal to memory and biographical details as a search for the moral sources of the self; the motive for self-knowledge, or its expression, is the desire to render one's experience intelligible to others and promote a self-image that can act as a paragon for future observers. In this sense, Guo has "translated" the Western autobiographical impulse into Chinese, substituting a notion of historical legacy for the early Christian search for the divine sources of individual identity.

In fashioning his anthology, Guo takes extensive biographical detail coupled with a desire for self-expression as his standard of selection. The resulting anthology is a diverse selection of texts drawn from earlier genres united by an editorial concept of a self that is both coherent and stable, supersedes earlier genre distinctions, and may be expressed within the formal characteristics of any literary style. The neologism of *zi zhuan* supposedly addresses the quality of the author's self-expression and not the particular mode of expression in which it originally occurred. Thus tomb inscriptions written by the deceased themselves, revealing personal letters, selected rhapsodies (*fu* 賦), and verse (*shi* 詩), and postfaces of major works are read as a single kind of self-expression despite the variations among these texts in terms of traditional genre or *ti* 體. Poetry, for example, generally tends to neglect the genealogy of the author, letters focus on affective bonds or their dissolution, and authorial postfaces are largely concerned with introducing the author's literary works. Yet from all of these genres Guo selects examples of "autobiography."

Omission, as much as inclusion, is the key characteristic of any anthology or literary collection, and it is extremely important in Guo's compilation. The anthology must necessarily exclude texts from each earlier genre that do not conform to the criteria of the new genre for self-presentation, namely, that they take the author as the subject and recount the life of the subject with enough biographical detail to warrant inclusion in the anthology. In his introduction, Guo writes:

> With regard to the "Postface" 序傳 of *Han shu* 漢書 (History of the Former Han) by Ban Gu 班固 (32–92), the "Authorial Postface" 自序 of the *Song shu* 宋書 (History of the Song) by Shen Yue 沈約 (441–513),

and the "Postface" to the *Bei shi* 北史 (History of the Northern Dynasties) by Li Yanshou 李延壽 (seventh century), all [of these works] recount the background of the author's ancestors in detail and recount their own background to a limited extent and are actually connected with the characteristics of family genealogy and definitely are not autobiography, and so they are not here recorded.[45]

Guo's definition of early Chinese autobiography is strongly rooted in the efforts of early-twentieth-century Chinese intellectuals to associate the autonomous construction of an individual—and by extension autobiography, which is the story of that individual—with a decisive break from traditional culture. In this regard, the anthology must exclude those texts that emphasize elements associated with traditional culture such as familial bonds, which, as we might expect, was contrary to the views of the postface genre espoused by Liu Zhiji in the early Tang dynasty.[46] Moreover, the texts that Guo rejected may implicitly challenge an autonomous construction of the individual by portraying their subject—imagined as the author—in terms of familial traditions or other social bonds. Guo implies that biographical detail about the individual subject is paramount in this regard, as a detailed life narrative focused on the individual would develop and help to convey a sense of autonomy for the subject.

Guo's anthology mirrors the more traditional Western notion of the genre by focusing chiefly on prose writing, a fact that reflects his reading of Western genres into the Chinese tradition. Although Guo includes a section devoted to rhapsodies and verse, the bulk of the collection consists of prose works. Early examples from the genres of rhapsody and verse include "Gui qu lai ci" 歸去來辭 (Upon Returning) by Tao Qian, a rhapsody that is no more ostensibly autobiographical than many of Tao Qian's other works. Indeed, in terms of biographical detail, the autobiographical content of this particular rhapsody lies largely in the prose introduction, which allegedly details the origins of the rhapsody. In this regard, the introduction functions as a kind of "authorial preface," or *zixu,* to the central work. However, unlike other examples of the authorial postface, this brief introduction does not provide a genealogy, family history, or personal history of the author. The rhapsody itself certainly is no more detailed than Tao Qian's well-known "Gui yuan tian ju" 歸園田居 (Returning to Live in My Gardens and Fields), a five-poem series of five-character 五言 verses that epitomizes the reclusive persona of the poet. Thematically similar to "Gui qu lai ci," both works describe the author's retreat from public life into the simple joys of home, family, and living in the country. From Guo's point of view, the distinction between the two may lie in the preface to the rhapsody, which states in the most transparent possible terms the autobiographical undercurrents of the work.

This limited reading of the autobiographical potential of poetry illustrates a turn toward Western prose models of autobiography in the early twentieth century and a rejection of more traditional hermeneutics of the Chinese poetic tradition. During the Han and medieval periods, many writers and readers of poetry adopted the well-worn idea that "verse expresses intention" 詩言志 first expressed in *Shang shu* 尚書 (Book of Documents) and elaborated on in the "Great Preface" 大序 of *Shi jing* 詩經 (Classic of Poetry). "The poem is that to which intention proceeds. In the mind it is intention. Emerging in words it is verse" 詩者, 志之所之也. 在心爲志. 發言爲詩.[47] During the period in which this concept was being established, it sometimes resulted in tortured interpretations of poetry as readers sought the "intention" of the poet through recourse to historical and biographical information. The author of the "Great Preface" provided the archetype for this kind of reading by interpreting the first poem in *Shi jing*, "Guan Ju" 關雎, as a celebration of the virtues of the queen consort of King Wen of the Zhou dynasty.[48] Perhaps more important for later generations of scholar-officials and authors of verse was Wang Yi's 王逸 (ca. 89–158) melancholy reading of the poem "Li sao" as the autobiographical suicide note of the legendary poet Qu Yuan. Wang Yi's interpretation of "Li sao" demonstrates the use of historical biography—in this case the biography of Qu Yuan as composed by Sima Qian—as the basis of literary criticism in an attempt to fix interpretation around an imagined, didactic intention on the part of the poet.

Thus a traditional reading of poetry would appear to demand a genre of autobiography so inclusive as to become meaningless, as an anthology that selects everything is not really an anthology at all. Whether or not historical and biographical interpretations of early poetry had any basis in reality is less important than the impact they had on later generations of poets, many of whom came to see their work as a venue for public reflection on their circumstances, ambitions, or successes and failures. Such works were not always transparently autobiographical but often used metaphor or allusion to canonical texts to create self-presentations that were veiled in seemingly innocuous language. Simple actions such as pouring a glass of wine could be read on many levels by an informed reader.[49] Moreover, early Chinese poets often obscured themselves behind allegorical identities such as hermits, wandering immortals, consorts, or abandoned wives. Thus more often than not the burden of understanding was placed on the shoulders of the reader, who required extensive knowledge of the relevant literary conventions and historical framework to interpret the poem. However, works that drew heavily on literary tradition for the purpose of self-presentation would not have been useful for an anthology created in the intellectual climate of early-twentieth-century China, in which the appeal to individuality and autobiography was precisely a rejection of traditional culture. Shifting allegorical self-descriptions would also undermine the notion of a stable and coherent self so desperately sought by readers, critics, and authors alike. Finally, because this traditional hermeneutic implies that it is quite possible to read most of the early Chinese poetic tradition as a densely packed historical and autobiographical document, a problem arises of how to select texts from a vast tradition that was conceived in the main as autobiographical.[50]

Guo's anthology illustrates how the adoption of a model of autobiography based on an apparently coherent, transparent self-presentation and an emphasis on prose subvert traditional genres of Chinese self-referential writing. Guo disassembles the Chinese poetic tradition in terms of a prose narrative of the self, thereby limiting the inclusion of the autobiographical subgenres of verse and rhapsody to a mere handful of works. Such limitations belie the fruitful and interesting work that remains to be done in terms of autobiographical verse, while demonstrating the extent to which early-twentieth-century Chinese intellectuals and literary critics such as Guo essentially created the genre of autobiography from a reading of the Western tradition.[51] Rereading the Chinese literary tradition to accommodate Western genres was not limited to poetry. As in the West, autobiographical writing also came to be seen in terms of a perceived connection with biography, and many works that adopted any of the formal features of historiography were viewed retroactively as autobiography regardless of their content.

Tao Qian's well-known essay "Wuliu xiansheng zhuan" illustrates how a connection—either real or imagined—between historiography and autobiography might have been used to further define the scope of the genre in the early twentieth century. This brief essay is generally seen as the earliest example of "formal" autobiography when it is defined as a biography written by the subject himself.[52] Long tradition supports the notion that Tao Qian's brief account of the reclusive yet virtuous hermit known only as Mr. Five Willows is nothing less than a self-portrait. With the word *zhuan* 傳, or biography, in the title of the work and a *zan* 贊, or appraisal, at the end, standard fare for biography, it seems clear that Tao consciously adapted (and perhaps lampooned) several of the formal features of state-sanctioned historiography. Indeed, from the perspective of early-twentieth-century Chinese critics one may argue that it is precisely these formal features that warrant its inclusion in an anthology of autobiography, or recommend it as biography of any kind, for the work lacks any transparent or specific biographical detail, one of the criteria for autobiography that Guo established in his introduction. Tao Qian's brief "autobiography" contains fewer biographical details than the comparatively shorter preface to his rhapsody "Gui gu lai ci." The subject, Mr. Five Willows, is anonymous, known only by an appellative derived from a description of his house. His origins, family name, and given name are all "unknown"; poor and without ambition, he seeks only wine, simple living, and to express himself in writing.[53]

Nevertheless, Tao's work has several features that make it well suited as an exemplary autobiography in the context of early-twentieth-century Chinese intellectual trends. Although Tao's subject is wrapped in the well-worn language of reclusion so prominent during the third and fourth centuries, he appears to be free of such traditional reference points as family, place of origin, name, or occupation, creating what Wendy Larson has called an "impressionistic" autobiography that is removed from the "orthodoxy of place, political power, and social structure."[54] He is thus "individualistic" in the most pedestrian sense of the word in that he is beyond conventionally accepted social constraints or customs. Moreover, the work seems to augment the persona Tao Qian so carefully crafted in his poetry, providing future readers with an archetype of behavior and character, a characteristic that Guo believed to be central to the purpose and meaning of early Chinese autobiography. Indeed, the appraisal links the subject to ancient sages, creating an identity based in timeless virtue that Tao inherits from past worthies.[55] By creating a subject that appears to live beyond social and familial ties, Tao constructs a relatively autonomous but socially meaningful identity, though ultimately it is Tao Qian's adaptation of the features of state-sanctioned historiography that marks the work as autobiographical. Assuming that the tradition is true that Tao himself is the subject of the work, then the biography meets the most basic requirement of autobiography according to Lejeune, namely, that the author and subject are the same. As a self-written biography, Tao Qian's text becomes autobiography by definition. Formal features such as the appraisal became useful to later critics who sought in the Chinese literary tradition a mirror of the Western tradition of autobiography that had become closely identified with biography and historiography in the preceding century.

Such formulations of the Chinese autobiographical tradition have continued to influence the study of the genre both in English and in Chinese by limiting the scope of the genre to a handful of texts that conform to a relatively narrow reading of the Western tradition. Generally speaking, this reading follows Guo Dengfeng's early anthology by privileging prose as the primary form of autobiography in early China, a fact that is largely due to the research objectives of the individual authors. More recent studies of Chinese autobiography have tended to focus on May Fourth writers of autobiography in the early twentieth century, who embraced modernity but rejected European colonialism. During this era, the popularity of Augustine's more traditional, confessional model of autobiography supported a view of the genre as largely composed of prose narratives, which in turn spawned a generation of imitators such as Lu Xun and Hu Shi and successors such as Eileen Chang 張愛玲 (1920–95) and Shen Congwen 沈從文 (1902–88). Studies of May Fourth writers naturally emphasize the prose autobiography produced during this era and consequently seek antecedents for such texts among early Chinese prose works. The view that autobiography must speak to the inner life of an autonomous, individual subject supports such a rigid emphasis on prose. If the subject's autobiography were to speak instead to his or her family genealogy, career, official titles, and so forth, then self-worth and identity can only be measured in relation to external terms. These "tradition-centered" or "relationship-centered" narratives are more concerned with portraying the subject as an exemplar of a stock type, a result that tends to negate any notion of an "inner self" within a web of outer affiliations.[56]

This strict construction of the genre of autobiography tends to negate the importance of poetry as well as drastically narrowing the scope of acceptable prose pieces. From this point of view, we could say that Sima Qian did not write an autobiography per se, even if the text has undisputed autobiographical elements. Sima Qian's autobiographical work can be said to create a "circumstantial" identity out of external factors, but it does not presume to describe the interior life modern critics might expect from the genre.[57] Therefore the lack of external reference points or obvious social ties might suggest to some readers that Tao Qian's "Wuliu xiansheng zhuan" is the first authentic autobiography in the Chinese tradition.[58] However, such an assertion fails to take into account the long literary tradition within which Tao constructs his ostensibly autonomous identity, creating a web of affiliation that is literary rather than social or familial in nature. Indeed, there is little about Tao Qian's autobiography that is individual at all; the author is rather a composite of well-worn images and tropes current during the era. Furthermore, the fact that Tao does not attach his identity to any interiority or individual development seems to challenge the idea that the work represents the first Chinese autobiography in any meaningful sense.[59]

More flexible genealogies of early autobiography tend to follow Guo Dengfeng's lead by placing Sima Qian's authorial postface and Tao Qian's "Wuliu xiansheng zhuan" on the same plane, implying that a tradition of diverse texts eventually culminated in or evolved into a recognizable genre of autobiography during the early twentieth century. Such studies reconcile differences between literary works by recognizing variation within the tradition. One approach is to describe texts that place the subject in a specific time and place, and within an orthodox social setting, as "circumstantial" autobiographies, as opposed to "impressionistic" autobiographies, which describe the subject beyond a realistic notion of time or orthodoxy of place.[60] This distinction creates an open-ended continuum in which it is not only possible to describe the texts of both Sima Qian and Tao Qian as early examples of autobiography, but also to recognize that authors create different kinds of texts under different circumstances. Nevertheless, it should be noted that whether or not a particular study of modern autobiography is bound by strict or flexible approaches to early texts the emphasis on prose remains constant and the number of texts identified as precursors to the modern genre remains small.

The influence of Guo Dengfeng's anthology of Chinese autobiography is not limited to studies of the modern genre but can also be seen in studies of premodern and early Chinese autobiographical texts. Guo's division of the autobiographical tradition into subgenres is generally used to illustrate the diversity of the textual record, with categories such as "Self-Written Necrologies" 自作墓誌鈔, "Authorial Self-Accounts" 附於著作的自序, and "Authorial Self-Accounts Independent of Books" 單篇獨立的自序.[61] Owing to the constraints of space and research goals, some subgenres, such as "Personal Letters of Self-Narrative" 書牘體的自序 and "Fu and Verse Self-Narrative" 辭賦體與詩歌體的自序, are generally omitted while categories such as "Annalistic Autobiography" 自序年譜 that are drawn from other collections and anthologies are often included in their place.[62] This selection process speaks to several issues in the study of premodern Chinese autobiography, not the least of which is the power of anthologies to act as a form of literary criticism and thereby shape the scope of later studies. For example, the foremost scholar of premodern Chinese autobiography, Pei-yi Wu, generally relies on the categories provided by collections such as *Ming ren zizhuan wen chao* 明人自傳文鈔 (Anthology of Ming Autobiographies) and *Wuxia zhong mu yiwen* 吳下冢墓遺文 (Necrologies Recovered from the Wu Area) in addition to those found in Guo Dengfeng's work.[63] This approach respects preexisting genres such as the "Authorial Postface" and "Annalistic Biography," which reflects a measured attempt to interpret or explain the texts within the context of their authorship. However, even Wu's groundbreaking study passes on an extensive discussion of the role of poetry within the early tradition, instead emphasizing prose antecedents to modern notions of the genre. Moreover, both early anthologies and studies of early autobiographical writing tend to "flatten" the tradition by treating each of these diverse prose forms as somehow representative of the larger genre of autobiography. In other words, even when distinctions are made among the various subgenres, the tendency is to imagine a psychoanalytic, modern model of a coherent and stable self that supersedes genre, which ultimately dissolves different prose styles into a single kind of self-expression rather than questioning whether the author even believed that there existed an autonomous self or coherent identity to be conveyed.

The idea that Sima Qian's *Taishigong zixu* is one of the earliest examples of Chinese autobiography illustrates Guo's central assumption that diverse modes of self-expression may be collapsed into a single genre. As we have seen, in his postface, Sima Qian attempts to explain the circumstances that led to the writing of his masterwork, *Shi ji* 史記 (Grand Astrologer's Record). Given the unprecedented nature of such a monumental history and the fact that during Sima Qian's time officials who held the post of *taishigong* 太史公 ("grand astrologer" or, more commonly, "grand historian") were actually responsible for the imperial calendar and not state historical writing, an explanation was probably in order. One of Sima Qian's goals in the postface was to equate his life with literary production in order to demonstrate the necessity of writing *Shi ji* in terms of the author's personal history. In the context of this explanation, Sima Qian uses biographical detail as a way to ground his text within a tradition of literary production by focusing on his filial duty to his father, Sima Tan 司馬談, who allegedly began the work that was completed by his son.[64] In this regard, the postface departs from Roy Pascal's "interested search for the self" through autobiography and becomes a search for the validation of literary production and represents a past more intimately connected to the text than to the author. In other words, the text rather than the author is the narrative subject of the postface, a fact that poses an interesting challenge to the idea that Sima Qian's work represents autobiography as such.

Scholars who uphold the position of Sima Qian as the progenitor of Chinese autobiography acknowledge the defensive or explanatory purpose of the work but define it as autobiography in terms of its biographical content and the precedent it established for self-narrative. Zhao Guoxi 趙國熙 writes:

> We recognize that the *Taishigong zixu* is Sima Qian's autobiography. . . .
> [I]ts publication not only shows that the genre of autobiography 自傳 had formed by the Han period but also reflects Sima Qian's affirmation of the value of his self-identity. . . . After Sima Qian's era, people continued to express their self-identity, and many people imitated Sima Qian and used autobiography to build up their own prestige.[65]

While Zhao acknowledges that the authorial postface serves as an introduction to and table of contents for *Shi ji*, he clearly emphasizes autobiographical features of the text and asserts that one of its primary functions was the "affirmation of the value of his [Sima Qian's] self-identity." Indeed, in Zhao's view Sima Qian established a trajectory for the genre as largely concerned with self-expression or self-narrative, a truism about the authorial postface that persists in most studies of early Chinese autobiography. Zhao's most striking claim is that Sima Qian's postface is representative of a genre of autobiography that had taken shape by the early Han dynasty, although the implications of this statement are unclear. Rather than arguing that Sima Qian's work was representative of a preexisting genre, Zhao seems to be saying that Sima Qian originated the form of the authorial postface as autobiography and that his innovation marks the inception of the genre in the Chinese tradition.

While the autobiographical aspects of the text cannot be denied, the presence of biographical details does not in and of itself imply a kind of uniformity between the postface and other autobiographical works within a single genre of autobiography. Not only does Sima Qian's focus on familial ties and authorship of *Shi ji* undermine the work as autobiography for some scholars, as we have seen, but also the text itself is not particularly revealing or detailed. In this regard, Zhao Guoxi seems to be embracing the truism rather than assessing the autobiographical features of the text or weighing the definition of the genre. Indeed, one could argue that Ban Gu's use of the postface in his "Biography of Sima Qian" 司馬遷傳 in *Han shu* (chapter 62), and his juxtaposition of the postface with Sima Qian's "Letter in Response to Ren Shaoqing" 報任少卿書 in the same chapter, are responsible in part for the autobiographical legacy of the text. The more personal and revealing letter illuminates the biographical details of the largely reticent postface by providing the background and circumstances of Sima Qian's castration and disgrace. The picture of the subject that emerges from the combination of this material speaks to the subject's interior life far more so than the image of the author formed by either text alone. Ban Gu's biography seems to suggest that neither of the texts was intended to stand as an account of an autonomous subject, which he instead created through recourse to several different autobiographical statements.[66]

Zhao's discussion of Sima Qian underscores the extent to which Augustine's model and modern notions of autobiography continue to dominate our understanding of the genre in both the Chinese and Western traditions. For Augustine, the notion of accurate memory is inseparable from its origins within Christian discourse. To confess without accuracy—or at minimum the fervent *belief* that the confession represents the truth—would have been useless, and consequently undesirable, because factuality was the portal to divinity. Only an accurate, historical confession is useful in religious terms. Modern critics of autobiography discarded the notion of transcendence but retained the emphasis on factuality, wedding accurate, historical confession to modern notions of individuality. Autobiography was considered well suited for the demands of modern identity in any national literature, and critical interest in the genre was and continues to be informed by similar assumptions of self-identity and individualism.

2

Reading Self-Narrative and
the Self in Early China

As we have seen, studies of early Chinese autobiography frequently cite the authorial postface as being among the earliest examples of the genre in the Chinese literary tradition. But the idea that the postface should provide an extensive narrative of the author's life was not widely accepted by premodern critics. Whereas Western autobiography emerged from within a Christian discourse of factual, individual confession, these postfaces originated from a literary and intellectual tradition that merged tradition with the present. The archetypes of behavior and ideal character lay in the past, and the representation of the present character in autobiographical writing was a matrix for the transmission of the ideal past, not necessarily an opportunity for expressing uniqueness or individuality. Consequently early authors of the postface often wrote with extreme self-effacement and considerable reticence.

The early Tang historian Liu Zhiji's description of the evolution of the authorial postface was not only the most extensive account of the subgenre up to that time but also a forceful rejection of the postface as a vehicle for an extensive, individualistic autobiography. Liu resists the type of self-expression that Guo Dengfeng and others would like to find in early China, which would establish the postface as a type of expression that stands up to the Western tradition well. In contrast to modern critics of autobiography—and what may have been common practice at the time—Liu Zhiji seems to have embraced a view of the authorial postface as a reserved record of the author, who is described ideally within a network of dependencies such as family lineage and public, political life, all expressed through traditional literary convention. This chapter will begin by exploring Liu's view of the postface and his criticism of its authors. As we shall see, his appraisal seems at odds with the function of the postface as it was understood by the authors themselves, who Liu claims gradually came to see the postface as an outlet for autobiographical self-promotion. Liu is only interested in forms of personal expression that fall into set didactic modes. However, we would be mistaken to identify Liu's criticism of Eastern Han and Wei-Jin authors with criticism of a freewheeling individualism that asserts an autonomous identity in any modern sense. To the contrary, I will attempt to show that even the most extreme examples of seemingly individualistic behavior were also deeply embedded within didactic modes meant to express a philosophical stance, political affiliations, or the good character of the subject. While such a reading of the postface may seem to rob the texts of Wang Chong, Cao Pi, and Ge Hong of their autobiographical weight, I will argue instead that by reading for the matrix of didactic modes we are able to reconcile traditional and modern readings of the postface and understand more completely those texts that have long been considered the earliest Chinese autobiographies.

Liu Zhiji on the Authorial Postface

It seems clear that Liu believed the genre of the postface had already begun to decline during the late Han and early medieval periods, becoming an exercise in authorial self-indulgence, but it is difficult to judge the extent to which Liu Zhiji's criticism had any traction among medieval literati or whether he was alone in his opinion. He states that the origins of the authorial postface extend into antiquity and lie with self-expression in verse. Since verse was considered self-expression by definition, and often made to serve didactic ends, Liu may be attempting to wed later genres with orthodox Tang literary theory and canonical literature both to find precedents and to create an ideal standard with which to judge later works. However, Liu is less interested in self-expression as such than the brief presentations of family genealogy that occur in poems such as "Li sao."

> In all probability, the authorial postface derives from middle antiquity. The precedent is Qu Yuan's classic "Li sao"; its first section narrates his clan [origins], then below enumerates his grandfather and father. First [he] narrates his birth and then provides his name and appellative. The emerging traces of the authorial preface in truth take this as the foundation.[1]

> 蓋作者自敘, 其流出於中古乎. 案屈原離騷經, 其首章上陳氏族, 下列祖考. 先述厥生, 次顯名字. 自敘發跡, 實基於此.

It is interesting that Liu Zhiji connects the genre of the postface—arguably a footnote in the history of Chinese literature—with the core of Chinese literary tradition by citing a canonical work long regarded as an autobiographical poem as the progenitor of this minor literary form. Different expectations for the level of self-disclosure appropriate for each genre temper the claim that Qu Yuan's epic lament may have initially inspired the form and function of the authorial postface. While Qu Yuan may have provided a model for brevity in genealogy and the circumstances of one's birth, Liu stops short of suggesting that the postface should imitate the dramatic self-expression of "Li sao."

The tradition that Qu Yuan wrote "Li sao" as a scholarly lament may have contributed to the development of the postface in a more oblique fashion by providing Qin and Han authors with the first true authorial persona that was suitable for imitation. Prior to the Qu Yuan tradition, authorship was relatively anonymous; even eponymous works such as the *Zhuangzi* were largely the work of disciples and editors. But, as Mark Edward Lewis argues, Sima Qian's establishment of Qu Yuan as the author of "Li sao" was a crucial step toward the invention of authorship during the Han period.[2] In Lewis's view, the biographical details of any subject become critical to retelling the life precisely because the life of the subject attains added dimension to future generations. Qu Yuan became a model for later scholar-officials as the archetypal scholar in exile, and the details of his life took on symbolic importance for later generations of failed scholar-officials and political exiles.[3]

In this regard Liu Zhiji is probably correct to cite "Li sao" as the oldest example of an autobiographical impulse in canonical literature. But if Qu Yuan epitomized the author who was possessed by the need to explain his life and work, the beginnings of the formal features of the authorial postface probably lie with authors from the Qin and early Han period such as Sima Xiangru and Sima Qian.

> Later was Sima Xiangru, the first to use the authorial postface as a biography, so that which he narrated was a record of his youth up to his maturity, establishing [a record of] his own conduct and service and nothing else. With regard to the origins of his ancestors, this is omitted and we hear nothing. Coming to Sima Qian, in addition to recalling the story of [Qu Yuan], he imitated the recent works of [Sima Xiangru], and, taking as a model these two writers, he rolled them into one [i.e., he embodied them both].[4]

降及司馬相如，始以自敘爲傳，然其所敘者，但記自少及長，立身行事而已．逮於祖先所出，則蔑爾無聞．至馬遷又徵三閭之故事，放文園之近作，模楷二家，勒成一卷．

Although the content of Sima Xiangru's postface is largely unknown, early Han era texts are probably a more realistic precedent for the genre than Warring States poetry. According to Liu Zhiji, Sima Xiangru's postface, unfortunately no longer extant, is the first example of the genre as an autobiographical work in its later, more recognizable form, that is, in imitation of the form of historical biography. Chief among the similarities seems to be an emphasis on creating a clear record of public conduct and official life, which by the early Tang period was the narrative style of historiography most conducive to creating the impression of an exemplary "type" of biography. In one sense, an official biography was the dissolution of the individual into the historical record; it was not meant to be a "complete" telling of an individual life but the placement of that life into a larger historical frame. This kind of orthodox, historical account stood in contrast to the interiority of Augustinian autobiography cast over and against historical contingency.[5] Liu regards Sima Xiangru's text as a record of his public conduct and "nothing else," an indication of its similarity to the ideal narrative style of late medieval historiography.

According to Liu Zhiji, Sima Qian's *Taishigong zixu* marked a new development in the genre by combining Qu Yuan's family genealogy with Sima Xiangru's account of his youth, maturity, and conduct. Liu seems to be following Sima Qian's authorial account to some extent, as the Han historian was the first to link his own writing to that of authors such as Qu Yuan. Sima Qian based his comparison on the observation that there was some continuity between his life and that of Qu Yuan, and he also named Confucius, Sunzi 孫子, and Lü Buwei 呂不韋, among others, as antecedents to his experience. In this sense, Sima Qian's life narrative follows the narratives of an exemplary stock type of his own creation, that of the protagonist who turns failure into tragedy by virtue of his good character. Character was the central theme of many of Sima Qian's biographies and was often the foundation of his historical judgments.[6]

For Sima Qian, similarity between the works of the poet and the historian in terms of formal features does not appear to be an issue; only the character of the author matters. In contrast, Liu Zhiji's comparison seems focused on the fact that both Sima Qian and Qu Yuan make similar declarations of their quasi-mythical ancestry, their births, and account for their official offices rather than any supposed similarity between the biographies of the two authors. Beyond this, the works could not be more different.[7] Whether or not the author of "Li sao" intended the opening lines as a preface to the rest of the poem is obviously a matter of interpretation, but Liu Zhiji seems to be suggesting at minimum that "Li sao" was among the earliest known models for authors who chose to introduce a life work through recourse to autobiography.

In any event, the subgenre seems to have matured with Sima Qian, whose fusion of genealogy and biography became the standard for the authorial postface. Liu Zhiji writes, "Thereupon Yang Xiong followed [Sima Qian's] wagon ruts, and Ban Gu ladled from his abundant wave. Indeed, [authorial postfaces] proliferated during this time. Although there were changes of style and language, the essential features remained unchanged" 於是揚雄遵其舊轍, 班固酌其餘波. 自敘之篇實煩於代. 雖屬辭有異而茲體無易.[8] Insofar as Liu Zhiji refers here to the basic narrative of such texts, he is essentially correct. Both Yang Xiong and Ban Gu use their postfaces to describe their ancestry, provide a brief account of their early years, include literary works such as rhapsodies, briefly describe their professional careers, and finally introduce the work to which the postface is appended.[9] Ban Gu wrote his "Postface" in two parts, with the second half almost entirely devoted to introducing *Han shu*. However, Liu is correct in pointing out that stylistically the two texts are quite different from their predecessor and are more similar to one another. Yang Xiong and Ban Gu replace the tragic protagonist of Sima Qian's narrative, weeping at the deathbed of his father, with a terse narrative that reveals very little of the subject's biography. Ban Gu's authorial account is remarkable in this regard as it devotes less than a few dozen characters to an account of his birth and early years.[10]

This reticent narrative style reveals an altogether different type of protagonist, that of the scholarly gentleman for whom it is impolite and at times impolitic to reveal too much of oneself. Humility may be regarded as a necessary pose for this exemplary stock type. Insofar as the postfaces of Yang Xiong and Ban Gu are otherwise concerned with demonstrating the good lineage, literary achievements, and official accomplishments of their subjects, they demonstrate little in the way of humility. Instead, the image of each author is revealed through descriptions of familial bonds and official conduct, as well as more typical forms of self-expression such as rhapsodies that speak obliquely to the character of the subject. Unlike Sima Qian, both authors avoid writing narratives with a transparently subjective point of view, which only adds to the reticent quality of each work. Given the influence of canonical Confucian works on both of these authors, this stock type may be said to have been inspired by models from the Confucian textual tradition.[11] Even in Sima Qian's authorial postface we may observe how the author's reliance on exemplars of the past leads to a life narrative of apparent terseness when judged by the standards of modern and postmodern autobiography.[12]

The stock type of the reticent and humble Confucian gentleman no doubt gained even more traction among early Tang historiographers, and it clearly found a sympathetic reader in Liu Zhiji, who regarded Yang Xiong and Ban Gu as exemplary authors of the authorial postface form. The impersonality of this kind self-expression appealed to later historians by providing the raw material for historical narratives that emphasized moral principle over illuminating the distinguishing characteristics of individuals. Indeed, by the Tang period such autobiographical writing had made its way into the hands of the historian through the efforts of the family and friends of the deceased. Immediate relatives or intimate confidantes of the deceased wrote "Accounts of Conduct," conceived as a posthumous report or extended curriculum vitae for the dead official. The writers of such accounts took great care in their composition, as favorable reports could result in a posthumous promotion or designation.[13] Hence the material was not simply a matter of record but represented an important document for the living friends and family. The accounts reflected the concerns of the living as well as the legacy of the dead because, quite simply, they were the same. Because of this, the temptation always existed to embellish such accounts and epitaphs with conventional fictitious incidents and actions designed to show the deceased as a role model. These social tropes played a role similar to that of most cautionary images in biography and probably were interchangeable and highly predictable from subject to subject.

Thus impersonality or reticence, if it ever existed as a feature of historical writing, was not solely the product of the didactic aims of the historian. These extremely formulaic passages were designed to link the deceased to older standards of conduct or public virtue rather than to provide merely a factually accurate account of the deceased.[14] From the point of view of Tang historiography, documents left behind as self-expression were often written with an eye toward this form of dogmatic historiography, and to some degree they support Wu Pei-yi's lament that Chinese autobiography, constrained by historiography and social taboos against writing the self, concealed more than it revealed.[15] Instead Wu argues that in Chinese literature authors more commonly used poetry or painting to express the inner, subjective experience that is typically associated with autobiography.[16]

From the perspective of the historian, because the subject's life served the ideological function of illustrating moral principles, the events of that life acquired a predictable and interchangeable quality.[17] Historians meant for biography to provide future generations with a mirror for their own actions, a model with which to confront their daily lives.[18] The imagery of the biography was in some ways without a specific context, in essence a mold for biographical details, and was readily available for reflection and use in any historical context within that tradition. In other words, the pedagogical aspects of biography as a mode of historical discourse marginalized the personality of the subject, rendering the actual, historical person peripheral to the telling of the biography. It is for this reason that impersonality of tone and an emphasis on political or other exterior qualities became central to retelling the subject.[19] Wu Pei-yi believes that during this process, biography acquired many of the distinguishing characteristics of classical historical narrative, particularly "the reticence and impersonality of Chinese historical discourse."[20]

Liu Zhiji's criticism of Ge Hong and several of his predecessors makes it clear that his expectations for the postface as a self-written biography were shaped in part by this model of dogmatic historical writing. The question of whether or not an authorial postface constitutes an accurate record is largely answered by the presentation of the subject in moral terms. In Liu's view, the portrayal of the subject's conduct should focus primarily on representing one's actions in ethical terms.

> Nevertheless, as for the principle of the authorial postface, only if it is able to conceal one's faults, and praise their strengths, then the words are not in error and it constitutes a true record. But Xiangru's authorial postface records his wandering as a guest in Ling Chong and his seduction of a woman from the Zhuo family, and so he took that which is taboo in *Chunqiu* [Spring and Autumn Annals] and advances it as lovely chit-chat. [21]

> 然自敘之爲義也，苟能隱己之短，稱其所長，斯言不謬，即爲實錄. 而相如自敘, 乃記其客游臨邛, 竊妻卓氏, 以春秋所諱, 持爲美談.

It seems evident from this critique of Sima Xiangru that writing an authorial postface is an act of concealment to a significant degree. At issue here is the question of what constitutes a truthful self-account, which Liu interprets as an admixture of orthodoxy and morality. This is considerably different from the parameters established by the Augustinian tradition, in which truth is not only an issue of verisimilitude but also one of correspondence to what may be called an "objective" notion of reality. This is also a strong rejection of Guo Dengfeng's confessional model of early Chinese autobiographical writing. Deng is essentially correct to argue that autobiographical texts had as part of their purpose the intention of providing future readers with a model of conduct by which they might confront their own lives; such a view of autobiographical writing parallels well-accepted notions of historical biography and appears to have been one possible interpretive strategy. But Deng's idea that authors sought to become models to future readers by recounting their own mistakes is substantially different from Liu Zhiji's view that such mistakes should be concealed. Here Liu seems to be saying that omitting lapses of judgment or conduct may be considered part of a true record so long as such omissions promote a sense of propriety. He continues, "[I]n affairs there may be some that are not false but a principle cannot be extracted [from them]. How could it not be shameful to record them in a biography?" 雖事或非虛, 而理無可取. 載之於傳, 不其愧乎?[22] The truth in this regard is not constituted of the facts themselves but rather in the appropriateness of their presentation.

The principle of omission also applies to accounts of family and distant ancestors, whose lives should be recorded only in the spirit of filial piety. In this regard Liu censures only Wang Chong, whose disparaging account of his family surely stands as the pinnacle example of filial impropriety from early China. According to Wang Chong's postface, he possessed a penetrating intelligence and the "will of a great man" from an early age, which was all the more remarkable for the fact that his family's lineage was characterized by violence, crime, and feuds with their neighbors. [23] Liu Zhiji writes:

> Now if one discusses his family within an authorial postface, certainly [the author] must take as central acclaiming his name and glorifying one's parents, and if there is no one [deserving of praise] then this part may be omitted. Going so far as to greatly extol oneself but widely disparage one's ancestors, how is this different from bearing witness against one's father for stealing a sheep,[24] or imitating the son who called out the name of his mother.[25] [Wang Chong] must be censured according to Confucian moral teaching [mingjiao] and is truly a criminal deserving [death].[26]

> 夫自敍而言家世，固當以揚名顯親爲主，苟無其人，闕之可也．
> 至若盛矜於己，而厚辱其先，此何異證父攘羊，學子名母？ 必
> 責以名教，實三千之罪人也．

The link between extolling the favorable points of one's ancestors and the cardinal virtue of filial piety seems obvious, and here again adherence to moral principle outweighs any obligation that the author should create a factually accurate account. Indeed, we may observe again that what constitutes verisimilitude is exactly that which corresponds to moral principle. A filial account of one's ancestors would serve to strengthen the author's self-presentation in paradigmatic terms insofar as ancestral presentation is assumed by Liu to be a key component of the authorial postface when it is wedded to the orthodoxy of filial piety. But rather than malign the memory of one's ancestors by recording their shortcomings, Liu prefers that the author omit the ancestral account altogether.

Liu Zhiji accompanies this emphasis on filial piety with an appeal for the qualities of reticence and humility, made specific through the example of Confucius. According to Liu, the self-description of the postface should be couched in modest and obfuscated language so as to avoid the appearance of self-promotion, making the soaring self-congratulation of Qu Yuan's "Li sao" unavailable to the author of the postface.

Now when the sages set forth their words, at times they also demonstrate their own talents. Sometimes [they do this] by relying on indirection to show their feelings or [they] select artful words and reveal their tracks. But they never pose and brag of themselves or stir up public talk. Moreover when [Confucius] commanded his disciples [by saying] "Each [of you] speak to your own ambition," Zi Lu was not modest and was criticized by Confucius for impropriety.[27]

則聖達之立言也, 時亦揚露己才, 或托諷以見其情, 或選辭以顯
其跡, 終不盱衡自伐, 攘袂公言. 且命諸門人"各言爾志," 由也
不讓, 見哂無禮.

By resorting to indirection and artful language, an author should convey himself through his work without lapsing into subjective self-expression or self-evaluation. While the conventions of poetic self-expression, however obscure, provided the means for promoting the character and virtues of the author, Liu Zhiji suggests that such language was not among the acceptable conventions of prose during the early Tang unless cast in the most reticent terms. Stephen Owen concurs, arguing that verse was the "privileged document of inner life" and, moreover, it was in verse and rhapsody that a person might hope to "be known at all or make himself known." Owen writes, "By its very definition, *shih* [verse] was the stuff of inner life, the person's *chih* 志, 'intent,' and *ch'ing* 情, 'emotions' or 'subjective disposition.'"[28] Based on the example of Zi Lu, Liu seemed to understand the postface in terms of *zhi*, intention, rather than *qing*, subjective disposition.

The idea that a person's interior life is comprised of distinct, nameable components is hardly surprising considering that medical theory had long divided and subdivided the anatomical system, including its more metaphysical or immaterial aspects. Donald Munro, citing *Mengzi* 孟子 (Mencius) (II.I.2/9, 10), describes *zhi* as the "active aspect of the mind"; it is that which mediates the mind 心 and the *qi* 氣, the material of the body, ensuring no violence is done either to the *qi* or to the mind.[29] In the context of Mencius, *zhi* seems to be related to qualities of self-control; the *zhi* seems to govern the *qi*, but both seem subsequent to the mind. In Liu we see the development of this concept into something more than either self-control or casual wishes but as a tendency toward action that reveals something of our character. His view of the postface implies that the author expressed intention (*zhi*) but not the self (*zi* 自 or *ji* 己 when the object of a verb), which was not an indivisible category but rather the sum of several components. Thus, paradoxically, although the reticence of orthodox discourse was self-negating in the modern sense of the term, it would not have been considered so in an intellectual environment in which a modern notion of self was never posited. Rather, we must see that the issue of self-expression is bound to the author's *zhi* or intention.

Liu condemns several later writers of autobiography, among them Cao Pi and Ge Hong, for giving free reign to their intention and twisting the postface into a document of self-promotion, thereby committing the sin of immodesty.

> When we come to the likes of Emperor Wen of Wei [Cao Pi], Fu Xuan [217–78],[30] Tao Mei,[31] and Ge Hong,[32] then they go even further than those [before, such as Yang Xiong]. How is that? If they themselves possessed the slightest goodness or in their actions had some minute talent, in all cases [these things] will be analyzed and comprehensively discussed, and they were sure to record a few such things. How can this be taken as one who models the previous sages or humbly governs himself?[33]

> 至魏文帝, 傅玄, 陶梅, 葛洪之徒, 則又逾於此者矣. 何則？身兼片善, 行有微能, 皆剖析具言, 一二必載. 豈所爲憲前聖, 謙以自牧者歟？

The criticism certainly seems fair for an individual of Ge Hong's position. Rare was the minister who spoke at length without couching his words in appropriate levels of false humility. Probably written after Cao Pi had been designated Cao Cao's 曹操 (155–220) heir, Cao Pi's text is traditionally considered to have been the postface of the *Dian lun*, although his itemization of a collection of his writing that included rhapsodies, essays, monographs, and verse raises the possibility that it may have initially introduced a more diverse anthology. That Liu Zhiji levels the same criticism at an emperor as he does a lowly official suggests the strength of the convention of modesty in prose by the early Tang period.

Much of Cao Pi's immodesty stems from a clear pride in his martial prowess, which his father began to develop in him at an early age. He explains that this was simply a result of his circumstances, for he often accompanied his father on campaigns even as a young boy and so learned horseback riding, mounted archery, and other skills befitting the son of a famous general. However, his skill was evidently not that of a gentleman, for whom archery and horseback riding were activities of friendly and humble competition.[34]

> Sometime afterward, the army went south on a campaign, encamping at Quli; Commander Secretary Xun Yu [163–212] was acting under orders to reward the troops.[35] He saw me, and at the end of our discussion Yu said, "I

have heard that you are able to shoot a bow either left- or right-handed; this is truly a rare talent." I said, "Has your honor heard of [a mounted archer in such harmony with his horse that horse and rider look up and down at the targets in perfect accord]?" Yu laughed merrily and said, "Is that so!" I said, "The field [for archery practice] has a fixed track and the target has a fixed position; even if one were to hit the target every time, this is not the utmost in skill. Now, as for riding across the plains, plunging into thick grass, chasing crafty beasts, leading swift birds, not wasting a single shot, and hitting the mark each time, this can be called skillful." [36] At that time the army libationer, Zhang Jing,[37] was sitting in attendance, and looking back at Yu he clapped his hands saying, "Excellent!" [38]

後軍南征次曲蠡，尚書令荀彧奉使犒軍，見余談論之末，或言：
"聞君善左右射，此實難能." 余言："執事未睹夫項發口縱，俯馬
蹄而仰月支也." 或喜笑曰："乃爾!" 余曰："埒有常徑,的有常所,
雖每發輒中. 非至妙也. 若馳平原,赴豐草,要狡獸,截輕禽,使
弓不虛彎. 所中必洞. 斯則妙矣." 時軍祭酒張京在坐，顧彧拊
手曰 "善."

The vivid image" of practical skill and experiential knowledge stands in striking contrast to the predictable ritual decorum of the archery field.[39] The anecdote not only expounds on the theme of Cao Pi's martial skills, but it also distances him from the expectation of humility and gracious competition that characterized archery as a gentleman's game and sets his skill apart from that of the scholar-official.

At other times Cao is even less oblique regarding his skill at arms, freely comparing himself favorably to other individuals. In one amusing anecdote he describes how he once settled a debate over proper technique with a long sword by humiliating an army officer with a reputation for swordplay.

Once I was drinking with Arbiter General Liu Xun, General Advancing Glory Deng Zhan, and a few others.[40] I had long heard that Zhan had powerful arms and had mastered the Five Weapons. It was also said that he could defeat an armed opponent with his empty hands. He and I discussed swordsmanship for quite a while, and I told him, "Your technique is wrong. I used to be fond of your technique, then I learned a better art." Then he asked to spar with me. At the time we were all very drunk and eating sugarcane, so we used the sugarcane as swords and descending from the hall we sparred for several rounds. Three times I hit him on his arm and everybody laughed. Zhan would not concede and asked to spar again. I told him, "My technique emphasizes speed, and it would have been improper to strike your face;

therefore I have simply struck your arms." Zhan said, "I still want to have another round." I knew he wanted to dash forward and strike my chest, and therefore I feigned an advance. As I predicted, he attempted to rush forward, and I stepped back and hit him square on the forehead.[41] Everyone there was startled to see this. I returned to my seat, laughing, and said, "Formerly Yang Qing [fl. 180 BCE] instructed Chunyu Yi [fl. 180 BCE] to abandon his old method and taught him with an esoteric technique.[42] Now I also wish General Deng to disregard his old skill and accept the essential Way." The assembled guests made merry and were all pleased.[43]

嘗與平虜將軍劉勳, 奮威將軍鄧展等共飲, 宿聞展善有手臂, 曉五兵, 又稱其能空手入白刃. 余與論劍良久, 謂言 "將軍法非也, 余顧嘗好之, 又得善術." 因求與余對. 時酒酣耳熱, 方食芋蔗, 便以爲杖, 下殿數交, 三中其臂, 左右大笑. 展意不平, 求更爲之. 余言 "吾法急屬, 難相中面, 故齊臂耳." 展言 "願復一交," 余知其欲突以取交中也, 因僞深進, 展果尋前, 余卻腳鄭, 正截其顙, 坐中驚視. 余還坐, 笑曰: "昔陽慶使淳于意去其故方, 更授以祕術, 今余亦願鄧將軍捐棄故伎, 更受要道也." 一 坐 盡 歡.

Despite the unabashed bravado and egotism of the piece as a whole, it seems clear that Cao Pi was at least aware of the conventions of humility but, for a number of possible reasons, chose to ignore them. Following this anecdote, Cao explains how he became such an extraordinary swordsman by recalling the skills of his teachers. He begins by stating, "Now, in any matter, one should not boast of one's own strengths," indicating at least a passing nod toward the convention of humility, perhaps in deference to the teachers he is about to mention. However, the rest of the account takes a predictable turn as Cao describes the deadly skill he inherited from each of his teachers, writing, "In an earlier day, if one had encountered [Yuan] Min on a narrow path, a person would have had no chance against him" 先日若逢敏於狹路, 直決耳.[44] By extension, Cao Pi's skill was equally deadly and without equal.

By the end of the Han period, proscriptions to avoid self-promotion in prose may not have been so firmly entrenched among the literati that they could not be cast aside by the political and intellectual upheavals of the second and third centuries. The breakdown of central authority meant that local officials were increasingly selected on the basis of reputation and social connections rather than proficiency in the classical canon, and self-promotion may have played some role in this process. The accompanying intellectual fad of character evaluation certainly raised interest in the question of individual self-worth and may have led, in turn, to broader acceptance of acts of self-promotion, although as I argue below, this stopped short of endorsing individualism in any modern, Western sense of the word. Nevertheless, it is interesting that Liu Zhiji directs his admonition against the postface as a vehicle for self-promotion at authors from the Wei-Jin era.

Like Cao Pi, Ge Hong displays an awareness of some expectation of humility and reticence in self-presentation, but beyond a passing reference he chooses to set it aside in favor of extensive self-promotion. Ge Hong, by citing Cao Pi and Wang Chong among his predecessors, establishes his essay within a consciously selected tradition of authors who also seemed to favor modes of self-narrative that stressed extensive biographical detail and life history. He makes no explicit claim that he is engaged in a project to describe his life as it "actually" happened, and in one passage his criticism of his predecessor, Cao Pi, implies that an autobiographical record should conform to some standard of humility regardless of its verisimilitude to lived experience. The concern with the convention of humility, or with any fidelity between the text and lived experience, seems less important than Ge Hong's condemnation itself, which is fairly clichéd in tone.

> [I] read the autobiographical postface to the *Dian lun* of Emperor Wen of Wei, the end of which recounted topics such as chess and swordsmanship, for he had the intention to outline that which he knew, but [his claims] did not match reality.[45] The skills one learns while young, they cannot [be employed] to emptily praise one's good points, and so here I will speak of that with which I am unfamiliar.[46]

> 洪見魏文帝典論自敘, 末及彈棋擊劍之事, 有意於略說所知, 而實不數. 少所便能, 不可虛自稱揚, 今將具言, 所不閑焉.

Like Liu Zhiji after him, Ge Hong seems more concerned with the appropriateness of self-presentation than with the veracity of the account. What is at issue is not whether skills such as swordsmanship or chess constitute a veritable record of an individual life but whether they ought to be considered at all.

Yet, despite Ge Hong's criticism of Cao Pi's unabashed egotism, we might say that he compounds the error by repeating it and reveals his criticism to be more literary posturing than genuine concern for the conventions of modesty. For example, the list of activities with which Ge Hong claims to be unfamiliar is nothing more than a list of activities he judged to be vices indulged in by those of low character.

[I] never engaged in cockfighting or racing dogs and horses. Seeing people gambling, I would not look on and ogle, but if someone compelled me and dragged me to come watch, still I could not get interested and felt that [this activity] was like sleeping in the daytime.[47] For this reason down to the present day I still do not know how many lines are on a chessboard, or the name of the dice used in *shupu*.[48]

未曾鬥雞鶩走狗馬. 見人博戲, 了不目眩, 或強牽引觀之, 殊不入神, 有若 晝睡. 是以至今不知棋局上有幾道, 樗蒲齒名.

Here every alleged defect of character is in fact a virtue, as exemplified by the reference to *Lunyu* 論語 (Analects) 5.9, in which Confucius criticizes Zai Yu 宰予 for sleeping in the daytime. By Ge Hong's era, the observation that lofty virtue in a world of bad character was a fatal flaw had become a common cliché and had roots in classical verse such as Qu Yuan's "Li sao." Like much of Ge Hong's self-description, the passage above bears a strong resemblance to Ji Kang's 稽康 (223–62) letter "Breaking off Relations with Shan Tao" 與山巨源絕交書 in which Ji Kang lists among his supposed defects his inability to flatter high officials.[49]

As we have seen, such expressions of individual virtue were more commonplace in poetry, which was considered the appropriate venue for authorial self-disclosure. Indeed, by Ge Hong's era it had become commonplace for poets to describe difficult circumstances or ostensible deficiencies in order to allude to other upstanding character traits.[50] Ge Hong seems to have preferred prose as a medium of self-description or self-promotion for, despite producing a fair amount of poetry when young, it seems that he was little interested in poetry as a genre. His attitude may reflect a distaste for the popularity of abstract or metaphysical poetry during the Jin period, but it also echoes Yang Xiong's opinion that *fu* and verse were a young man's pursuits and not worthy of a serious scholar.[51] In *Waipian* 32, "Extolling Broad Learning" 尚博, Ge Hong writes, "Some value and love the shallow and detailed writing of poetry and rhyme prose, and disregard and despise the deep beauty and rich breadth of philosophical writing, and consider words that cut to the heart of the matter as foolish and stupid, and take the vacuous elegance of petty argumentation as refined and skillful" 或貴愛詩賦淺近之細文, 忽薄深美副博之子書, 以磋切之至言爲騃拙, 以虛華之小辯爲妍巧.[52] Ge Hong compares the relative virtues of the two genres several times and consistently advocates the superiority of prose in terms of both style and content.[53]

His general disapproval of verse—or what it had become during his era—helps explain his prolific output of essays and biographies and may also explain his willingness to take more liberties for self-expression in prose. At times Ge Hong is far bolder in his self-promotion, echoing the tone of Cao Pi in a description of his military prowess during Shi Bing's 石冰 rebellion in 303 CE.

> Formerly while in military service, I once shot with a bow at a pursuing cavalryman. The bowstring came back, and the arrow shot forth. I killed two of the enemy and a horse, and thus escaped death. I was also trained to use a saber and shield, a single saber, and double halberds, all of which employed formulas in their art; for employing surprise on a selected target, I had an esoteric technique, and my skill was uncanny. If this technique was employed against someone unsuspecting, then you could achieve total victory, and nothing would stand in your way.[54]

> 昔軍旅, 曾手射追騎, 應弦而到, 殺二賦一馬, 遂以得免死. 又曾受刀楯及單刀雙戟, 皆口訣要術, 以待取人, 乃有秘法, 其巧入神. 若以此道與不曉便可以當全獨膀, 所向無前矣.

The passage recalls Cao Pi's description of his teacher, Yuan Min, a resident of the state of Chen 陳, whose skill was also considered "uncanny" 神.[55]

Whether the unabashed self-promotion of Cao Pi and Ge Hong are the exceptions that prove the rule of reticence and humility or an example of the distance between literary theory and practice is a question that may be impossible to answer. At minimum we might say that verse and rhapsody had long been seen as a genre that, by definition, implied self-expression, while humility and reticence were qualities that were generally expected in prose biography. Liu Zhiji's criticism of Ge Hong's detailed, almost Augustinian approach to his authorial preface claims that the narrative is bound to the intention of the author and was neither self-expression as such or symptomatic of an emerging notion of "individuality" or "self" during the early medieval period that conveniently matches Western notions of autobiography. As I argued at the beginning of the chapter, in modern, conventional terms, the modesty of speech and extreme reticence expected by Liu Zhiji almost demands self-negation. According to Liu, the conventions of prose self-narrative allow an author to omit the need for an Augustinian "self" narrative, which thus explains his inclusion of Ban Gu's family history, Yang Xiong's exposition of his rhyme prose, and—perhaps the most startling—the first few lines of "Li sao" in a single genre.

The abbreviated autobiographical sketches of Ban Gu and Yang Xiong, along with Liu Zhiji's critique of Cao Pi and Ge Hong, suggest a kind of self-conception that was deeply embedded within the different contexts of family lineage, political life, and textual production. Rather than a full picture of an individual life, we are left with the fading impression of an individual that practically disappears into a web of interdependencies and contexts. As we might observe in Guo Dengfeng's exclusion of Ban Gu's postface by arguing that it is simply family history, in the eyes of early Chinese critics the self of the postface is almost postmodern in its diffusion. It is no surprise, then, that in fashioning his ample self-narrative Ge Hong would find few precedents beyond Wang Chong and Cao Pi. Modern readers of early Chinese autobiographies are simply repeating Ge Hong's sense of the postface as including only those texts that disclose a substantial biography of an individual subject. However, we must bear in mind that most authors of the postface before Ge Hong failed to address the self as the subject of autobiographical writing, having been primarily concerned with accounting for the creation of other literary works or a family lineage. As we shall see in chapter 3, even within the most substantial, autobiographical self-narratives, biographical features still submerged the subject within textual traditions, cultural expectations, and literary conventions.

The Vanishing Subject: Literary Subjectivity in Early Medieval China

Before moving on to consider Ge Hong's self-narrative and those of his predecessors in detail, I would like to examine the meaning of self-disclosure within literati society. Cao Pi and Ge Hong did, after all, write during the Wei-Jin era (ca. 220–420), a period often seen as a hotbed of unprecedented individualism that drew a sharp dichotomy between the individual and society. Radically antisocial behavior that violated the ritual norms of elite society was common among some social elites. As with autobiography, many modern scholars have judged these actions to be expressions of a unique identity rather than viewing the values of individuality and uniqueness as modern concerns. Modern ideas of subjectivity are superimposed onto the rhetorical patterns of the early Chinese textual tradition.

This idea of subjective identity is sometimes reinforced by a tendency to bifurcate Chinese philosophy into distinct sectarian traditions of a Confucian social philosophy that stands opposed to a Daoist-Buddhist philosophy of individual transcendence. For example, in a chapter entitled "The Romantic Literature of Individualism" 個人主義的浪漫文學 from his *Wei-Jin sixiang lun* 魏晉思想論 (Discussions of Wei-Jin Thought), Liu Dajie 劉大杰 establishes a strong dichotomy between the individual and society in the opening paragraph. Moreover, Liu states that the "individualist" literature he surveys was heavily influenced by Buddhism and Daoism and consequently "departed from real social norms and fully expresses a kind of transcendent romanticism."[56] Ying-shih Yü, though wary of using categories such as individualism in the study of early China, ironically embraces a definition of the term during the Wei-Jin era that creates a sharp distinction between "collectivism" and "individualism" or between society and the individual.[57] Both authors seem to suggest a belief within Wei-Jin elite culture in an autonomous, private self that could function separate from society. But this formulation of the individual naturally tends to exclude or render unintelligible modes of self-portrayal that emphasize social, political, or familial dependencies at the expense of a seemingly autonomous, individual identity. However, I believe strategies of self-identification in early China support reading more reticent texts as autobiography and also raise the question of whether more revealing self-narratives, such as those of Ge Hong or Cao Pi, even reflect a cultural value of an autonomous self.

Because of the dramatic breakdown of traditional Han social structure, the growing popularity of Buddhism and Daoism, and flourishing intellectual trends that reinforced eccentric behavior among the scholar-official class, scholarly interest in the subject of individuality in early China tends to focus on the Wei-Jin era. Foreign invasion, civil war, and court factionalism accompanied by violent purges forced many members of the scholarly elite out of public life and into a premature and unsatisfying life of retirement. Scholars who might otherwise have enjoyed positions in the imperial administration often embraced the role of the hermit, long established in the Confucian textual tradition but embellished with the new vocabulary of worldly transcendence borrowed from Buddhism and Daoism. Moreover, debates by participants of "Pure Conversation" 清談 over the relationship between "Naturalism" 自然 and "Ethical Teaching" 名教, and the relationship between being 有 and nonbeing 無, inspired modes of behavior that redefined social norms and conduct.[58] In particular, proponents of *xuan xue* 玄學 ("abstruse learning" or perhaps "metaphysics") advocated the expression of one's spontaneous inner nature, which, arising from nonbeing, expressed itself through being. Being became associated with traditional, canonical Confucian public etiquette, social roles, and social hierarchy and was the chief concern of so-called ethical teaching, while Daoism (and later Buddhism) were associated with the state of nonbeing out of which arose one's natural self or spontaneous nature.[59] The distinction between the two groups was extremely fine and often only discernible in philosophical terms or between the discussants themselves. Moreover, the philosophical positions of the two groups changed over time in ways that underline the instability of either as a fully articulated school of thought.[60] For example, those who advocated naturalism accepted the importance of the proper correlation between an empirical object and its designation, but they stressed the importance of expression of the spontaneous nature in every being without which a proper designation could not be properly decided.[61] Because the spontaneous nature of two individuals would not be identical, the metaphysicians identified with abstruse learning advocated modes of self-expression that would express the unique qualities of spontaneous being.[62] Using another term from the period, we can say that Wei-Jin era scholars emphasized *shen* 神, or "spirit," as the totality of individual personality through which one demonstrates inner quality in tangible manifestations such as behavior.[63]

The outward manifestation of an individual's inner nature is the theme of *Shishuo xinyu* 世說新語 (A New Account of Tales of the World), written—though more likely edited—by the Liu-Song 劉宋 (420–79) dynasty author Liu Yiqing 劉義慶 (403–44).[64] *Shishuo xinyu* is an anthology of brief anecdotes about individuals from the Wei-Jin period; these anecdotes are largely concerned with how an individual's character and virtue could be expressed in behavior and conversation. Some of the issues surrounding being and nonbeing, inner character, and its outward expression in outward behavior can be summarized with the following anecdote.

> When Ruan Ji [阮籍, 210–63] was mourning for his mother, Pei Kai [裴楷, 237–91] went to pay him a visit of condolence. Ruan was drunk at the time and sitting with disheveled hair, his legs sprawled apart, not weeping. When Pei arrived he put down a mat for himself on the floor, and after his weeping and words of condolence were completed, he departed. Someone asked Pei, "Generally when one offers condolences, the host weeps and the guest simply pays his respects. Since Ruan was not weeping, why did you weep?" Pei replied, "Ruan is a man beyond the realm of ordinary morality and therefore pays no homage to the rules of propriety. People like you and me are still within the realm of custom, so we live our lives after the pattern set by etiquette." His contemporaries all sighed in admiration over the way both men had found their true center.[65]

> 阮步兵喪母, 裴令公往弔之. 阮方醉, 散髮坐床, 箕踞不哭. 裴至, 下席於地, 哭弔唁畢, 便去. 或問裴: "凡弔, 主人哭, 客乃爲禮. 阮既不哭, 君何哭?" 裴曰: "阮方外之人, 故不崇禮制; 我輩俗中人, 故以儀軌自居." 時人歎爲兩得其中.

Ruan Ji, an exemplar of Wei-Jin naturalism, is not bound by social etiquette, which lies within the "realm of ordinary morality." His "true center," which proceeds from nonbeing, must find its natural expression, in this case through unseemly behavior that defies social convention.[66] His behavior, as an expression of his natural self, not only lies beyond the realm of ordinary morality, but also beyond that of conventional public opinion; Ruan's behavior is an individual expression of his unique nature and must be judged in terms of its success as such. However, although Pei Kai and his interlocutors are bound by the morality rejected by Ruan, Pei Kai in turn adheres to social conventions as an expression of his own inner nature. Here Pei Kai's ritual conformity is also a form of naturalism. Furthermore, his statement places him in a moral hierarchy in which unfettered naturalism possesses the most moral currency. Pei Kai places himself below Ruan Ji but above his fellow ritual conformists. Although the anecdote—and the rest of the chapter—seems biased toward the unconventional naturalism of Ruan Ji, the idea expressed here that all behavior must ultimately express a natural self implies that both men are laudable for the depth of their self-knowledge and their ability to express themselves in terms of their "true centers."

As shown in this anecdote, character was almost always comparative and superiority of one individual over another was established through a dialogic approach by pitting two character types against each other. Even if the goal was to express one's unique character, the act of expression was hardly the battle cry of autonomy and individuality but proceeded from recognizable, shared conventions. In other words, character appraisal was carried out through an appeal to other individuals.[67] This form of character evaluation had some basis in contemporary political culture. In his *Hou Han shu* 後漢書 (History of the Later Han), Fan Ye 范曄 (398–445) writes that the emperor "entrusted the state's destiny to the eunuchs, with whom scholars felt ashamed to associate. Therefore commoners protested with anger, and private scholars criticized [the government] without fear. They exalted their own reputations, appraising and upholding on another" while criticizing others.[68] The identity of a political faction was composed of individuals who required the same characteristics, and the faction as a whole thus required favorable comparisons of virtues that would contrast with those of their political opponents. Moreover, unique behavior became one way to attract the partisan attention of certain factions. Cao Cao, first ruler of the Wei, was widely reputed to select men based on reputation and talent rather than erudition in the classics. Fierce competition among the gentry to distinguish themselves thus nurtured the trend of "individuality" in a political world in which old standards of evaluation had lost their importance.

As the terms of comparison grew more abstract, the avenues of self-expression continued to expand. In *Shishuo xinyu* we read:

> Zu Shishao loved money; Ruan Yaoji loved wooden clogs. Both men pursued their obsessions, yet both were equally burdened by their labors, so that it was never settled who was superior and who was inferior. Once someone went to visit Zu and found him counting his money. When the guest arrived, the process of storing the cash had not been completed, so there still remained two small bamboo chests tucked away behind him. [While the guest was there,] he tilted his body to conceal them, and his mind was not at ease. Someone went to visit Ruan and saw him personally blowing on the fire and waxing his clogs [to repair them]. Ruan sighed and exclaimed, "I would never have known that in one lifetime I would wear so many pairs of clogs!" His spirit and demeanor were leisurely and at ease. It was only after this that it could be determined who was greater than the other.[69]

祖士少好財, 阮遙集好屐, 並恆自經營, 同是一累, 而未判其得失. 人有詣祖, 見料視財物. 客至, 屏當未盡, 餘兩小簏箸背後, 傾身障之, 意未能平. 或有詣阮, 見自吹火蠟屐, 因歎曰: "未知一生當箸幾量屐?" 神色閑暢. 於是勝負始分.

This anecdote shows an increasingly "open-minded approach to knowing others and knowing the self . . . insisting upon the idea that each person can excel in his or her own way."[70] Ruan Yaoji's obsession with wooden sandals may seem at first glance like an odd entryway into the evaluation of his character. However, matching close pairs together, in this case two gentlemen obsessed with material objects, can achieve a comparison of character. Ying-shih Yü is correct that the basic assumption of Wei-Jin character evaluation was that character and ability differed from individual to individual. The point of character evaluation was to capture the essence of an individual's spirit, which could only be achieved through a process of comparison.[71]

However, it would be misleading to equate the above expressions of Wei-Jin "individualism" with a kind of freewheeling social freedom, as do Ying-shih Yü and Liu Dajie. In both of the anecdotes from *Shishuo xinyu*, individual evaluation and self-definition occur within a social setting using terms agreed on by a larger group. As Richard Mather states, people "were individualists only to the extent that they insisted on defending the inviolability of themselves as individual persons, and they refused to bend to political and social pressures to conform to shallow and meaningless regulations. But they were not radically challenging the basic values or the hierarchical structure of the society to which they belonged, with its built-in network of mutual obligation."[72] I would add that any expression of "spontaneous nature" that is subject to peer evaluation and must furthermore be defined vis-à-vis another individual also constitutes a kind of pressure to conform to a public standard no matter how unspecific. The very existence of peer evaluation implies that some models of self-expression were deemed "inauthentic" or otherwise unacceptable; moreover, the typology of character evident in both *Shishuo xinyu* and the earlier *Renwu zhi* 人物志 (Treatise on Human Abilities) by Liu Shao 劉邵 (fl. 220–50) implies that self-expression did follow precedents or evolving standards no matter how nebulous or broad. In the anecdote of Ruan Ji and Pei Kai, we see that the evaluator is also at pains to offer the correct evaluation of the subject. Ruan Ji's behavior is *performative*. It evokes a judgment from his peers based on the assumption made by all the parties involved—including Ruan Ji—that his character is intelligible through his actions. Pei Kai's judgment of Ruan Ji is also subject to public scrutiny. Both the evaluated and the evaluator fall under the gaze of public judgment in a reciprocal relationship of expression and evaluation.[73] Ruan Ji and Pei Kai establish their individual identity in terms of one another through different, socially significant expressions of their "authentic selves." The anecdote of the wooden clogs also supports the idea that one's individuality was a socially mediated quality during the Wei-Jin era. Here public opinion also finalizes the comparison between two individuals, Zu Shishao and Ruan Yaoji. The men are compared not by the objects of their obsessions but on their level of comportment when engaged in their passions. The quality of their characters is a matter of public discourse not the lone assertion of an autonomous individual or of the subjects of evaluation themselves. In this regard, the individual cannot exist without a social group from which an observer can differentiate him; nor can he exist without the public recognition of his individuality.[74]

The continuity between society and the individual observed in *Shishuo xinyu* implies a definition of individuality as a quality achieved within the arena of public judgment and social discourse. Such a definition stands in contrast to modern, Western notions of individuality as a quality, action, or state of being that lies beyond the purview of society. Both anecdotes demonstrate that one could be more or less successful in the expression of one's individuality. The authors of *Shishuo xinyu* seem to uphold the view that each individual is unique and has the potential to realize and express his or her uniqueness in life.[75] Clearly the degree to which one is worthy of respect depends on whether individuals fully express their unique character. Only with thorough self-knowledge could individuals accurately perform their inner character. This public performance of character had moral and political connotations, as a life that expressed the "authentic self" within the parameters of acceptable or known character types was laudable in the eyes of peers. In real terms, a positive character evaluation could lead to social and political rewards such as an official position or, at the very least, lead away from political dangers. Wei-Jin proponents of individualism saw the individual as a project that was revealed within a scheme of socially sanctioned archetypes.

This formulation of subjectivity allows us to see autobiography in early China as a self-narrative composed of meaningful, social-political terms and not the vacuum of autonomous experience. The ostensibly "free and unrestrained" self-expression of the Wei-Jin period anticipates Liu Zhiji's interest in didactic modes of self-narrative by measuring individuality in terms of public acclaim and the embodiment of socially meaningful standards of evaluation. We might say that here we see the kinds of ideological restraints that operated against the development of extensive, prose self-expression. Moreover, because the expectation for self-expression varied among literary genres, the quality of self-disclosure was often a product of literary convention rather than an interest in the individual as such. Such an approach to literary subjectivity frees us from the details of the biography by seeing them as tropes of self-expression rather than historical facts.

3

Hidden in Plain Sight
Creating "The Master Embracing Simplicity"

Ge Hong's explicit references to Wang Chong and Cao Pi suggest that he understood his own self-narrative in the postface to *Baopuzi Waipian* in terms of these earlier texts while at the same time adding new features to the genre from his own context in the Wei-Jin period. The postface to the *Waipian* is ostensibly an example of what some scholars term a circumstantial autobiography, which is an attempt at a transparent act of fidelity to the life of the subject. While the text does convey an enormous amount of biographical information, it also possesses many features that more literal readings fail to address such as instances in which the author's self-presentation exaggerates or contradicts historical and biographical detail. Ge Hong's autobiography is an example of a text that only becomes intelligible when read as what Olney would describe as a metaphor of the self, an interested self-presentation that relies on literary tropes and culturally significant archetypes. Rather than attempting to understand the text as a narrative in which strict verisimilitude to lived experience reveals the subject, we might say that self-definition occurs by referring to a defining community that functions as a "web of interlocution" among other selves.[1] Above all else, the text does not describe a subject whose lived experience constitutes the raw material for a claim of unique, individual identity.

Ge Hong's use of multiple archetypes and literary tropes to define his subjective identity implies that his narrative does not stand as an effort of individualistic self-representation as some might expect of a modern autobiography but instead must be seen as an attempt to map the subject onto preestablished narratives and typologies of character. Thus, although scholars of Chinese autobiography frequently cite Ge Hong's account as a precursor to modern autobiography, we must acknowledge that the individual subject of modern narrative is simultaneously present and not present; he or she is present insofar as we are able to read correctly the archetypes used by the author, but in terms of specific biographical detail we cannot see the ontologically real person we hope to find. The resulting narrative is a subjective identity created of a meaningful juxtaposition of cultural and literary tropes as Ge Hong prioritizes different modes of character. Instead of a personal life story recounting events as they might have actually occurred if seen from an omniscient perspective, Ge Hong combines images from previously established literature and weaves them into a coherent self-representation in order to convey the kind of self-image he believes is significant for his audience. While his selection of archetypes reveals much about who Ge Hong was and, perhaps more important, how he wanted to be perceived, it is nevertheless not a substantial statement of biographical or historical fact.

The use of historical precedents and cultural archetypes to create a meaningful literary persona or subjective identity was hardly an innovation of Ge Hong. As we have seen, historical and literary figures such as the doomed scholar-official Qu Yuan provided precedents for later writers of verse and rhapsody and inspired early authors of autobiographical texts such as Sima Qian by establishing a meaningful rhetoric of self-identity. Successful self-representation drew on both traditions of individual identity and other reference points such as familial bonds or other social ties. Ironically, this form of self-presentation often obscures the individual as a discrete object of knowledge and tends to defy modern notions of autobiography. Stephen Durrant notes of Sima Qian that "the most pervasive feature of [Sima's] autobiographical notes, is the degree to which the individual repeatedly disappears into the patterns of tradition. It is almost as if [Sima Qian] could not locate himself, could not even interpret his most intense experiences, outside a network of historical relationships and precedents."[2] We might say that Sima Qian lacked any alternative frame of reference for self-identification other than to locate himself within textual and familial traditions. This tendency is even more pronounced in the autobiographical works of Ban Gu and Yang Xiong, for whom subjective identity was intimately linked to familial ties and direct references to the author are limited to a mere handful of words.

This chapter is a close reading of Ge Hong's autobiography and is divided according to literary tropes. When possible I have followed closely the narrative of Ge Hong's text, beginning with his ancestry and early life and ending with his self-reflection on the nature of his scholarship. We shall see that Ge Hong aggressively employs a wide variety of cultural archetypes in his authorial self-presentation even more so than his predecessors, but it would be misleading to characterize the subjective identity created in his authorial postface as entirely derivative. Models of individual character such as the recusant official or hermit (*yimin* or *yinzhe*) possess qualities that reflect both tradition and Ge Hong's historical context. Other stock character types such as the philosopher (*zi* 子) or the martial hero (wu xia 武俠) existed in a more diffused form prior to Ge Hong, who attempted to codify them in more meaningful terms than had been previously attempted. In such instances, Ge Hong shows some innovation by pointing to recent exemplars such as

Wang Chong or Cao Pi—significantly by drawing on their autobiographical works—as well as more mainstream traditions such as that of Confucius. By combining all of these archetypes, Ge Hong is attempting to become more than simply the sum of several different images; he is trying to multiply the depth of his literary persona and create something new and unique. Indeed, we might say that not only do such exemplary models frequently conflict with historical or biographical details, but they also conflict with one another. Thus Ge Hong's literary persona and authorial self-presentation is not just another repetition of a standard pedigree or empty recasting of stereotypical qualities but the combination of disparate elements into a new kind of persona. Unlike modern expectations for autobiography, which assume an interested search for the self among the narrative details of lived experience, Ge Hong gives depth to his subjective identity through this combination of exemplary character types and archetypes rather than resorting to a detailed narrative of biographical or emotional truths. Indeed, he seems to reject a chronological narrative in favor of juxtaposing different archetypes at intervals within the text. While ultimately we may not be able to think of Ge Hong literally the way he presents himself, we can begin to understand both his context and his life by understanding that this is how he wanted to be seen and would like to have been remembered.

Southern Origins

It is nearly impossible to judge the veracity of Ge Hong's account of his early family history as found in the postface because details are few and mired in the literary and social conventions of the time.[3] Ge Hong claims that in ancient times a distant ancestor had controlled "all under Heaven," possibly a reference to Ge Tian 葛天, first mentioned in the chapter "Ancient Music" 古樂 in *Lüshi chunqiu* 呂氏春秋, (Annals of Lü Buwei) who, according to later sources such as Ban Gu's *Han shu*, was an ancient ruler or local lord, possibly during the pre-Zhou era.[4] According to Ge Hong, the descendents of Ge Tian became the rulers of one of the various states and lent their dynastic name to the state, where it was disseminated as a surname. The account recalls Liu Zhiji's criticism that writers of authorial postfaces prior to the Tang frequently cited ancient figures from classical texts to fluff their family tree. Liu writes, "Moreover, according to the ethics of the recent past, people are fond of claiming an eminent clan [for their ancestry]" 又近古人倫, 喜稱閥閱.[5] Ironically, Liu condemns Yang Xiong and Ban Gu, two staunch Confucians, for making false claims of eminent ancestors based on erroneous citations from classical texts. According to Liu, the problem with false claims of ancestry is that they are fundamentally unfilial, for "if one offers respect to another's relatives, then the people will be immoral" 致敬他親, 人斯悖德.[6]

> In all these cases, they do not make use of true records and make no use of their lives of leisure and wealth, but only rely on classics and histories and themselves produce contradictions. Thus we know the Yang clan resided in Xi Shu [Sichuan province], and the Ban family dominated the northern frontier, those who falsely claim to be descendents of Bo Qiao are the Yangs, and those who falsely claim Xiong Yi as their ancestor are the Bans. I fear they themselves are the ones who made it ancient, and pushed it back into the past further and further![7]

> 斯皆不因真律, 無假寧楹, 真據經史, 自成矛盾. 則知揚姓之寓西蜀, 班門之雄朔野, 或冒纂伯僑, 或家傳熊繹, 恐自我作古, 先之彌遠者矣.

In some cases the illustrious ancestor may serve to counterbalance the actions of more recent family members, framing them as aberrations that are uncharacteristic of the family history as a whole. Liu's criticism underlines the fact that the authorial postface as a source of family history is not free of problems such as exaggeration or outright fabrication and should probably be read as documents whose purpose is to attach the author and his family to culturally significant figures from canonical texts rather than as attempts at genealogy as such.

Ge Hong's account of his more recent ancestry is no less archetypal but is perhaps more plausible. One nameless ancestor who held the post of regional inspector 刺史 of Jingzhou 荆州 during the Former Han resisted the usurpation of the Han dynasty by "the bandit" 國賊 Wang Mang 王莽 (33 BCE–22 CE) and was exiled to Langye 琅邪 in modern Shandong province after an unsuccessful insurgency. According to Ge Hong, the exile was largely voluntary for, although Wang Mang spared his ancestor's life, he subsequently pleaded illness and retired from the world rather than returning to public service under a usurper.[8] The account generally reflects later Han historiography, which was extremely hostile to Wang Mang's reign of Confucian reform. There is no compelling reason to doubt the veracity of Ge Hong's version of events, for it seems possible that many officials loyal to the Han found themselves in retirement south of the Yangzi River during Wang Mang's reign. However, the notion of loyalty to legitimate rule is a recurring theme among Ge Hong's ancestry and should be seen in the context of the Jin absorption of Wu in 280 CE.

The sons of this ancestor, Pu Lu 浦盧 and his younger brother Wen 文, fought together to assist Emperor Guang Wu 光武 (r. 25–57) to restore the Han dynasty. Because of his official status in the government army, Pu Lu received rich rewards and an official appointment while Wen, who followed his older brother into battle as a private soldier, did not. This situation was unacceptable to Pu Lu, who according to Ge Hong's account eventually secured for his younger brother both estate and position and subsequently retired south of the Yangzi River to become a farmer in Jurong 句容, located in Jiangsu province near present-day Nanjing. The account may be historically accurate and still serve the purpose of demonstrating the loyalty and filial piety of Ge Hong's ancestors; indeed, loyalty and reclusion for moral and ethical ends seem to run in the family. Ge Hong also uses the story of Pu Lu to move his narrative geographically, relocating his family to the south; of the descendants of Wen in the north we hear nothing.

Ge Hong's family remained in the south for generations and occupied official positions in the kingdom of Wu 吳 (220–80), which ruled southeastern China after the final dissolution of the Han dynasty in the early third century. According to Ge Hong, his grandfather, Ge Xi 系, was an erudite scholar who governed several counties in modern Jiangsu and Zhejiang provinces, including present-day Hangzhou. He eventually rose to the rank of Junior Mentor to the crown prince of Wu 太子少傅 and occupied numerous posts within the central administration.[9] Ge Hong describes his father, Ge Ti 梯 (d. 295), in similar, laudatory terms as a scholarly gentleman of model conduct. Ge Ti served in various civil and military positions and was eventually appointed governor of Kuaiji 會稽 prefecture (modern Zhejiang province). Around the time of this appointment the Jin dynasty, which had already succeeded in unifying northern China around 265, invaded Wu under the command of the famous literatus and Jin general Du Yu 杜預 (222–84).[10] Because the Jin administration attempted to check the power of the southern gentry by giving them positions of little authority, Ge Ti initially lost prestige and power under Jin rule.[11] He was appointed to various posts at the Jin capital of Luoyang as well as positions in several counties. Ge Ti's administrative skills were eventually rewarded with a promotion, and he died while in office serving as the governor of Shaoling 邵陵 in modern Hunan province, an area of relatively modest size.

Because the Jin victory changed the fortunes of his family, it may have been a cause of resentment or frustration for Ge Hong. He tells us that his father, a Wu loyalist, was placed in "supreme command of military expeditions and garrisons [in five prefectures] and had to defend the area" from the Jin invasion.[12] Quoting *Zuozhuan* 左傳 (Zuo Commentary), Ge Hong states, "That which heaven destroys, man cannot assist" 天之所壞, 人不能支.[13]

The reference to *Zuozhuan* recalls the dissolution of the ailing Zhou dynasty at the hands of various princes, and the destruction of Wu takes on the tone of an epic historical tragedy as his father fights in vain to save his home state. The air of fate and epic tragedy is even more manifest in Ge Hong's description of Sun Hao's capitulation to the conquering Jin, which states, "The former ruler of Wu respectfully followed [Heaven's command], and the nine regions submitted" 故主欽若, 九有同賓.[14] The phrase *qin ruo* 欽若, used here to mean "surrender," may refer to a *Shang shu* passage from the "Canon of Yao" 堯典 in which Yao instructs his officials to follow (*qin ruo*) the principles of Heaven to create the calendar.[15] This is not to suggest that Ge Hong viewed Sun Hao as a sage, but the rhetorical gesture expressed in light of the sympathetic description of his father's wartime efforts to defend Wu distinguishes Sun Hao and Wu from Wang Mang; Sun Hao is no usurper but a legitimate ruler whose mandate has come to an end. Such expressions of loyalty or sympathy to Wu may indicate that Ge Hong felt a certain level of disquiet over the decline of his family's fortunes, but at the same time it did not seem to diminish his opportunities under China's new masters, as we shall see. Indeed, by providing the proper framework for these expressions of loyalty—in this case the will of Heaven and the role of fate—Ge Hong transforms a potentially troubling issue into a statement of great piety that would be well regarded by the Jin. However, given the strong tradition within historiography of using the past to criticize the present, such expressions of loyalty might also have cast the Sima family in the role of the usurper, condemning the Jin while providing Ge Hong with an avenue of rhetorical retreat.

A third possibility is that Ge Hong is expressing in political terms the cultural divide that may have come to separate the south from the north during the preceding two centuries. David Knechtges argues that the reunification of China under the Jin and, perhaps more important, the relocation of the Jin court south of the Yangzi after 311 CE, led to a distinct clash of cultures between the north, which had developed a more libertine culture, and the south, which had remained fairly conservative.[16] Knechtges bases his argument on a close reading of several literary figures who migrated to the capital in search of official positions after the fall of the Wu, focusing on Lu Ji 陸機 (261–303) and his younger brother Lu Yun 陸雲 (262–303), who both arrived at the capital under the patronage of Zhang Hua 張華 (232–300) around 289 and soon became enmeshed in the literary coteries of northern China.[17] According to Knechtges, Lu Ji and Lu Yun identified strongly with Wu culture, which had an origin story that went back to Taibo 太伯 and Zhongyong 仲雍, who were sons of a venerable Zhou ancestor King Tai 太王. According to legend, Taibo and Zhongyong renounced any claim to the throne to clear the way for

King Wen of Zhou and moved south, an event commemorated in Lu Ji's verse the "Ballad of Wu" 吳趨行.[18] Moreover, *Shi ji* refers to Confucius' disciple Zi You 子游 as a "man of Wu," a tradition to which Lu Yun refers in a letter to his uncle.[19] Knechtges believes such literary references suggest Lu Ji and his brother not only saw Wu as a political entity they fought to defend from the Jin invasion but also as a cultural tradition that, though related to northern culture, was distinctive in a number of ways.

Thus the Lu brothers would have been horrified to arrive at the capital and find the intellectual fad of "untrammeled remoteness" (*ya liang* 雅量) to be a common practice that endorsed a reaction to excessive Han ritualism that included inopportune speech and behavior. Indeed, their patron, Zhang Hua, was even known to have neglected the proper customs for his own mother's funeral.[20] Such impolite and nonritual expressions would have been out of step with the more conservative current of southern culture. In one incident, recorded in *Shishuo xinyu*, the Lu brothers take offense at the use of the taboo names of their father and grandfather.[21] Knechtges writes, "I wish to suggest, then, that Lu Zhi's use of the taboo names of Lu Ji's father and grandfather, or Liu Bao's insolent questions, were not necessarily intentional slights directed at Lu Ji because he was a southerner, but simply conventions of the social discourse of the time that included deliberate breaches of the code of etiquette and ritual. That Lu Ji took umbrage shows that he did not subscribe to this social discourse, and considered such conduct as a terrible offense."[22] This kind of conduct only entered into public discourse in the south after northerners fled over the Yangzi to escape the invasion of the north.[23]

In addition to his account of his ancestors, there is other evidence to suggest that Ge Hong, like Lu Ji, identified not only with Wu as a political unit but also with the south more broadly as a distinct cultural entity. As Knechtges observes, in his *Waipian* 15, "Examining Promotions" 審舉, Ge Hong argues that southern scholars are no less fit for official appointments than their northern counterparts because rigorous Confucian learning never declined under the Wu. To further his point, Ge Hong points to a tradition of southern scholars that includes both Zi You and Wang Chong, who was from Shangyu 上虞 in modern Zhejiang province.[24] Indeed, as we have seen, Ge Hong refers to Wang Chong as a precedent for his own autobiographical postface and took him as an important model for imitation. Moreover, Ge Hong greatly admired the work of Lu Ji and Lu Yun. The fact that the two brothers, like Ge Hong's father, had resisted the Jin invasion may have also fueled his admiration, and Ge Hong sought to imitate Lu Ji as a writer and a southerner who aspired to go north and gain an official position.[25]

Like Lu Ji, Ge Hong condemned various behaviors associated with libertine circles of intellectual society, chief among them excessive drinking of alcohol. The use of alcohol and other drugs, such as "five-minerals powder" 五石散 (also known as "cold victual powder" 寒食散), by the literati had become so common by the end of the Jin period that intoxication was a salient feature of the literary personae of many historical figures, chief among them the so-called Seven Sages of the Bamboo Grove 竹林七賢 and their imitators. The use of five-minerals powder became widespread after its importation by northern émigrés, and there is little evidence to suggest that Ge Hong either condemned or endorsed its use.[26] Ge Hong's condemnation of drinking alcohol is more evident despite that fact that wine was widely touted among libertines as "just the thing to make every man naturally remote from the world."[27] Remoteness from the world and subsequent violations of social etiquette may have been precisely what offended Ge Hong's southern, conservative disposition.

> So it is that in all cases where petty, trifling men have some wealth and power, they in no way resume living in the manner of mourning but are often in other accommodations, with high beds and thick quilts, rich food and plentiful drink, sometimes in the company of good friends, filling cups to the brim and emptying them to the point of becoming very drunk. They say, "This is the manner of the capital, Loyang." Is this not a pity![28]

> 於是凡瑣小人之有財力者，了不復居於喪位，常在別房，高床重褥，美食大飲，或與密客引滿投空，至於沈醉. 曰："此京洛之法也". 不亦惜哉!

Moreover, at the beginning of *Waipian* 24, "Admonitions on Alcohol" 酒誡, Ge Hong states, "The Gentleman on account of it corrupts his virtue, and the petty man on account of it hastens his vices" 君子以之敗德, 小人以之速罪.[29] As a whole, the chapter refutes the notion that inappropriate behavior resulting from intoxication can be seen to liberate the imbiber from the constraints of Confucian formalism in any positive way; in Ge Hong's view it is simply a petty indulgence excused with a weak philosophical justification. He counters a libertine interlocutor by invoking examples of behavior by Confucius and the Duke of Zhou (Zhougong 周公).[30] Such condemnations of the libertine lifestyle aesthetic may indicate that Ge Hong identified more closely with a relatively conservative southern culture that found violations of earlier Han, Confucian social norms—as imagined by Wu traditionalists—to be anathema to social order.

Early Life and Poverty

Ge Hong's account of his early life begins after his family history and blends seamlessly into the description of the author's character and reclusion that follows it. The narrative of both his early life and his disengagement from worldly affairs illustrates the way in which the archetypal self-presentation eclipses the importance of accurate biographical details for Ge Hong's authorial postface. Tropes from his childhood are intended to create a self-image that, like the early life of Augustine, establishes a context for interpreting the author's life in moral terms. Unlike autobiographies in the Augustinian tradition, Ge Hong sets aside any notion that the account of his early life and development must be accurate from an imagined, objective perspective; although he presents his early life and the quality of his reclusion in vivid detail, little of it corresponds to what is known of his historical circumstances. Ge Hong's self-image suggests that accuracy or truth in autobiography corresponds to the position of the protagonist in moral space rather than being revealed through the details of time and place. We may say that despite the overwhelming detail presented in Ge Hong's autobiographical writing it remains more impressionistic than circumstantial and has more in common with Tao Qian's abstract self-presentation than the narration of a life as a historical biography.

Biographical details concerning Ge Hong's early life are slight and quickly give way to hyperbole and fabrication. He was born in 283 in Jurong just three years after the Jin conquest of Wu. He was the youngest of three sons, but no information exists concerning his older brothers except for a nephew, Ge Wang 葛望, who moved south with him after his retirement and is briefly mentioned in Ge Hong's official biography.[31] By his own account Ge Hong possessed a serious demeanor as a child, declining to play with other children or to participate in activities such as chess, gambling, or cock fighting.[32] He was equally uninterested in serious study and states that his indulgent parents never compelled him to pursue the kind of academic training that was probably expected of the offspring of an influential gentry family.

Ge Hong was only twelve years old when his father died in 295, an incident that seems to have inflicted some hardship on his family.[33] He states that he personally engaged in plowing and planting and suffered from cold and hunger. The destruction of his father's library by soldiers during a period of civil strife worsened Ge Hong's plight, and in one colorful passage from his postface he describes how he used his meager income earned from chopping firewood to underwrite his education.

At times when I could rest from working in the fields I had no books to read. I would shoulder my satchel and go on foot to borrow them. When finally I came to a household [in possession of some books], I rarely received a complete volume. Every day I spent my time in this way. In the daytime, I cut firewood and sold it in order to buy paper and brushes and worked in the fields; by firelight [at night] I would copy the books. Because of this, early in life I did not immerse myself in fine arts and literature. I often lacked paper and would write on both sides, so that few people could read what I had written.[34]

農隙之暇無所讀．乃負笈徒步行借，又卒於一家，少得全部之書．益破功日伐薪賣之，以給紙筆，就營田園處，以柴火寫書．坐此之故，不得早涉藝文．常乏紙，每所寫反覆有字，人尠能讀也．

Ge Hong's claim of extreme poverty is generally regarded as an exaggeration. It has been rightly observed that a distinguished family with such a long and prestigious record of government service would not have declined so quickly into economic ruin.[35]

The death of Ge Hong's father is dissimilar to that of Sima Qian, whose father on his deathbed charged Qian with completing *Shi ji*, a task he claims to have undertaken out of filial devotion. We might say that Ge Hong imitates more closely Wang Chong's iconoclasm by defining himself in contrast to his family lineage, though not so willingly as his predecessor and with considerably less rancor. The personal tragedy removes Ge Hong from a fundamental social norm, accentuating the scope of his predicament. The death of Ge Hong's father provides a basis for his noncanonical education, an important step for his image as an author as we shall see in the next section, for the absence of more traditional family instruction allows him to highlight a different intellectual and religious aesthetic. The passage may also point to the difficulty of Ge Hong's position in the Jin political climate. Although he studied assiduously, "few people could make out what he had written," perhaps an indication of his lack of opportunity to make himself known and advance under the Jin regime.

It is probably true that the death of his father was a blow to Ge Hong's aspirations for a career in the central administration, for it might have meant losing some (or all) of his father's network of friends and allies who might have helped him find an official position. However, the idea that Ge Hong was reduced to such a state of poverty that he sold firewood to buy books is hyperbole that few critical readers take seriously. Several modern scholars have correctly pointed out that ordinary farmers could ill-afford such luxuries as books or the leisure time to read them.[36] The possibility that Ge Hong subsidized a broad education with manual labor is remote at best. Regardless, it is not hard to imagine that upon his father's death Ge Hong's family underwent a period of relative hardship during which he may have personally supervised the family estate, an activity that took time away from his studies.

The impressive range of Ge Hong's early education and his youthful literary endeavors also cast doubt on claims of extreme poverty. According to his own account, as well as his biography in *Jin shu* 晉書 (History of the Jin) it was during this early period that he began his study of the canon of texts generally associated with *Ru jia*, a term often translated simply as "Confucianism." Ge Hong states that he began to read classics such as *Shi jing* at fifteen without the benefit of a tutor, could recite from memory those books he studied, and could grasp their essential meaning. His extensive reading approached "ten thousand chapters," a number meant to suggest the dizzying scope of his education.[37]

In reality his formal education probably began much earlier, as elsewhere in his autobiographical postface Ge Hong states that he had already begun to write poetry, rhapsodies, and other miscellaneous works by the age of fourteen or fifteen (ca. 298), all of which he later destroyed.[38] His statements regarding early poverty and belated studies convey the sense that his education was largely the product of his own acumen and determination rather than his privileged social status. The claim that Ge Hong advanced his education despite the difficulties of poverty would have differentiated him from the children of more powerful, aristocratic clans (*menfa* 門閥) for whom birth would have provided high social status. Such exaggerations may be regarded as literary conventions intended to show the unique nature of his education in the face of financial difficulties brought on by his father's death. Moreover, they establish a background for the trope of poverty and reclusion that dominates the rest of the first half of the authorial postface.

It seems clear from Ge Hong's image of the hermit in the first chapter of the *Baopuzi Waipian,* "Praising Eremitism" 嘉遯, that Ge Hong's reclusion is a literary pose expressed in idealized terms, for he shares most if not all of the identifying characteristics of the fictional recluse. The recusant scholar of Ge Hong's chapter conceals himself behind a grass gate, and his brilliance is unknown in his own time. Rather than call on the influential and powerful, he engages in the art of Daoist alchemy and keeps to the company of other hermits.[39] "He calls glory and eminence unlucky and regards jade and silks as grass and dirt" 謂榮顯爲不辛, 以玉帛爲草土.[40] He takes Laozi and Zhuangzi as his companions and prefers tranquility to worldly engagement: "The myriad things could not upset his harmony, [and even] the four seas could not disturb his spirit" 萬物不能攖其和, 四海不足汩其神.[41] Accordingly, Ge Hong's recluse chooses seclusion and constancy to the inconsistencies of public life and the morals of popular society, which are seen as complementary aspects of worldly engagement.

Ge Hong liberally employs the same tropes of reclusion throughout the *Waipian zixu,* and the resulting image of the author from the first half of the text is not only remarkably similar to the fictional hermit of the first chapter but both are drawn from earlier sources. Indeed, aside from a few details in his account of his early life, Ge Hong's self-presentation in this first section is devoid of any biographical information of even modest historicity. The dwelling of the hermit may reflect either a sense of withdrawal to the countryside or solitude in the midst of society; the residence of the Master Embracing Simplicity belongs to the latter category. According to the text, he lives near high officials, but has no commerce with them, and as a result there are no carriage tracks in front of his home.[42]

> My clothes cannot keep out the chill, my house does not keep out leaking water, my food does not fill my emptiness, and my fame does not extend beyond my dwelling, but I do not feel worried [about the situation]. So poor I have no servants, my fence fallen and broken, brambles crowd the roof of my house, blackberries clog the stairs and gutters, [so that I must] part the thicket to leave and clear away weeds to enter.[43]

> 衣不辟寒, 室不免漏, 食不充虛, 名不出戶, 不能憂也. 貧無僮僕, 籬落頓決, 荊棘叢於庭宇, 蓬莠塞乎階霤, 披榛出門, 排草入室.

By the beginning of the fourth century, a ramshackle dwelling had become standard issue for any reclusive hermit or retired official, so much so that less than a century later Tao Qian would build his oeuvre around returning home to his "thatched hut of eight or nine rooms" (草屋八九間) in the countryside. Ge Hong's leaky (*lou* 漏) roof and bramble-choked doorway recall an exchange between two students of Confucius, Yuan Xian 原憲, who was poor, and Zi Gong 子貢, who was relatively wealthy, recorded in the *Zhuangzi* chapter, "Yielding the Throne" 讓王.

> Yuan Xian lived in the state of Lu, in a tiny house that was hardly more than four walls. It was thatched with growing weeds, had a broken door made of woven brambles and branches of mulberry for the doorposts; jars with the bottoms out, hung with pieces of course cloth for protection from the weather, served as windows for its two rooms. The roof leaked and the floor was damp, but Yuan Xian sat up in a dignified manner, played his lute

and sang. Zi Gong, wearing an inner robe of royal blue and an outer one of white, and riding in a grand carriage whose top was too tall to get through the entrance to the lane, came to call on Yuan Xian. Yuan Xian, wearing a bark cap and slippers with no heels, and carrying a goosefoot staff, came to the gate to greet him. "Goodness!" exclaimed Zi Gong. "What distress you are in, Sir!" Yuan Xian replied, "I have heard that if one lacks wealth, that is called poverty; and if one studies but cannot put into practice what he has learned, that is called distress. I am poor, but I am not in distress!" Zi Gong backed off a few paces with a look of embarrassment. Yuan Xian laughed and said, "To act out of worldly ambition, to band with others in cliquish friendships, to study in order to show off to others, to teach in order to please one's own pride, to mask one's evil deeds behind benevolence and righteousness, to deck oneself out with carriages and horses, I could never bear to do such things!"[44]

原宪居鲁, 环堵之室, 茨以生草, 蓬户不完, 桑以为枢而瓮牖, 二室, 褐以为塞, 上漏下湿, 匡坐而弦歌. 子贡乘大马, 中绀而表素, 轩车不容巷, 往见原宪. 原宪华冠纟徙履, 杖藜而应门. 子贡曰: "嘻! 先生何病? "原宪应之曰: "宪闻之, 无财谓之贫, 学而不能行谓之病. 今宪贫也, 非病也." 子贡逡巡 而有愧色. 原宪笑曰: "夫希世而行, 比周而友, 学以为人, 教以为己, 仁义之慝, 舆马之饰, 宪不忍为也."

Yuan Xian's humble, naturalistic lifestyle emphasizes individual virtue rather than worldly success. Hypocrisy and duplicity are the hallmarks of public advancement, but one may live in poverty and yet follow Confucius's exhortation to "study and when appropriate practice what one has studied" (學而時習之), thereby living a transcendent, moral life.[45] It is to this traditional aesthetic that Ge Hong lays claim as a sign of his lofty, ethical character.

Ge Hong closes the first half of the *Waipian zixu* with a brief appraisal that transforms his seclusion into an act of ethical criticism. He laments the deteriorating social mores accompanied by increased factionalism at court, characterized by the readiness of his contemporaries to criticize one another.[46] He closes by referring to Confucius and the Duke of Zhou as examples of men who suffered anxieties because they could not completely achieve their goals, which should serve as a warning not to criticize others lightly.[47] The reference reinforces the notion that Ge Hong faces similar frustrations because he lives outside the norms of his own era, which we may observe through his living space, reiterating the connection between isolation and moral virtue.[48]

Thus in an autobiographical postface individuation or isolation is used to justify the act of writing by associating the author with a tradition of writers who retained their moral integrity through their isolation from the corruption of society regardless of whether such isolation was the result of individual choice or circumstances beyond the individual's control. In this regard, Confucius became the most famous example of unrecognized virtue and untapped talent. Authors who so justified their works did so with an appeal to their own unrecognized or misunderstood character; their autobiographies therefore play on the themes of isolation, difference, and individuality. Sima Qian defended his work as a filial act within a long tradition of neglected authors, including Confucius and the quasi-historical poet Qu Yuan.[49] "In all these instances, men had ideas that were stifled and did not manage to disseminate their doctrines; thus they narrated past events and thought of those to come" 此人皆意有所鬱結, 不得統其道也, 故述往事, 思來者.[50] Wang Chong distanced himself from his family lineage in his autobiographical essay, comparing himself to a precious jewel or phoenix that had been overlooked by fate and circumstance after the manner of Confucius. At the close of his postface, he writes, "In talent, none surpassed Confucius, but his talent was not appreciated and he was exiled" 材鴻莫過孔子, 孔子才不容, 斥逐.[51] Similarly, Ge Hong uses the persona of the recluse in his autobiographical postface to distinguish himself from his own era in moral and intellectual terms.

> Styles of fashion change suddenly and often. Sometimes they have a broad neck and large belt, sometimes they fit tightly and have long sleeves; sometimes they are long a sweep the ground, sometimes they are so short as not to cover the feet. At all times I preserved constancy and did not follow the changes of the age. In speaking, I stuck to the truth, refraining from abusing and mocking others. If I did not have an appropriate companion, I would remain silent all day long. Since among the people of my district there were those who called me "The Scholar Who Embraces Simplicity," when I wrote this book I called myself this.[52]

> 俗之服用, 俄而屢改. 或忽廣領而大帶或促身而修袖, 或長裾曳地, 或短不蔽腳. 洪期於守常, 不隨世變, 言則率實, 杜絕嘲戲, 不得其人, 終日默然. 故邦人咸稱之為抱朴之士, 是以洪著書, 因以自號焉.

Despite such assertions to the contrary, there is enough evidence to suggest that Ge Hong remained in government office—and therefore firmly entrenched in contemporary society—for most of his adult life. Ge Hong's self-narrative serves as a statement of the author's unique and individual moral character, recognizable through signs of behavior and speech agreed to by society as a whole.

Eremitism as a Political Theory in Ge Hong's *Baopuzi*

The idea that liberty from social norms played a strong role in Wei-Jin notions of reclusion has been discussed elsewhere, as has the idea that retreat from public life was an action of social and political criticism.[53] The appeal of this literary aesthetic was strong for Ge Hong, who used his literary persona of the reclusive philosopher for a kind of social criticism that reveals in turn his suitability for public office. We might say that the creation of new standards of character, virtue, and self-expression, however they may have appeared to be modeled on ostensibly solitary individuals such as the recluse, was a form of social and political engagement, not the hallmark of an anarchic individualism based on an ideal of autonomous individuality. Ge Hong's reclusive persona as found in his autobiographical postface may reflect a period during which he did not seek office and turned his attention to other matters, but it also reflects his desire to parlay the virtues associated with reclusion into an official position as the Jin court fled south across the Yangzi in the face of foreign invasion.

By Ge Hong's time, eremitism was intimately linked to well-known archetypes of retreat from the public sphere. Such retreat was often predicated on the recluse's self-perception as a moral being and the inability to assimilate his or her morality into the larger social and political landscape. Bo Yi 伯 夷 and Shu Qi 叔齊, for example, were lionized during the Warring States era and the Han dynasty for their loyalty to the Shang dynasty and their unwillingness to taint their virtue by serving the conquering Zhou. While some commentators quibbled over whether their decision might be criticized as tantamount to suicide, the story is unambiguously rooted in moral self-preservation.

According to some, the *Ru* (Confucian) textual tradition was instrumental in infusing reclusion with the potential for social-political significance. In *Lunyu* 16.12 we read, "Duke Jing of Qi had a thousand teams of horses, and yet on the day he died, the people could find no reason to praise him. Bo Yi and Shu Qi starved to death at the foot of Mt. Shouyang, and yet to this day the common people still praise them" 齊景公有馬千駟, 死之日, 民無德而 稱焉. 伯夷叔齊餓於首陽之下, 民到于今稱之.[54] Confucius himself was said to remark, "In the empire, if the way prevails then show yourself, but if it does not then hide" 天下有道則見, 無道則隱, lending a quasi-cosmic overtone to the issue of holding government office.[55] Reclusion was thus flavored to various degrees by implications of possible political defiance that increased the level of personal danger to the scholar who chose to retreat from official life.[56] Expressed in ideal terms, the trajectory of the hermit oscillated between engagement and disengagement; one might leave public life in protest only to return when the Way was restored to the empire.

Ancient recusants continued to serve as models of behavior for Wei-Jin literati who wished to abstain from official life. For example, the official biography of Xie An 謝安 (332–85) in *Jin shu* portrays the Eastern Jin statesman as a reluctant official who is slowly coaxed out of his premature—and self-imposed—retirement and into official life at the age of forty. While in retirement, Xie An enjoyed the company of others who did not wish to be sullied by public life, and his biographer alleges that Xie drew on ancient models of reclusion: "Once [Xie An] was traveling in the mountains of Lin An and he sat in a stone grotto and looked out into the deep valley. Sighing, he sadly exclaimed, 'From here it is so far to Bo Yi'" 嘗往臨安山中, 坐石室, 臨濬谷, 悠然歎 曰：'此去伯夷何遠.'[57] Whether or not the reclusion of Xie An was substantial in any way and constituted true political retreat, an aesthetic choice, or simply a literary pose, the social and political implications of eremitism provided by earlier precedents were impossible to ignore.

As suggested above, more important than the hermit's physical proximity to the central court was his location in moral space. According to Guo Xiang 郭象 (d. 312), the famous commentator on the *Zhuangzi*, even at court the mind of the sage should "not be any different as if he were in the mountains," uncorrupted by worldly affairs and the influences of peers.[58] Sun Chuo 孫綽 (314–71), echoing this view, supposedly stated, "For those who embody the Mysterious and understand the Remote, public life or retirement amounts to the same thing" 體玄識遠者, 出處同歸.[59] The ability to maintain a spirit of lofty remoteness and thereby transcend a corrupt world was a hallmark of the champions of abstruse learning such as Xie An. Remoteness was thus an abstract measure of character whose coordinates were located on the plane of public morality. As Ralph Waldo Emerson states in his essay "Self Reliance," "It is easy in the world to live after the world's opinion; it is easy in solitude to live after our own; but the great man is he who in the midst of the crowd keeps with perfect sweetness the independence of solitude."[60] Through his untrammeled remoteness, a recluse offers his own example as a judgment on the status quo. Reclusion and inner moral independence was thus a sign of moral authority with regard to society but was not exclusive from it. In this regard, we might say that the counterpart of the recluse was neither the gainfully employed scholar-official nor society as a whole but the ruler, who often referred to himself as *gua ren* 寡人, a term that means something like "I, one of little virtue" but is more literally translated as "the orphan." Solitude or individuation was considered a maneuver of political power that was intimately linked to moral authority.[61]

Because of his moral authority, the hermit's very existence was a commentary on the character of the ruler. Emperors and warlords were frequently at pains to coax hermits back to court life and government service as a symbol of the legitimacy and virtue of their regimes. Rulers thus attempted to conflate moral and physical space by centralizing moral authority in the centers of political power: "The support of reclusion was a measure of the magnanimity of the ruler, if not a calculated pretension of the legitimacy and security of the rule."[62] Rulers who thus beckoned hermits from retirement hoped to negate the moral authority implied by reclusion that challenged their own.

In early China, the hermit's relationship with society and political power was one of reciprocal reflection. Famous figures such as Tao Qian and Ji Kang who expressed an interest in giving rein to their "true selves" through eremitism hoped in part to preserve their good character in the face of political adversity and perhaps to comment on their contemporaries. Thus Ji Kang's refusal to assume office on the recommendation of his friend Shan Tao 山濤 (205–83) was not a challenge to the validity of court protocol as such but an assertion of his orientation in the moral landscape in relation to a central court increasingly dominated by factions that he refused to serve.[63] His execution was a significant object lesson for other famous intellectuals who refused to serve the ambitions of the Sima clan.[64] Similarly, Tao Qian's poetry reveals a concern with a sense of personal congruity, his ability to live life on his own terms, something the poet believed impossible in his contemporary social and political landscape.

This description of reclusion is not intended to exhaust the limits of the topic, which has been analyzed elsewhere with more subtlety and nuance.[65] Alan Berkowitz, for example, has attempted to delineate differences between substantive reclusion and reclusion as an aesthetic, and he has identified distinct models within a tangle of terminology and vocabulary that early Chinese writers applied to specific forms of eremitism. My own view is that any record of reclusion may constitute eremitism as an aesthetic even if it is in regard to those who may have actually practiced reclusion. As Berkowitz has shown, all such descriptions tend toward tropes of one kind or another, becoming in essence literary descriptions that are no more objective than their authors. True hermits would probably be unknown to the general public and not subject to any record. Indeed, whether or not anyone ever engaged in substantive reclusion is ultimately irrelevant, for what is most important in the description of eremitism is the *performance* of reclusion and its subsequent reception by a third-party observer such as a reader.

There is considerable evidence to suggest that Ge Hong was deeply invested in the aesthetic of reclusion as a form of social engagement because it constituted a clear and public sign of inner virtue. The recluse is one of the most prevalent archetypes found in *Baopuzi*. There are at least six hermits in the *Waipian* who defend or justify their reclusion to interlocutors such as government officials who encourage them to return to public life either by characterizing the actions of recusants such as Bo Yi as futile and suicidal or by appealing to the expectation that the hermit will return with the onset of social and political order. "I hope [you] will give up the caves of dragons and serpents,[66] advance on the path of opportunity, [and] abandon your residence of solitary purity. . . . Bo Yi was only one man; how is plucking ferns sufficient to bring admiration?" 願先生委龍蛇之穴, 升利見之 塗, 釋戶庭之獨潔...柏成一介之夫, 採薇何足多慕乎.[67] However, the recusants of *Baopuzi* refuse to return and serve as officials, justifying their reclusion with an interpretation of the eremitic tradition that esteems the role of the recluse as a political actor for whom a return to public life is largely irrelevant.

In Ge Hong's view, the hermit was not merely a critic of the status quo but an individual who at times is empowered to act as a teacher even to the wisest rulers. Conversely, a ruler who understands the position and function of hermits honors them as teachers but does not press them into official positions.

> The recluse said, "As for the Duke of Zhou, he was a great sage; although he was of high rank, he put himself below the common people. Spitting out the food in his mouth and holding his wet hair, he was afraid of losing talented men.[68] He followed seventy scholars from poor families and received ten scholars wearing commoner's clothes; he personally met them with gifts as if receiving a teacher and treated twelve scholars in commoner's clothes as friends, and in all of these instances they were not forced to appear at court. Hypothetically, assuming Lu Shang had lived in the Duke of Zhou's land, all such people would become bodies displayed in the market or the court or rotting flesh in ditches and ravines!"[69]

> 逸民曰: "夫周公大聖, 以貴下賤, 吐哺渦髮, 懼於失人, 從白屋 之士七十人, 布衣之徒親執贄所師見者十人, 所友者十有二人, 皆不逼以在朝也. 設令呂尚居周公之地, 則此等皆成市朝之暴 尸, 而溝澗之腐骴矣."

Here the relationship between ruler and subject is juxtaposed with the relationship between master and student, and the ruler's ostensible subordination to the wisdom of the recluse demonstrates the elevated status of the latter within this model relationship.

However, the relationship simultaneously reaffirms the status of the ruler, for in the transaction between ruler and recluse the ruler loses corporeal power over the subject but gains new authority by enacting the political ideal of virtuous conduct. The ruler appropriates the moral authority of the recluse and in turn acquires greater temporal authority over his subjects. In this scenario, the ruler rejects the toxic moral atmosphere of the central court and seeks his authority on the periphery of political power.

> Although [recluses] are of no practical quality, and their talents are not equal to [those of] outstanding officials at court, is this not better than shrugging shoulders and casting down brows [to appear humble], flattering the powerful, bearing gifts and concealing valuables, traveling at night to the homes of the powerful, to race one another for access to the powerful, to buy famous treasures in the market place, abandoning the basis of virtuous action and the basis of study and knowledge while proceeding to the gratuitous end of forming cliques among their own kind?[70]

> 雖器不益於旦夕之用, 才不周於立朝之俊, 不亦愈於脅肩低眉, 諂媚權右, 提贄懷貨, 宵征同塵, 爭津競濟, 市買名品, 棄德行學問之本, 赴雷同比周之末也?

The link between physical isolation and moral authority seems clear, as recluses are able to avoid the cliques and political snares of court life and remain morally pure. The argument that a recluse has no "practical use" is perfunctory; the statement quoted above advocates unequivocally for the superiority of the recluse in moral terms, which had clear, practical implications during the Wei-Jin era when enacting the role of recluse was essentially a vocation.

The duration of Ge Hong's reclusion was more than a decade and may have benefited his official career by allowing him to cultivate a literary image that corresponded to the ideal of reclusion as outlined above. This may have permitted him to move away from his early military career into the more prestigious appointments befitting a member of the literati. One must admire the way in which Ge Hong cultivated an air of virtuous eremitism and promoted it with a body of philosophical work and other literature, emerging from his abrupt retirement, which began with the violent end of his benefactor, Ji Han 嵇含 around 306. As Berkowitz states, "During the Six Dynasties the nomination of candidates whose sole forte was dissembling the lofty conduct of a man-in-reclusion continued as a sort of mutated vestige of the earlier recommendatory system. And a sizable number of aspiring officials did in fact gain recognition and suitable employment through a stint 'in reclusion.'"[71] The attention paid to recluses was not isolated but part of a larger policy to create cohesion within literati society—atomized and ravaged by years of conflict—under the auspices of the emperor's court. In *Shishuo xinyu* 18.15, we read:

> Every time Chi Chao [336–377] heard of someone living in lofty retirement, he would always put up a subsidy for him of a million cash, and in addition would build a residence for him.[72] While he was living in the Shan Mountains he once constructed a house for Dai Kui [d. 396] that was extremely refined and genteel.[73] When Dai first went there to live he wrote letters to all his intimate friends, saying, "Recently when I arrived in the Shan Mountains, it was like coming to an official mansion."[74]

> 郗超每聞欲高尚隱退者, 輒爲辦百萬資, 并爲造立居宇, 在剡爲戴公起宅, 甚精整. 戴始往舊居, 與所親書曰: "近至剡, 如官舍."

Thus we must conclude that Ge Hong's autobiography, which he probably wrote while only in his early thirties, functioned as an extended character resume and contributed to a public reputation that would result in an official position. This adds a new wrinkle to the tradition of early Chinese autobiography by recognizing a text written at a young age, for public consumption, that required verisimilitude only in terms of the author's family history but did not insist on the historicity of the author other than to testify to elusive qualities of character that would be useful for advancement in office.

Shortly after emerging from reclusion and returning to his family home of Jurong around 314, Ge Hong received an appointment as clerk 府掾 to the prince of Langya 琅邪王, Sima Rui, who served as prime minister 丞相 from 313 until 316.[75] The exact date of the appointment is unclear, but it certainly occurred either after Ge Hong's return to Jurong or as an incentive for his return and probably occurred early in Sima Rui's tenure as prime minister. Sima Rui used the position of clerk, which was for the most part an honorary appointment, to woo talented officials and bring them into his administration. He appointed over one 100 (some sources say 106) in this way, and the appointments were probably an indication of his growing political power.[76] In 317, the Western Jin collapsed after years of civil conflict and an invasion by non-Chinese people to the north. Sima Rui stepped into this power vacuum, moving the Jin court south to Jiankang 建康 (near present day Nanjing) and taking the title of king of Jin 晉王 as a preliminary step toward claiming the mantle of emperor.

The refugee court in Jiankang was eager to solidify its position among the southern gentry families on which it now depended for its survival and granted numerous official appointments and honorary titles. In 317, Ge Hong was recognized for his previous military service with the honorary title Marquis of the Region within the Pass 關中侯 and awarded an income of two hundred households in Jurong, an official honor recorded at the end of his authorial postface.[77] Finally, in 318 Sima Rui proclaimed himself Emperor Yuan (r. 318–23), becoming the first ruler of the Eastern Jin (317–420).

Among the prerogatives of a new dynasty was writing the history of its predecessor. Around 318, the influential minister Wang Dao 王導 (276–339) commissioned Gan Bao 干寶 (fl. 340), the author of *Soushen ji* 搜神記 (Inquest into the Spirit Realm), and other accomplished literati to write the *Jin ji* 晉記 (Record of the Jin).[78] Wang Dao and others in his coterie would exert considerable influence over Ge Hong's later official career. Gan Bao already knew of Ge Hong, as the two men shared a common literary and intellectual interest in arcane subjects. In 324, Wang Dao was made regional inspector of Yangzhou 揚州刺史. According to his official biography, sometime during this period, between 318 and 326, Ge Hong was summoned to fill a variety of appointments in Wang Dao's administration such as recorder 主簿 of Yangzhou, clerk to the minister of education 司徒掾, and the military post of administrative adviser 諮議參軍.

Ge Hong's official biography states quite clearly that he refused all such positions, including another offer by Gan Bao to work on his staff as senior recorder 散騎常侍, and remained reclusive to the end, interested only in pursuing elixirs of longevity or *waidan*. Reaction to this assertion is mixed, but the weight of general opinion leans toward accepting the *Jin shu* account as true. However, there is some evidence to suggest that Ge Hong did accept at least the position offered by Gan Bao. The *Sui shu* 隋書 (History of the Sui) "Bibliography" 經籍志 contains an entry for a work called *Han shu chao* 漢書鈔 (Notes on *Han shu*) attributed to Senior Recorder Ge Hong.[79] Furthermore, tradition later credits him with editing a volume of Han dynasty history entitled *Xijing zaji* 西京雜記 (Miscellaneous Record of the Western Capital). According to William Nienhauser, this tradition is probably spurious, but the attribution seems logical given the nature of potential appointments under Wang Dao and those he patronized.[80] Ge Hong's official biography, which closes with the assertion that his contemporaries believed him to have become transcendent, suggests that by the early Tang his reclusive literary persona had merged with the aesthetic of the solitary Daoist practitioner. This biographical tradition would naturally underline his pursuit of longevity techniques and deemphasize his official career. Regardless, the possibility exists that he accepted any or all of the positions, contrary to official accounts.

If Ge Hong did in fact accept any of these official positions, the fact that his autobiographical writing does not mention any actual duties performed in them suggests several possibilities, the most likely of which is that he had completed a final draft of his authorial postface before taking up the positions. Ge Hong takes care to mention specifically the event of his early association with Wang Dao and Sima Rui. If he had accepted a prestigious position such as clerk to the minister of education before completing the text, he probably would have mentioned it in addition to his previous honors. However, if it is true that Ge Hong's authorial postface was intended for self-promotion, then there would be no reason to amend the text after his advancement had been achieved. Another possibility is that Ge Hong, aware of his growing profile, wished to preserve the veil of virtuous reclusion that obscures his autobiographical account and therefore did not edit the text at a later date.

Conflict between an official career and Ge Hong's reclusive literary persona and interest in longevity techniques may also have been an invention of later biographers and hagiographers. During Ge Hong's lifetime the two aspects may have been mutually supportive. For example, while living on Mount Luofu 羅浮山 after Ji Han's death, Ge Hong probably met the Governor 太守 of Nanhai 南海, Bao Jing 鮑靚.[81] Both Ge Hong's and Bao Jing's biographies describe the latter as interested in alchemy; for this reason he valued Ge Hong very much and married a daughter to him.[82] For his part, Ge Hong seems to have benefited from Bao Jing's tutelage, valued him greatly as a teacher, and even received the *Sanhuang wen* 三皇文 (Text of the Three August Ones) from him.[83]

A stance of seclusion and disengagement stood as ironic testimony to Ge Hong's suitability for office. Like Chi Chao after him, Wang Dao seems to have been a collector of famous recluses, perhaps out of a desire to project an image of virtuous authority. In *Shishuo xinyu*, 18.4, we read that Wang Dao attempted to lure Li Xin 李廞 (d. ca. 350) out of retirement and into public service with the appointment of clerk just as Sima Rui had earlier appointed Ge Hong. When Li received the summons, he reportedly laughed and exclaimed, "Wang Dao is once more conferring a title on a man" 茂弘 乃復以一爵假人.[84] According to the *Jin shu* biography of Ge Hong's contemporary Guo Wen 郭文, Wang built a garden in which Guo resided as a kind of hermit in residence, entertaining Wang Dao's entourage with philosophical debates and clever conversation.

Wang Dao had heard of Guo Wen by reputation and sent someone to extend an invitation. Wen steadfastly refused boat or carriage, but shouldering his pole he walked there. At the time he arrived, Wang placed him in the western courtyard, in the middle of which the fruit trees had grown into a [veritable] forest, and there lived birds and beasts and elk and deer, and so [Wang] housed Guo Wen there. Thereupon the court gentlemen all came together to see him, but Guo Wen sat limply with his legs sprawled, as if there was no one present.[85]

王導聞其名, 遣人迎之, 文不肯就船車, 荷擔徒行. 既至, 導置之西園, 園中果木成林, 又有鳥獸麞鹿, 因以居文焉. 於是朝士咸共觀之, 文穨然踑踞, 傍若無人.

Ironically, Guo Wen's biography suggests that Ge Hong acted in collusion with state officials and ventured into the wild to collect Guo, who dressed in animal skins and communed with wild animals.

The Prefect of Yu Hang, Gu Yang, together with Ge Hong, called on [Guo Wen], and carrying him aloft took him back. Because Wen traversed the wilds and wore skins for clothing, Yang gave him gifts of fine leather trousers and lined garments to honor him, but Wen refused them and excusing himself returned to the mountains. Yang subsequently sent an emissary to fetch the clothes and deliver them to Wen's dwelling. Wen did not say a word, but the fine clothing thereupon rotted away just within the door and to the end was never worn.[86]

餘杭令顧颺與葛洪共造之, 而攜與俱歸. 颺以文山行或須皮衣, 贈以韋褲褶一具, 文不納, 辭歸山中. 颺追遣使者置衣室中而去, 文亦無言, 韋衣乃至爛於戶內, 竟不服用.

Thus, in addition to his past services on behalf of the Jin court, Ge Hong's self-consciously crafted image of eremitism may have contributed to his success within Wang Dao's administration. It was, after all, only following the composition of *Baopuzi* that Ge Hong received the first of his honorary appointments by Sima Rui. Regardless, it seems clear that Wang Dao knew Ge Hong by reputation and sought to bring him into the fold of his personal staff.

Military Career

In terms of style and content, we may say that the conclusion of Ge Hong's pose of eremitism marks a division within the text, with the latter portion taking up his military service as a young man and ambitions as a scholar and philosopher. James Ware has surmised that the second half of the text was written as many as fifteen years after the first, around 335, making Ge Hong about fifty years old when he concluded the autobiography.[87] While it is possible that Ge Hong wrote the autobiographical postface at an older age, nothing within the text itself requires this to be true. The military service to which Ge Hong refers had already concluded by 306, while the latest honorific mentioned is Ge Hong's title of marquis of the region within the pass, bestowed in 317. As I indicated in the previous section, it seems unlikely to me that Ge Hong would have omitted mention of any later honors he received during Wang Dao's administration. If Ge Hong wrote the chapter around 318, the acknowledgment that he is about to receive an official appointment makes more sense, for it may refer to any of the numerous opportunities his biography claims he rejected.[88] Since it was around 318 that Gan Bao received his commission to begin work on the *Jin ji*, this may refer to the appointment of senior recorder.

Two statements about his age hint that Ge Hong was likely in his midthirties when he wrote both halves of the text, around 313 at the earliest (accounting for exaggeration), but probably not much later than 323. While establishing his reclusive persona in the first portion of the postface, Ge Hong writes, "Now I am approaching the age of 'no doubts,' and my energy and determination are declining. I think only of decreasing and decreasing, taking no action" 今齒近不惑, 素志衰頹, 但念損之又損, 爲乎無爲.[89] The second half of this line is a quotation from *Daode jing* 道德經 48, which states, "Studying is to increase daily, while the *dao* is to decrease daily, decreasing and decreasing to the point of inaction" 爲學日益,爲道日損,損之又損以至於 無爲, a reference that augments his reclusive pose.[90] The phrase "no doubts" (*bu huo* 不惑) originates from the "autobiography" of Confucius in *Lunyu* 2.4 in which Confucius measures his age in terms of specific markers of moral maturation.

> At fifteen I set my heart on learning, at thirty I was confident in affairs, at forty I had no doubts, at fifty I knew heaven's decree, at sixty my ear was attuned [to truth and falsehood], at seventy I could follow that which my heart desired without overstepping established practice.[91]

> 吾十有五而志于學, 三十而立, 四十而不惑, 五十而知天命, 六十而 耳順, 七十而從心所欲, 不踰矩.

Ge Hong quotes *Lunyu* 2.4 one more time at the end of the postface, when he uses the device of the hostile, fictitious interlocutor in imitation of Sima Qian, who questions the timing of Ge Hong's authorial postface by referring to him as only thirty years old and about to take up office.[92] Splitting the difference between the two quotations, we might guess that Ge Hong completed the postface sometime after the age of thirty-five, in 318, when he received the honorific of marquis of the region within the pass but before the age of forty in 323. If a sharp difference in dating explains the difference between the two sections, it seems more likely to me that Ge Hong may have written the first half while still in forced, early retirement before 314 and initially utilized the postface as a character resume. When his career began to advance between 318 and 323, he may have amended the text for posterity to reflect recent successes but did not return to it again.

The earliest of Ge Hong's successes in public life came from military service around 303, when he participated in a campaign to put down Shi Bing's rebellion under the command of Gu Mi 顧祕.[93] In addition to his skill at arms, Ge Hong recounts in some detail his ability to command troops, and his disciplined leadership style even saves the day in one anecdote.

> The commanders loosed their troops for looting [after the defeat of the rebels] and in succession chariots were filled. I alone led with discipline and did not allow [my men] to break ranks. [I said that if] any soldier joined the mob I would execute him and display his head [as a warning], and no one dared to disobey. In consequence, several hundred rebels who lay in ambush emerged and attacked the disorganized and defenseless armies. Horses were loaded with loot, and men lacked the will to return to battle. The result was terror and confusion, and in the pandemonium many were killed; [the situation] was nearly beyond salvage. My company alone maintained ordered troops and readied chariots. Without a single casualty, it thus saved the rest of the army from total collapse. Here I showed my ability.[94]

> 諸軍莫不放兵收拾財物, 繼轂連擔. 洪獨約令所領, 不得妄離行陣. 士有摭得眾者, 洪即斬之以徇. 於是無敢委杖. 而果有伏賊數百, 出傷諸軍. 諸軍悉發, 無部隊, 皆人馬負重, 無復戰心, 遂致驚亂, 死傷狼藉, 殆欲不振. 獨洪軍整齊轂張, 無所損傷, 以救諸軍之大崩, 洪有力焉.

His success against Shi Bing's rebellion was a catalyst for later official appointments, for it was precisely this early service that brought him to the attention of Sima Rui and proved his worth to the refugee Eastern Jin court. Significantly, his skill at arms and military strategy belies the claim, made elsewhere in the postface, that his physique was so scrawny he could barely draw a bow.[95] The contradictory claims speak to the collision of various literary tropes in Ge Hong's autobiographical writing and a natural, logical tension that emerges between them. Through the device of the fictitious interlocutor, who challenges his alleged poverty, physical weakness, and reclusion, Ge Hong demonstrates that these different archetypes were not inherently comfortable with each other, that a certain logic with regard to lived experience still persists, and that Ge Hong may have anticipated some resistance to his unprecedented melding of disparate character archetypes.

Eclectic Scholarship

Besides reclusion, the most dominant character type reflected in Ge Hong's autobiographical postface is that of the philosopher, which is rooted in his defense of the importance and utility of philosophical works. Strands of thought within both the Confucian and Daoist textual traditions have at various times, especially during the Warring States period, undervalued the importance of literary works. For example, *Zuozhuan* states that there are three things that do not decay 三不朽 and may therefore establish an individual's legacy; among the three, virtuous action 立德 is considered more important than establishing words 立言.[96] The *Zhuangzi* chapter "The Way of Heaven" (Tian dao 天道) also remarks that the writings of past philosophers are just the dregs (*zao po* 糟粕) of dead men.[97] According to Pu Youjun 浦友俊, it is in this sense that we may say that in the pre-Qin era both Confucianism and Daoism deemphasized writing in favor of whatever action was prescribed by each textual tradition.[98] Early authors were frequently at pains to justify their literary accomplishments, a common function of the authorial postface prior to Ge Hong's time.

By Ge Hong's era, philosophical writing had acquired a higher profile more central to the literary tradition and had become a recognizable genre for contemporary literary critics such as Cao Pi.[99] Ge Hong did not separate literature and action but saw them as two sides of the same coin.[100] Indeed, Ge Hong believed that literature and philosophical writing might also be considered a virtuous action of its own.

> Virtuous action is a concrete action, [and] good and bad are thus easy to distinguish; writings are subtle and mysterious, [and] their relative worth is difficult to comprehend. Now that which is easy to see is coarse; that which is difficult to comprehend is delicate. When the flavor is coarse, there is a set way to weigh it out, but when the flavor is delicate it is difficult to comprehend. I therefore forsake the course and easy to see and discuss the delicate and hard to comprehend; can this not also be done?[101]

德行爲有事, 優劣易見; 文章微妙, 其體難識. 夫易見者, 粗也; 難識者, 精也. 夫唯粗也, 故銓衡有定焉; 夫唯精也, 故品藻難一焉; 吾故捨易見之粗, 而論難識之精v.不亦可乎?

According to Ge Hong, writing is ethically proscriptive and morally instructive in an era of social and political instability, analogous to Zhuangzi's fish trap. When the fish is caught, the trap may be discarded, but "when the Way has not yet been put into practice, we cannot do without writings" 文可以發, 而道未行, 則不得無文.[102] Thus, even during the Warring States era, in which writing was relatively undervalued and viewed with suspicion in texts such as *Zhuangzi*, space existed for philosophical works because they had an immediate social and political function.

Ge Hong's defense of philosophical writing is accompanied by his insistence that contemporary writing is at least as good as that which comes from the past, an argument that was clearly intended to support his own literary undertakings. This assertion was not as radical as it seems, for Ge Hong recognized the authority of canonical writing and defined contemporary writing as an extended commentary on the classics: "The Master Embracing Simplicity said, 'The orthodox classics are the pools and seas of moral righteousness. The writings of the philosophers are the flowing rivers that increase the profundity of the former. . . . Although they differ in beginning steps, they come together in promoting change. Thus the man of clear understanding embraces the root and includes the flowering branches" 正經爲道義之淵海, 子書爲增深之傳流... 雖離於舉趾, 而合於興化. 故通人總原本以括流末.[103] As commentary on the classics, recent philosophical writing surpasses traditional Han exegesis or *zhang ju* 章句, a commentary strategy in which individual characters are glossed in great detail at the expense of a broad understanding of the larger work. Ge Hong argues for something altogether more expansive that will "widen men's thoughts" and, though not as monumental as the classics themselves, may by their accumulated weight become something "as heavy as mountains and hills" 重於山陵.[104]

Ge Hong also points to traditional claims that portions of *Shi jing* and *Shang shu* originated from among the common people as an analogy to his claim that not all important literature originates with sages either in the past or in the present. In Ge Hong's view, because the classics, as anthologies, contain the wisdom of both sages and common people, "[S]imply because a book does not come from the sages we should not disregard words in it which help us in teaching the way" 不以書不出聖, 而廢助教之言.[105] By arguing on principle that canonical, classical wisdom originated from both what is traditionally valued and what is typically overlooked, Ge Hong attempts to assert the value of contemporary philosophical prose, which generally suffers in comparison to the great works of antiquity.

It may be for this reason that Ge Hong devotes an entire chapter of the *Waipian*, "Clarifying Obscurities" 喻蔽, to defending the relatively recent work of Wang Chong. We should recall that Ge Hong might have felt some affinity to Wang Chong as a fellow southerner, and his eclectic *Lunheng ziji pian* likely served as a model for Ge Hong's own work; both are broad in scope, are critical of tradition while living in its midst, and blur sectarian and canonical divisions. Ge Hong's defense of Wang Chong focuses on rebutting criticism of eclecticism and pragmatism, demonstrating how Ge Hong might have anticipated criticism of his own work. In driving home his point, Ge Hong largely draws examples from the Confucian canon by pointing out its own inconsistencies and explaining them as a pragmatic eclecticism: "Formerly the feudal lords asked about government, and the disciples asked about benevolence. When [Confucius] answered them, he used different words to each one. In all probability this was due to the particulars of each situation, and so according to the time there is that which is most important" 昔諸侯訪政, 弟子問仁, 仲尼答之, 人人異辭. 蓋因事詫規, 隨時所急.[106] Ge Hong seems to imply that his approach to scholarship is analogous to that of Confucius, who was himself no slave to dogma. However, by operating from within the traditional canon of historical figures and classical texts, Ge Hong shows that Wang Chong's work—and by extension his own—was rooted in the core principles of the literary and philosophical tradition. Like Confucius in the preceding example, practicality and flexibility addressed the inevitability of changing circumstances and did not call for the abandonment of traditional values and concepts.

The inevitability of historical and material change simply bolstered his argument that recent writings offered more insight into contemporary circumstances than the classics, but this was not a rejection of traditional categories.[107] In this way, Ge Hong creates a complex, critical stance toward the classics that insists on the value of contemporary philosophical works: "If we employ [contemporary authors], there would be favorable omens in the heavens above and lucky signs on the earth below" 施之可以臻徵祥於天上, 發嘉瑞於后土.[108] Thus the work of Ge Hong and his contemporaries borrows the authority of the canon but simultaneously insists on the validity of newer works, a strategy that would have had broad implications for Ge Hong as he promoted his own literary corpus.

The extent of Ge Hong's writing and the timing of its composition suggest that this body of work, in conjunction with the trope of virtuous reclusion, acted to establish his eligibility for an official position. His long decade in reclusion afforded him the opportunity to create a reputation as a literatus and demonstrate his merits for more prestigious civil appointments; the bibliography of his own writing, as Ge Hong describes it, appears to have taken shape by 317, around the time he was awarded the largely honorary title marquis of the region within the pass.

> By the middle of the Jianwu period [ca. 317 CE], altogether [I] had written twenty "inner chapters," fifty "outer chapters;" stone inscriptions, eulogies, poetry, and rhyme prose in one hundred chapters; military correspondence, dispatches, essays, charts, and commentaries and notes in thirty chapters. [I] also composed the *Shenxian zhuan* in ten chapters, a text uninteresting to the layman. Additionally, [I] wrote about eminent men who did not serve in government called *Yinyi zhuan* [Traditions of Recluses] in ten chapters, and furthermore copied the five classics, seven histories, and the words of the [philosophers], military affairs, divination, and miscellaneous writing on strange phenomena. In all, [my] writing totaled 310 chapters.[109]

> 至建武中乃定, 凡著內篇二十卷, 外篇五十卷, 碑頌詩賦百卷,
> 軍書檄移章表　箋記三十卷.　又撰俗所不列者爲神僊傳十卷,
> 又撰高尙不仕者爲隱逸傳十卷, 又抄五經七史百家之言, 兵事
> 方伎短雜奇要三百一十卷.

It is unclear whether this extensive body of work is in addition to writing that began in Ge Hong's late teens, a period in which he was especially active. Of the verse, rhyme prose, and other writings he composed at an early age, he claims to have discarded nearly all of them by the age of twenty, preserving only philosophical works (*zi shu* 子書) and a few miscellaneous texts.[110]

Ge Hong's rejection of verse and rhyme prose may represent a conscious attempt to craft a public image as a philosopher during a period in which poetry was deeply infused with metaphysical language and flattery and largely written on commission.[111] As we have seen, the rejection of verse in favor of prose was a hallmark of Yang Xiong's transformation into a serious philosopher later in life. Likewise, Ge Hong claims that around the age of twenty he came to feel that the composition of minor writings (*xiao wen* 小文) was "not comparable to establishing one school of discourse" 未若立一家之言, a sentiment that echoes Sima Qian's own postface.[112] The very appellative "Master Embracing Simplicity" connotes the masters of antiquity, and the *Waipian* contains several references to disciples and students that are likely an exaggeration.[113] While Ge Hong clearly did not reject entirely the possibility that verse might play some role in enhancing his literary reputation—it does, after all, constitute a full third of his total output—it appears that at some point during his tenure on Mount Luofu he elected to craft his literary persona as the Master Embracing Simplicity, a reclusive philosopher and social critic who pursued esoteric pharmacology. His rejection of verse may speak to a trend toward abstract verse during the Western Jin era and underscore his view that the genre should embody social and political critique. Regardless, Ge Hong's emphasis on literature as useful for ordering society is at the core of what became the Han Confucian textual tradition and seems to lie at the heart of the portrayal of his literary works.[114]

Rhetorical Self-Creation

Ge Hong's autobiographical writing as described in the preceding pages does not represent an empirically factual record on the level of ostensible biographical detail and resists a literal reading. As we have seen, to the degree that it constitutes autobiography it is intelligible in terms of literary tropes or modes of behavior in rhetoric. The text is a record of Ge Hong's ethical life; it is the performance of his character. His various autobiographical personae are his character rendered in signs intelligible to his readers, suggesting that subjectivity in early China was not necessarily a coherent experience of a narrative self but was synthesized from various modes of self-expression. As Habermas states:

> I must choose myself as the one who I am and want to be. *Life history* becomes the principle of individuation, but only if it is transposed by such an act of self-choice into an existential form for which the self is responsible. This extraordinary decision to posit oneself which as it were retroactively places the historicized self under one's own direction, results in the claim of the individual to be identical with himself in ethical life.[115]

What is fascinating in Ge Hong's case—and perhaps in early China as a whole— is that the chosen modes of self-expression need not be complementary. He is both sickly and heroic, a hermit on the verge of serving Emperor Yuan, and a Confucian gentleman who yearns to fabricate elixirs of transcendence. Ge Hong moves freely between modes and styles, weaving tropes into a unique fabric.

Yet the text was not intended as an act of individuation in the conventional sense, one that loudly proclaimed the uniqueness of the author as did Rousseau. Insofar as the author identifies more strongly than his peers with a cluster of ethical virtues, he may *appear* unique, but that individuation only takes place with reference to traditional, canonical values and culturally significant archetypes. What is unique or original is the summary performance.

However, regardless of whether any of the tropes selected by Ge Hong conveyed what his contemporaries might have considered his authentic self, it is clear that the act of self-expression carried deep political and cultural significance. Differences in style and content within the text have suggested to many that the chapter may be composed of two halves written at different times. The first traces his family history, early life of poverty, and reclusive persona as a kind of resume prior to the opportunities of 314 CE. Empirical accuracy was largely irrelevant; the larger question was whether the text provided him with a measure of dignity or social recognition. In this regard, the autobiography represents an accurate self-narrative on an altogether more meaningful level for Ge Hong and his contemporaries. The second section, if it is indeed that, may have been added several years later, after the appointments of 317, to grease the wheels of further advancement or perhaps for the benefit of posterity once he had risen to a relatively secure position on Wang Dao's staff. Like the work of most apologists, Ge Hong's literary activity had, at its core, an intense focus on the future as well as the present.

4

Soteriology of the Text
Transcending History through Autobiography

Modern autobiographies, like their early Chinese counterparts, reflect the internalized needs and external pressures that come to bear on the author but defy reduction to a single motivating principle to write a life narrative. As we saw in the previous chapter, the forces governing an act of self-representation are often fragmentary, contradictory, and poorly understood even by the author. William Least Heat Moon, in his autobiographical travel log *Blue Highways*, writes, "I had hopes of writing a few small stories someone might publish, [but] I primarily wanted to put myself on a new path toward wherever it turned out to lead."[1] The fact that Least Heat Moon laid the foundations for his journey and subsequent best seller some four years prior to his departure betrays the ostensible spontaneity of his autobiography as he describes it in the opening pages. His meticulous forethought and careful attention to the tropes of autobiography and travel writing suggest a dense complex of motivations and social pressures not dissimilar to those of early Chinese writers, impossible to untangle, ranging from self-discovery to careerism.

The genre of the authorial postface also reflects an irreducible tangle of elements that give rise to and justify authorial self-narrative.[2] In Ge Hong's predecessors, the chief aim of autobiography was to justify the act of writing another text; a personal narrative, sometimes detailed and always in the form of a postface or introduction, plays a supporting role to a larger work of self-expression such as a historical work or collection of essays. Unlike Sima Qian's *Taishigong zixu*, the autobiographical detail given by Ge Hong in the *Waipian zixu* is not used only to explain the creation and function of the larger text. Ge Hong's *Waipian zixu* differs from its predecessors by taking the self as a legitimate subject. Ge Hong hoped to craft his own legacy through self-narrative, a text that would define and constrain how he would be "read" by future generations. He radically reinterpreted the act of authorial self-narration, placing autobiography and history in dialogue with one another in a struggle over the privilege to record the narrative of an individual life. He was also deeply invested in esoteric techniques of longevity—particularly pharmacology—and appears to have pursued them with considerable energy late in life. In this sense we might regard Ge Hong as an individual interested in different yet overlapping ways to immortality. To understand this shift in the function of the autobiographical writing within the authorial postface, I will discuss the relationship among traditional historiography, literature, and self-narrative by comparing Ge Hong's formulation of the genre—consisting of the autobiographical essays by Sima Qian, Wang Chong, and Cao Pi—with his own work, the postface to the *Waipian*.

Traditional Historiography

Casting aside the irresoluble dispute about whether the *jiaguwen* 甲骨文, or "oracle bones," constitute the earliest form of historical writing, we may see the privileged position of the scribe, or *shi* 史, to shape historical legacy in the earliest work of Chinese historiography, *Shang shu*. In this early anthology, the scribe appears less concerned with history as such than with performing a specific function to record and store ritual documents related to divination. For example, in the well-known *Zhou shu* 周書 (Book of Zhou) chapter "The Metal Bound Coffer" (Jin teng 金縢), the Duke of Zhou, minister to the ailing king Wu of Zhou, prays to the "former kings" 先王 to save the life of his ruler: "He stood facing north [on the platform], and grasping the ritual implements, he thus prayed to Tai Wang, Wang Ji, and Wen Wang. The scribe thus recorded [the prayer]" 北面, 周公立焉, 植璧秉卦, 乃告太王, 王季, 文王. 史乃冊.[3] Once the prayer is recited and the judgment pronounced (the passage is not clear as to whether the Duke of Zhou says the prayer or another ritual officer, the *zhu* 祝, recites what the scribe has transcribed), the scribe's record is stored in the metal-bound coffer. Later, when political intrigue casts doubt on the Duke of Zhou's loyalties to the Zhou house and the new ruler, King Cheng and his ministers don ritual garments and open the metal-bound coffer only to discover the record of the Duke of Zhou's prayer for the king's well-being: "The two ministers and the king then asked the scribes about this matter, and they replied, saying, 'It is true! The [Duke of Zhou] commanded us not to dare speak of it'" 二公及王乃問諸史與百執事, 對曰: 信. 噫! 公命我勿敢言.[4] Amending his behavior in accordance with the record of the previous divination, the king thus saves Zhou from the retribution of Heaven (representative of "natural law" or the normative order), presumably aroused by intrigues at the court. This episode suggests that the scribe initially operated as a religious functionary, preserving a record of religious rituals and presiding over an archive consisting of ritual pronouncements and the judgments of spirits and ancestors. Though not strictly what we might consider a historical record, the divination and subsequent judgment recorded certain qualities of experience, such as illness, loyalty, and character, that intersected with ritual and were subject to future verification, becoming a de facto historical document. Because the judgment of the ancestors or spirits was believed to correspond to an authoritative, higher level of reality, the record of divination as a historical account acquired the ambiguous quality of "accuracy" on the level of what may be tentatively termed "objective reality." More important, perhaps, the divine judgments also guaranteed the longevity of the individual through periodic renewal of memory; the occasional addition to the cache of stored divinations and judgments through new rituals was a rite that recalled previous divinations and their outcomes. This record of ritual and divine judgments held tremendous power, including the ability to circumscribe the behavior of the political elite.

Based on this example, it is possible to argue that historians possessed a quasi-sacral and officially sanctioned power either to confer on individuals a lasting name or to obliterate them from the historical record. Xu Fuguan 徐復觀 suggests that the importance of historical writing may stem from the evolution of the scribe from a religious office to the secular function of "historian." According to Xu, the office of the scribe initially oversaw at least six religious and semireligious functions, including offering prayers, managing divinations, managing the calendar, explaining calamities, recording official appointments, and recording genealogies.[5] Gradually, other experts and occupations took over some of the more esoteric functions of the historian such as divination, which became the function of the *bu ren* 卜人, or "dream interpretation," also performed by the *wu* 巫, often liberally translated as "shaman."[6] This change in the office of the scribe coincided with a shift in the quality of the scribe's record away from religious judgments to a record of lived experience and marks the basis of the historian's authority. Because historical reporting of an individual's life overtakes religious notions of judgment, "[H]istory comes to replace religion as the ideal of longevity."[7] In *Zuozhuan*, Xiang 襄 24, a minister from the state of Jin 晉, inquires as to meaning of the phrase "To die and not decay" 死而不朽. The minister from Lu 魯 replies that if one establishes virtue, meritorious deeds, and good words, and "after a long time these are not discarded, this is what is called 'not to decay'" 雖久不廢, 此之謂不朽.[8] We need not visit Xu's "either/or" dichotomy between religion and history to grasp the point that historical writing became one method among many by which an individual could achieve a kind of immortality. Moreover, the scribe's authority to subject the individual to the rigors of historical judgment supported the state's monopoly to recognize talent and virtue. Stephen Durrant and Steven Shankman observe, "In a culture that places much more emphasis upon this world than on the other, to be remembered became a major means of immortality."[9] While divination remained the privilege of the court magician, or *wu*, the scribe retained at least one aspect of his former authority, the power to subject the individual to the rigors of a historical judgment that would survive for future generations.

The tradition that Confucius was the author of *Chunqiu* supported the idea that historical judgment possessed both a sacral and a secular function. Confucius was seen as the heir to both the traditional categories of knowledge of the historian and the responsibilities of historical judgment.[10] Further, "Confucius' intention or aim in writing *Chunqiu* does not lie in the contemporary category of 'historiography' but rather in promoting the classical historian's solemn charge to replace the judgment of spirits with the judgments of the historian."[11] Mencius provides the most succinct expression of this sensibility, arguing that Confucius also uses *Chunqiu* to replace the rewards and punishments of the ruler:[12] "In ancient times, Yu repressed the floodwaters and all under Heaven was made peaceful; Zhougong annexed the territory of the Yi and the Di and drove off the wild beasts and the people were free from worry; Confucius completed *Chunqiu*, and seditious ministers and unfilial sons were afraid" 昔者禹抑洪水而天下平, 周公兼夷狄, 驅猛獸, 而百姓寧, 孔子成春秋, 而亂臣賊子懼.[13] Here the writing of the *Chunqiu* is an act of mythic proportions, counted among the accomplishments of cultural heroes and sage kings. Confucius not only records the past, but the record itself becomes a blueprint for contemporary social and political order, regulating fundamental social relationships with an almost imperial prerogative by threatening "malefactors [with] the permanence of written historical records, in which their crimes will be preserved for everlasting condemnation."[14] Sima Qian seems to sympathize with Mencius's view, stating that Confucius used *Chunqiu* to "clarify the way of kings" 明王道.[15] Thus by the Warring States period the occupation of the historian had evolved from the religious functions evident in *Shang shu* into a secular scribe modeled on the figure of Confucius. Historical records such as *Chunqiu* not only recorded the past but were seen, at least by some, to possess the power to admonish the living.

The tradition that *Chunqiu* possessed the gnostic historical judgments of Confucius not only elevated the status of the scribe but also privileged their position as interpreters and keepers of the past.[16] As David Schaberg observes, the authors/historians of *Zuozhuan* closed the Spring and Autumn period with the death of Confucius, an act that marked the end of an era and hinted at the social and intellectual origins of their craft.[17] The portrayals of historians within *Zuozhuan* demonstrate the secular turn of the occupation during the Warring States period and underscore the claim of the authors that the scribe is the sole arbiter of the past.[18] The authority of the historian persists even when the scribe's record places him at odds with political authority. In *Zuozhuan*, Xiang 襄 25, we read:

> The Grand Scribe wrote, "Cui Zhu murdered his ruler." Cui killed him. The scribe's younger brothers wrote the same thing, and two of them died. Another younger brother again recorded it, and Cui let him go. When Nanshi, the Scribe of the South, heard that the Grand Scribes had all died, he took his bamboo slips and departed. When he heard that it had been recorded, he returned.[19]

> 大史書曰, 崔杼弒其君, 崔子殺之. 其弟嗣書, 而死者二人. 其弟又書, 乃舍之. 南史氏聞大史盡死, 執簡以往. 聞既書矣, 乃還.

Cui Zhu, clearly disturbed by the scribe's version of events, violently disagrees with the record of his regicide. Here we are asked to believe that Cui Zhu's anxiety stems from the threat of a written historical judgment beyond the authority of even the most powerful political figures to amend. Schaberg writes, "Historical writing, in the historiographers' understanding of it, is the most perfect form of enunciated judgment. It survives beyond the reach of the judged individual and continues to reward and punish indefinitely."[20] We may also observe from this account that the prerogative to record history belongs to the scribe alone, who ideally labors to transmit accurate information to posterity even in the face of murderous suppression.[21] However, Cui Zhu is clearly not concerned with the opinions of his ministers but with the threat of the potential longevity of a historical judgment that over time had become a substitute for the immortal judgment of the spirits.

Many of the *Zuozhuan* entries indicate that early Chinese historiography was concerned with representing reality on both a literal and a ritual (and hence moral) level. Early Chinese historians recorded the past as a deviation from ritual, or timeliness, a fact perhaps explained as the residue of the scribe's early function as a recorder of religious ritual. Histories such as *Zuozhuan* thus constitute a record of untimely action; without untimely events there would simply be nothing to record. As Schaberg states, "The elimination of ritual aberrations and the complete ritualization of time would bring the end of history."[22] The representation of ritual reality was the paramount concern of early Chinese historians, surpassing the need to distinguish the fine division of categories such as "fact" and "fiction." In *Zuozhuan*, Xuan 宣 2, we read:

On the *yichou* day, Zhao Chuan killed Duke Ling at Taoyuan. Xuanzi returned before crossing the mountains. The Grand Scribe wrote, "Zhao Dun killed his lord" and displayed [the record] at court. Xuanzi said, "[The account] is not accurate." [The Scribe] replied, "You are the *zhengqing*; when you fled you did not cross the border [of the state], and returning you did not punish the culprit. If you are not responsible, then who is?" Xuanzi said, "Alas! *Shi jing* says, 'My longing brings me such sorrow'; this describes me indeed!" Confucius said, "Dong Hu is a good scribe of ancient times; his record does not conceal. Xuanzi is a good minister of ancient times; because of the law he received evil [judgment]. A pity! Had he crossed the border, he would have been absolved.[23]

乙丑, 趙穿攻靈公於桃園. 宣子未出山而復. 大史書曰, "趙盾弒其君," 以示於朝. 宣子曰, "不然." 對曰, "子爲正卿, 亡不越竟, 反不討賊, 非子而誰." 宣子曰, "嗚呼! 詩曰: '我之懷矣, 自詒伊慼,' 其我之謂矣.'" 孔子曰, "董狐, 古之良史也. 書法不隱, 趙宣子, 古之良大夫也, 爲法受惡. 惜也, 越竟乃免."

Confucius praises Dong Hu for his frank account of events but not because he records what actually occurred from an omniscient, objective point of view. Zhao Dun did not personally kill Duke Ling, a fact Dong Hu does not dispute. As *zhengqing*, or prime minister, Zhao Dun is nevertheless responsible for the crime and punishing the perpetrators. Zhao Dun's submission to the judgment of history marks him as a "good minister of ancient times" by Confucius, who gives the overarching resolution and interpretation to the conflict between what we might call objective reality and the historical record. The judgment of Confucius, the paragon of the early Chinese historiographer, provides Zhao Dun with his immortal cultural relevance and on one level exonerates him for his complicity in the crimes of Zhao Chuan by citing his accordance with ritual. We might think of people such as Zhao Dun from early historical texts such as *Zuozhuan* in terms of character "types" found in the commercial fiction of later periods acting out tropes of behavior within a formal setting. History in this regard becomes a record of an idealized lived experience, not experience itself, in which each event or person is subject to the demands of the historian's conception of proper morality and ritual. Zhao Dun's submission to Dong Hu's judgment marks a submission to the authority of the historian to record and judge, but it ultimately represents his submission to ritualized political order, the *oughtness* of the situation as seen through the lens of historiography. In this context, the audacity of autobiography lay in its challenge to state authority. Claiming authorial agency to script one's self potentially undermined the state's monopoly to recognize talent and virtue by attempting to create a durable name beyond the authority of state sanctioned history. For this reason, early writers of autobiography such as Sima Qian were very careful to cast their self-narrative in terms other than authoritative self-representation.

Sima Qian: Self-Narration and the Tragic Persona

As we have seen, a few scholars generally credit Sima Qian, grand astrologer of the court of Han Emperor Wu 漢武帝 (r. 140–87 BC), with the first autobiographical writing in the Chinese tradition. Guo Dengfeng's enormous compilation of Chinese autobiographical writing lists Sima Qian's *Taishigong zixu* and "Letter in Response to Ren Shaoqing" as the earliest known examples of Chinese autobiographical prose.[24] The postface narrates Sima Qian's life in chronological order, beginning with his distant ancestry, but in a fairly reticent fashion, casting the author in terms of his genealogy rather than as a historical agent. In contrast, Sima Qian's letter is rich in autobiographical detail, essentially fleshing out the story of his disgrace over supporting the defeated general Li Ling 李陵 (d. 74 BCE), an event barely alluded to in his authorial postface. Although the postface is very personal at times, the more revealing letter complements the postface, and together they provide a well-rounded picture of the subject that is missing from either text alone.

The most important formal feature of the Sima Qian's authorial postface is its attachment to a larger work, *Shi ji*. Sima Qian uses his postface on one level to anticipate and counter objections to the writing of *Shi ji*, particularly his dangerous association between his own work and *Chunqiu* of Confucius, which, by implication, casts his own era as an epoch of political disorder:[25] "That which I do can be called *transmitting* ancient matters and *to put in order* hereditary traditions; it is not what is called *to create*. But you, sir, compare it [*Shi ji*] to *Chunqiu*, [and] this is mistaken" 余所謂述故事, 整齊其世傳, 非所謂作也; 而君比之於春秋, 謬矣.[26] Because history and record keeping were the privilege and responsibility of the state, such justifications were necessary to temper the implicit challenge to state authority by private records such as *Shi ji*. Sima Qian uses his autobiographical sketch to explain the origin and purpose of his comprehensive history through anecdotes that define his work as a filial act within a tradition of tormented authors, including Confucius and the poet Qu Yuan:[27] "In all these instances, men had ideas that were stifled and did not manage to disseminate their doctrines; thus they narrated past events and thought of those to come" 此人皆意有所鬱結, 不得統其道也, 故述往事, 思來者.[28] In Sima Qian's text, biographical information establishes the authorial persona as a circumstance of literary production, creating an image of the self that is in turn a literary product. In James Olney's words, the "self that was not really in existence in the beginning is in the end merely a matter of the text."[29]

The death of his father marks the moment in Sima Qian's postface when his own story is equated with literary production: "Qian bowed his head and wept, saying, 'I, your son, am ignorant, but I shall discuss in full your reports of antiquity; I must not fail" 遷俯首流涕曰, 小子不敏, 請悉論先人所次舊聞, 弗敢闕.[30] The figure of the father is important, as it grounds Sima Qian in a tradition of historical writing and serves to authorize his own literary production.[31] In addition to his father's admonition, the personal tragedy of Sima Qian's castration for the crime of offending Emperor Wu plays a critical role in his writing. Sima Qian justifies his textual production with notions of frustration and personal hardship. As suggested by Mark Edward Lewis, authors made claims to social, political, and philosophical isolation to authorize their writing; the convention of total isolation justifies the individual's effort to give rise to his concerns in writing. The individual voice "was not a matter of social converse, but a sign of disaster and disintegration."[32]

Providing that an individual is unlike any other, isolation need not be physical but is often established through reference to a personal tragedy or by similar means. Sima Qian, writing to his friend Ren Shaoqing long after his castration, states, "If {my work} is disseminated among all the people. . . . Though I suffer a thousand mutilations, what regret would I have? These matters may be discussed with a wise man, but it is difficult to explain them to ordinary people" 傳之其人通邑大都. . .雖萬被戮, 豈有悔哉. 然此可爲智者道, 難爲俗人言也.[33] Sima Qian's careful and close association with various other tragic literary figures, such as Qu Yuan, further indicates that he felt his personal tragedy isolated him from "ordinary people" and led to the writing of his masterpiece.

Wang Chong: Self-Narrative and the Role of Fate

While adopting Sima Qian's association between frustration and literary output in his own autobiographical postface, Wang Chong goes even farther than Sima Qian in emphasizing his failure to attain worldly success rather than any specific personal tragedy. On many levels, the "Chapter of Self Record" of the *Lunheng* establishes a more solitary subject simply by giving the reader far more detail than Sima Qian's essay, for Wang here depicts himself as lacking any kind of membership in a grouping that could define his identity whether this consists of ties to family, ties to the world of officialdom, or some other social affiliation. Wang Chong knows that his isolation is far from a source of misery but rather sets the stage for greatness: "A bird without lineage is a phoenix, an animal without a breed is a unicorn, a person without ancestry is a sage, an object of rarity is a precious jewel" 鳥無世鳳皇, 獸無種麒麟, 人無祖聖賢, 物無常嘉珍. [34] He claims that his productivity stems from his unsuccessful career as a scholar-official, for which he takes Confucius as his primary role model. In one very interesting passage, he employs Sima Qian's rhetorical device of an interlocutor who questions his impulse to produce literary works, including, it should be noted, the autobiographical postface. Wang Chong's interlocutor acknowledges his miserable official career but argues that it is only through high position, not literature, that one may advance his ideas and be heard. "Of what use to yourself are these beautiful words you have written down," he asks. "Where is all this [writing] leading you?" 著記美言, 何補於身? 眾多欲以何趨乎. [35] Wang Chong replies, "In talent, none surpassed Confucius, but his talent was not appreciated and he was exiled" 材鴻莫過孔子, 孔子才不容, 斥逐. [36] Aside from comparing his own work favorably to that of Confucius, Wang Chong's reply implies that unrecognized talent must find other avenues of expression.

Consistent with his overall philosophical stance, Wang Chong emphasizes the role of fate in achieving worldly success and recognition. Based on the example of Confucius, he concludes that success is not a reward for talent but a matter of timing and chance.

> Moreover, those who succeed are not necessarily clever, while those who fail are not necessarily stupid. Those who are lucky thus succeed, and those who are unlucky lose everything. Therefore, if fate is liberal and fortune good, a mediocre person becomes noble and respectable. If fate is light and fortune poor, then a remarkable person declines and is unlucky. [37]

> 且達者未必知, 窮者未必愚. 遇者則得, 不遇失之. 故夫命厚祿善, 庸人尊顯. 命薄祿惡奇俟落魄.

It is clear from the rest of the passage that Wang Chong feels bad fortune may be a safe place to lay the blame for his lackluster career. His answer to bad luck is literary output, which, in his view, is a way to transcend the vulgar world of success and failure.

> If somebody lives in honor and comfort, after a hundred years, like all other things, this, too, is gone. His name does not come down to the next generation; his words are not left on any document. Although he may have a store of riches, his literature and virtue are not abundant, and this is not what

I value. Deep and exemplary virtue, abundant and extensive knowledge, a writing brush dripping like rain, an overflowing spring of words, rich talents and enviable knowledge, noble action and a respectable mind, [with such qualities] a man's body exists in one generation, but his name will be transmitted for a thousand years; that is what I call extraordinary.[38]

身尊體佚, 百載之後, 與物俱歿, 名不流於一嗣, 文不遺於一札, 官雖傾倉, 文德不豐, 非吾所臧. 德汪濊而淵懿, 知滂沛而盈溢, 筆瀧漉而雨集, 言溶窟而泉出, 富材羨知, 貴行尊志, 體列於一世, 名傳於千載, 乃吾所謂異也.

This passage exemplifies the shift in the position and social value of literature by the end of the Western Han. As Lin Lixue has commented, "Based on traditional Confucian notions, virtuous action was considered most important, while literature existed on the periphery. This kind of concept for the most part was transmitted down to Wang Chong's era, by which time it began to change. He [Wang Chong] recognized literature as the expression of virtue . . . [and] literature and virtue were of equal importance."[39] In Wang Chong's view, literary output embodies the author's virtue, imparting to the author a measure of immortality unmatched by wealth or high office.

Although Wang Chong mentions his autobiographical postface among his other works in the dialogue with his interlocutor, it is worth pointing out that nothing in the contemporary concept of the value of literature necessitates a life story or autobiography in order to preserve the virtue of the author for posterity. Following Lin Lixue's argument, the *Lunheng ziji pian* itself is sufficient to express Wang Chong's virtue to future readers. In this sense, an autobiography expressing the character or virtue of an author would be redundant. Yet, as did Sima Qian's *Taishigong zixu*, the *Lunheng ziji pian* uses autobiographical detail, in this case a description of professional failure, to rationalize the production of the larger work. When timing and chance abandon those who possess virtue, their only alternative is to turn to future generations for vindication.

Cao Pi: The Narrative of Worldly Achievement

By rejecting self-deprecating modes of description, Cao Pi's "Authorial Postface" to his *Dian lun* is unique among early autobiographical essays for its unabashedly positive view of the author's life and accomplishments. Cao Pi's postface is essentially a brief record of the heroic exploits of a precocious warrior, who, following his father Cao Cao's example, mastered "the ways of literature and warfare" 文武之道 at an early age.[40] Cao Pi's education and literary achievements are largely inconsequential in his biographical sketch, which is rich in details about his military career. His cleverness and good character are intimately tied to his capacity as a man of action and his skill in battle. Only in the last few lines does Cao Pi attempt to convey how he came to write literature.

> His Majesty [Cao Cao] is fond of poetry, books, and classics, so that even among his troops he always has a book in hand. After every battle he would calmly intone, "When people are young and fond of studying their thought is very focused, but as they mature the joy is forgotten. Among those who are older but are able to study industriously, there is only myself and Yuan Boye."[41] Because of this I learned poetry and their commentaries at an early age, and when I was older I thoroughly explored the Five Classics, the Four Categories, *Shi ji, Han shu*, and the words of the various Masters and the hundred Schools, all of which I comprehensively read. Of the works I have written, including essays, monographs, poetry, and *fu*,they are altogether sixty chapters.[42]

> 雅好詩書文籍, 雖在軍旅, 手不釋卷, 每每定省從容, 常言 "人少好學則思專, 長則善忘, 長大而能勤學者, 唯吾與袁伯業耳." 余是以少誦詩, 論, 及長而備歷五經, 四部, 史, 漢, 諸子百家之言, 靡不畢覽. 所著書論詩賦, 凡六十篇.

Cao Pi frames his self-description in moral terms, coyly stating, "As for whether I have been wise but able to appear foolish, brave but able to retreat when need be, benevolent with others, or compassionate with my inferiors, this I leave for a good historian in a later time [to decide]" 至若智而能愚, 勇而能怯, 仁以接物, 恕以及下, 以付後之良史.[43] Of course, he has just finished explaining how he is in fact all of these things. The veneer of modesty is meant to conform to the expectations of the reader and may have been tempered by other expectations of martial and literary prowess appropriate for an individual of Cao Pi's position.

Unlike the autobiographical essays of Sima Qian and Wang Chong, Cao Pi's postface is related to the text it introduces almost as an afterthought. However, although the tone of the postface lacks the defensiveness of his predecessors, it nevertheless serves to justify his literary and martial accomplishments while conveying a sense of the author through a self-written history. In this regard, Cao Pi's submission to the authority of the historian seems almost a perfunctory statement as he has already described his lofty character in full detail. Cao Pi seems very conscious of the role history will play in shaping his legacy. He elaborates on this notion in his "Lun wen" 論文 (Discourse on Literature), stating,

"So writers of ancient times entrusted their persons to ink and brush, and let their thoughts be seen in their compositions; depending neither on a good historian nor on momentum from a powerful patron, their reputations were handed down to posterity on their own force."[44] Together these two texts show Cao Pi's awareness of the occupation of historian as one pitfall among many in establishing an enduring legacy, a hurdle that can be overcome by writing great literature.

Ge Hong and the Creation of Autobiography

Similar to the works of Sima Qian, Wang Chong, and Cao Pi, Ge Hong's *Waipian zixu* defends the idea of literary production as a means of achieving lasting fame. While suggesting that his autobiographical essay itself might create a durable legacy, Ge Hong's chapter "Equalizing Generations" (Jun shi 鈞世) devotes considerable attention to the far-reaching effects of writing in general.[45] In the autobiographical postface, he states:

> When we examine the scholars from the distant past, some used writings to soar like dragons,[46] some used military prowess to crouch like tigers, [their] great merit recorded in official chronicles,[47] their sonorous virtue proclaimed by pipes and strings. Although physical forms sink into the earth, praise [of good men] continues to circulate and be recorded. Thus, whether a hundred or a thousand generations pass, people still remember [great men] this way.[48]

> 歷覽遠古逸倫之士，或以文藝而龍躍，或以武功而虎踞，高勳著於盟府，德音被乎管絃，形器雖沈鑠於淵壤，美談飄飆而日載，故雖千百代，猶穆如也.

Similar to Wang Chong, Ge Hong claims that literary accomplishment is equivalent to virtuous action in perpetuating a good reputation.

Lacking Cao Pi's high position, Ge Hong imitated Sima Qian and Wang Chong by playing on the trope of failure and isolation as an inspiration for his prodigious literary accomplishments. Several passages in the *Waipian zixu* overstate the case that he was a failure in his official life and furthermore lacked political allies or any recognition for his virtuous actions. Throughout the autobiography, Ge Hong speaks to his moral isolation as well; he even draws parallels to Confucius and the Duke of Zhou, whose virtues set them apart from their contemporaries.[49] As Hu Fuchen 胡孚琛 points out, Ge Hong spends considerable energy casting himself as a "gentleman who does not follow the trends of the world but embraces simplicity" 不隨世變的抱朴之士.[50] According to the claims made in the autobiography, Ge Hong refused to participate in gambling, drinking, and gossip and rejected the fashion of his times by keeping to himself in a rundown house at the end of a quiet lane. Although Hu Fuchen interprets these biographical details literally, I see them more as literary tropes with a narrative function. Like Sima Qian and Wang Chong, his clear models in this regard, Ge Hong finds it necessary to demonstrate to the reader a certain level of uniqueness in order to justify a reclusive lifestyle spent in the pursuit of literary accomplishments.[51]

Although Ge Hong's *Waipian zixu* resembles its antecedents in form and function, it advances autobiography as a genre that captures the significance of an individual life and transmits it to future generations. I do not wish to imply that Ge Hong replaces literature or religious transcendence with autobiography as a means of either achieving immortality or transmitting his virtue to posterity. Rather, by emphasizing autobiographical writing as such, he elevates the status of such works as a genre and addresses the issue of memory and immortality on yet another level. We might say that Ge Hong's treatment or interpretation of his predecessors *creates* the genre of autobiography out of a collection of texts meant only to justify literary accomplishment. Whereas Wang Chong's *Lunheng ziji pian* emphasized the production of literature within the context of a life marked by unrecognized virtue, Ge Hong sees autobiography as another way to perpetuate his name and reputation. After recounting his literary talent and military achievements, Ge Hong closes the text using Sima Qian's convention of a hostile interlocutor who challenges the author's literary authority.

> Hong wrote the chapter of his autobiography, and someone criticized him, saying, "Formerly, when Wang Chong was sixty years old,[52] his ideals could not be carried out, and his hopes were cut off. He was fearful that both his body and his name would be extinguished, so he wrote an autobiography to conclude his work. Now you are but thirty years old,[53] and live while the Way is in effect, . . . [so] how can you deplore the fact that your virtue[54] has not been made known and work so studiously on an old man's occupation?[55]

> 洪既著自敘之篇. 或人難曰: "昔王充年在耳順, 道窮望絕, 懼身名之偕滅, 故自紀終篇. 先生以始立之盛, 值乎有道之運... 何憾芬芳之不揚, 而務老生之彼務."

Ge Hong added several new elements to this formulaic dialogue. He recognizes that Wang Chong's basis for literary accomplishment was political frustration and contrasts Wang Chong's time—probably for the sake of his personal safety—with his own age, "when the Way is in effect." As in Sima Qian's postface, Ge Hong's interlocutor questions the timing of his writing based on the alleged existence of an enlightened ruler.[56] However, in Ge Hong's postface the interlocutor narrows his criticism specifically to the writing of autobiography and reinterprets Wang Chong's text as a document designed to perpetuate the name of the author rather than explain the genesis of a body of literary work. The dialogue gives new meaning to the act of autobiography. In the view expressed here, self-narrative—with the exception of poetry—is an act intended to fix or control the legacy of the author during times of political turmoil or personal failure. Added to this is the notion of appropriate timing, the idea that an individual undertakes autobiography not only at a specific historical moment but also near the end of his or her life. Here Ge Hong's interlocutor questions the timing of his autobiographical chapter by quoting Confucius, who famously set forth the stages of his personal development in *Lunyu* 2.4. The allusion augments Ge Hong's defense of his autobiography by claiming a precedent within orthodox Confucian tradition.[57] Moreover, the association reinterprets Wang Chong's autobiographical writing as an act of self-revelation and personal narrative rather than a rationalization for his literary works such as the *Lunheng*.

Ge Hong displays more urgency than his predecessors to establish a lasting account of the details of his life and ensure that his biographical details will be remembered according to his own standard of interpretation. Such anxiety may reflect his relatively low social and political position in a time of seemingly unending turmoil and upheaval when historical writing had flourished to a new, greater degree.

> I am ordinary and mediocre, stifled and without expression,[58] useless for the times; my way of doing things runs against the world. . . . Within [the court] I do not have the assistance of Jin and Zhang Tang.[59] Beyond [the court] I lack the friendship of men who dust off their caps.[60] Although the way is flat, my feet are not those of the *qi lin*;[61] although the six directions are vast,[62] my wings are not those of the great *peng*.[63] As far as high affairs of state are concerned, I cannot set the country right, and in lesser ones I cannot leave a good reputation to honor my parents. My goodness has not been entrusted to a good historian. My reputation does not adorn bells and tripods.[64] Thus, in addition to my writings, I composed this autobiography. Although it cannot amend my failure or success in life, still it will give an account [of myself] for future generations.[65]

> 余以庸陋, 沈抑婆娑, 用不合時, 行殊於世 [...] 內無金張之援, 外乏彈冠之友, 循塗雖坦, 而足無騏驎, 六虛雖曠, 而翼非大鵬, 上不能鷹揚匡國, 下無以顯親垂名, 美不寄於良史, 聲不附乎鍾鼎. 故因著述之餘, 而為自敘之篇, 雖無補於窮達, 亦賴將來之有述焉.

Lin Lixue argues that this passage demonstrates the extremely high esteem in which Ge Hong held literature, eclipsing even the value of virtuous actions while alive: "In this case the writing of the *Waipian* stems from [Ge Hong's] encounter with times of misfortune, and having had few accomplishments [he] had no alternative but to hope for the next generation to know him by means of [his writing]."[66] I agree with Lin Lixue's assessment of the importance of literature to Ge Hong, but I believe the passage emphasizes the author's desire to establish his name and reputation specifically through autobiographical writing. Ge Hong states that his autobiography will explain his worldly successes and failures, much like Wang Chong and Sima Qian's view that literary works are intended to transcend misfortune. However, I would go further by arguing that the passage differs from the writing of Sima Qian and Wang Chong by forcefully asserting autobiography as a means of crafting a record of virtuous conduct. Ge Hong is more interested in telling his own story than framing the text as a defense of the writing of *Baopuzi*. In this sense he introduces a new wrinkle by creating a persona that possesses its own biography and is, moreover, present throughout the text "in character."

Ge Hong's interest in controlling and conveying the details of his life is in part an outgrowth of his distrust of traditional, Confucian historiography and the historical record. In one sense, this attitude may be an evolution of Wang Chong's notion that a virtuous life is, in itself, not enough to grant one a good name after death. An individual must provide a lasting expression of virtue in the form of literary works to ensure one's reputation and legacy. We could say that Ge Hong furthers Wang Chong's idea by arguing that an expression of virtue is also not enough; an individual must provide a durable record of that virtuous life as well.[67] Ge Hong had any number of reasons to turn to autobiography. In my view, the most obvious is that he saw autobiography as the antithesis of historiography: a history of the self, written by the subject, that addresses a potentially unjust or even nonexistent historical record. The importance of the "good historian" (*liang shi* 良史) to Ge Hong's concept of autobiography may reflect the growth of historical writing into a veritable cottage industry during the Jin era. It also seems to reflect the influence of Cao Pi's *Dian lun xizu*. While Ge Hong shared this concern with Cao Pi, his narrow focus on the self as a legitimate subject of discourse marks a significant break with his influential predecessor.[68] Ge Hong's explicit goal of anticipating the criticism or neglect of a future historian marks an evolution in the scope and purpose of autobiography that underscores the position of historical writing as a powerful arbiter of memory and lasting judgment.

Ge Hong and Historiography

Despite his distrust of the historical record, Ge Hong's attitude toward traditional historiography was one of ambivalence. As I discussed in the previous chapter, Ge Hong's literary activity may have included a supporting role in writing an annalistic history of the Jin era after the manner of *Zuozhuan* or *Shi ji*. By his own account his erudition in the classics included extensive knowledge of Han historiography. As we have seen, in his autobiographical postface Ge Hong describes his copious literary output in a remarkable 310 chapters, including *Baopuzi, Shenxian zhuan* "stone inscriptions, eulogies, poetry, and rhyme prose in one hundred chapters; military correspondence, dispatches, essays, charts, and commentaries and notes in thirty chapters . . . and furthermore copied the five classics, seven histories, and the words of the [philosophers], military affairs, divination, and miscellaneous writing on strange phenomena."[69] Presumably, the 20 "inner chapters" and 50 "outer chapters" also mentioned in this passage represent *Baopuzi* in a form very similar to what we have today. Ge Hong's poetry, rhyme prose, eulogies, military correspondence, dispatches, and commentaries are all lost. A text entitled *Shenxian zhuan* still exists, and is assumed by many to be the work described here,[70] but sadly the *Yinyi zhuan* is among his lost works. The "five classics" Ge Hong copied refers to the *Yi* 易, *Shu* 書, *Shi* 詩, *Li* 禮, and *Chunqiu*. The identity of the "seven histories" is probably impossible to determine. Ge Hong's official biography in *Jin shu* 晉 書 72 sheds little light on the problem, repeating almost verbatim the above list of works, clarifying only that Ge Hong had indeed copied *Shi ji* and Ban Gu's *Han shu*,[71] while the *Neipian* postface only lists *Baopuzi* itself, though in a startling 116 chapters![72] As we have seen, by the mid–seventh century a tradition had developed that Ge Hong copied, edited, and added a brief postface to the *Xijing zaji*, a text that was possibly the work of Liu Xin 劉 歆 (50[?] BCE–23 CE). William Nienhauser's argument against Ge Hong's authorship of the text tends to track the editors of the *Siku quanshu* 四庫全 書 on the issue, which also explains "Ge Hong's" postface to the *Xijing zaji* as most likely a forgery.[73] Yang Mingzhao suggests that four of the "seven histories" referred to here may be *Shi ji, Han shu, Dongguan Hanji* 東觀漢記 (Han Records of the Eastern Lodge), which in part formed the basis of Fan Ye's *Hou Han shu*, and *Wu zhi* 吳志 (Record of Wu). Yang quotes the *Siku quanshu* entry for the *Dongguan Hanji tiyao* 提要, which states, "During the Jin dynasty, [*Dongguan Hanji,*] together with *Shi ji* and *Han shu,* constituted the 'three histories'" 晉時以此書與史記漢書爲三史.[74] Histories of the Han era appeared in great numbers during the Three Kingdoms 三國 (221–65 CE) and Western Jin periods, including Sima Biao's 司馬彪 (240–306) *Xu Han shu* 續漢書 and perhaps more than a dozen other works with the title *Hou Han shu, Hou Han ji*, or some variation thereof.[75] The sheer glut of possibilities has led Jay Sailey to observe simply that it remains "unclear which histories are being referred to,"[76] a conclusion that seems hard to escape.

While the extent to which Ge Hong engaged in historical writing is unclear, two chapters of the *Waipian*, "The Faults of Han" 漢過 and "The Failings of Wu" 吳失, demonstrate his understanding of the role and authority of the historian by providing caricatures of classical historiography. The conflict in *Zuozhuan, Xuan* 2 between Dong Hu's ritualized version of Zhao Dun's alleged regicide and what "actually happened" illustrates a fundamental tension in classical Chinese historiography between the past and the historical record. While the authors of *Zuozhuan* insert the judgment of Confucius in a bid to explain this discrepancy, Ge Hong skirts the issue by failing to include even the barest historical narrative in either chapter. He begins both chapters by stating his desire to examine the failings of the Han and the Wu eras as cautionary tales for his contemporaries and their descendants, but the essays quickly become a flood of historically unspecific political sentiments that suggest Ge Hong was interested in models of formal or perhaps ritualized political and social behavior rather than historical narrative. The conspicuous lack of historical detail supports Sailey's reading of the two chapters as engaged in the time-honored Confucian tradition of "using the past to criticize the present."[77] Ge Hong did not intend these chapters to be specific historical narratives of the Han and Wu periods but considered them to be political commentary—possibly aimed at his contemporaries—wrapped in the rhetoric of historiography.

Ge Hong frames his discussion of "The Faults of Han" within the Confucian paradigm of declining political and social order. From antiquity to the present, the ancient way has declined and been lost: "Examining the record of the past on down to the present day, the Way has become obscured and customs have become vulgar; there is no [example of this] more severe than the end of the Han" 歷覽前載, 逮乎近代, 道微俗獘, 莫劇漢末 也.[78] Curiously, this view seems to contradict a "Legalist" trend in his writing that supports a paradigm of material and social progress,[79] best expressed in the *Waipian*'s "Equalizing Generations" 鈞世 chapter. Here Ge Hong rhetorically asks, "Everyone knows things are better now than in past eras, [so] why only in literature are we not equal to antiquity?" 世人皆知之快於 曩矣, 何以獨文章不及古邪.[80] My own explanation, irrespective of which thread may represent Ge Hong's "true" opinion, is that writing contemporary political criticism disguised as historiography requires him to fulfill certain tropical expectations of the genre, including the widely attested assertion that deep antiquity was a golden age. This strategy allows the author to construct the recent past as an age of decline, which is always useful as a thinly veiled metaphor for the present.[81] A fairly abstract discussion of political and moral propriety follows, immersed in literary and quasi-historical examples that frequently predate the Han period such as Zang Wen 臧文 and Liezi 列子.[82] Because the examples and allusions are not bound by time, place, and specific events, the criticism takes on a broader relevance and is less of a historical narrative than purely an essay of political opinion. Ge Hong concludes "The Faults of Han" by writing:

> The lives of common people were as if they were scorched and drowned in pools and fires. Families suffered misfortune, and the kingdom met with calamity.[83] Crimes were recorded on bamboo and silk, good historians had no words of praise, and tripods and stone inscriptions lacked the ring of virtue.[84] What brought this about? The loss of [talented] men was the cause.[85]

> 生民燋淪於淵火. 凶家害國. 得罪竹帛, 良史無褒言, 金石無德音. 夫何哉? 失人故也.

The dismal statement is a strong warning that the ruler's neglect of talented men not only marks the decline and end of a dynasty but also signals the enduring judgment of the historian, who will record only crimes and misfortune. Ge Hong aims the admonition at his contemporaries with a reference to his own marginal position as a member of the southern literati under the Jin, using the commonplace trope of the neglected but competent official.[86] In *Lunyu* 15.8 we read, "Not speaking to a man one should, this is wasting talented men; speaking to a man one shouldn't, this is wasting words; those who know [the difference] waste neither talented men nor words" 可與言而不與之言失人, 不可與言而與之言失言; 知者不失人亦不失言.[87] Furthermore, the phrase "metal and stone" refers to the *Lüshi chunqiu* chapter "Seeking Men" 求人, in which we read:

> In his search for worthy men and his desire to exploit fully the benefits of the land, [Yu] worked until his face turned black, the seven facial opening and five organs of his body were clogged, and he walked with a limp. These are extreme examples of making the greatest effort. In the end, Yu won the assistance of five men, Gaoyao, Huayi, Zhen Kui, Heng Ge, and Zhi Jiao. Thus, his merits are inscribed in metal [tripods] and stone and written on bowls and trays.[88]

顏色黎黑, 竅藏不通, 步不相過, 以求賢人, 欲盡地利, 至勞也. 得
陶, 化益, 真窺, 橫革, 之交五人佐禹, 故功績銘乎金石, 著於盤盂.

It was precisely Yu's ability to identify, attract, and use talented men that marks not only the success of his labors but his historical legacy as a sage ruler.

In "The Failings of Wu," Ge Hong more clearly departs from the pretense of historical narrative and lapses into broader political criticism. The chapter consists of two lengthy quotations from two teachers in his esoteric lineage, his own teacher, Zheng Yin, and Zuo Ci 左慈 a *fangshi* 方士 at the Cao-Wei court and teacher to both Ge Hong's uncle Ge Xuan and Zheng Yin.[89] According to Yang Mingzhao, several astrological references at the beginning of the chapter lauding the conquered state of Wu suggest more strongly that Ge Hong intended the chapter as criticism of the Jin court.[90] The content of the criticism, like that of "The Faults of Han," is fairly indistinct and lacks the historical context we might expect from a chapter dealing with Wu. For example, Ge Hong, quoting Zheng Yin quoting Zuo Ci, writes:

> Therefore the lofty and profound wear coarse clothing and embrace jade,[91] preserve tranquility[92] and a pure will, having no worldly desires, hiding their tools away in the depths,[93] attaining their intention they abandon the world, acting only with propriety[94] seen only when the time is right.[95] In hardship they have no misery,[96] in poverty they do not regret,[97] happy with their fate bestowed by Heaven,[98] honor and shame are all the same to them.[99]

> 然高概遠量, 被褐懷玉, 守靜潔志, 無欲於物, 藏器淵涔, 得意遺世,
> 非禮不動, 非時不見. 困而無悶, 窮而不悔, 樂天任命, 混一榮辱.

The passage is relatively unsurprising, constituting a fairly straightforward commentary on neglected but talented scholars. Ge Hong's use of orthodox Confucian sources gives the statement a clichéd and impersonal quality, although strong parallels with the *Daode jing Heshanggong* 河上公 commentary support Tang Yijie's 湯一介 claim that Ge Hong based his understanding of fundamental Daoist principles on the *Heshanggong* 河上公 text.[100] Again the broad relevance of such statements may suggest contemporary events.

Perhaps because the sentiments of this chapter are directed at a more recent historical target, the state of Wu, Ge Hong cautiously defers responsibility for the critical remarks by marking them as hearsay. However, the evasion seems too slight, too thinly constructed, to be anything other than the sentiments of the author toward his contemporaries. At the close of Zheng Yin's lengthy quotation we read:

I was born in an inauspicious age, neither earlier nor later,[101] and witnessed the land of Wu become the frontiers of the Jin, [and] southern people become the servants of the north. These words are as if I am hearing them now, and the Sun clan presents a cart with a coffin.[102]

我生不辰, 弗先弗後, 將見吳土之化爲晉域, 南民之變成北隸也. 言猶在耳, 而孫氏輿櫬.

We can only wonder at Ge Hong's boldness—or foolishness—in offering such transparent criticism of his own era. As a political figure, he was not entirely off the radar, having served the Jin in both civil and military posts. Perhaps he never meant for some sections of the text to be shown to contemporaries; there is certainly no record of Ge Hong presenting his work to the imperial court after the manner of Liu An 劉安 and *Huainanzi* 淮南子. Without a clear picture of the text's early distribution, we can only guess what reaction readers might have had to Ge Hong's assessment of the Jin conquest however much he appears to embrace the traditional role of the court historian as one who censures and admonishes.

Baopuzi questioned this and said, "The words of these two gentlemen can be used to remonstrate," and so he wrote this chapter, desiring that later generations will know [that] Han and Wu losing the kingdom was not the result of Heaven.[103] If we shun [speaking of] the ills of the state,[104] and fail to condemn even the smallest points, then should the honest judgment of Dong Hu have no value and Jia Yi receive ridicule for "The Faults of Qin"?[105]

抱朴子問之, 曰: 二君之言, 可爲來戒, 故錄于篇, 欲後代知有吳失國, 匪降自天也, 若苟諱國惡, 纖芥不貶, 則董狐無貴於直筆, 賈誼將受譏於過秦乎?

In this passage Ge Hong compares two seemingly contradictory statements from *Zuozhuan* about the role of the scholar-official. The phrase "shun [speaking of] the ills of the state" 諱國惡 comes from *Zuozhuan*, Xi 僖 1, where we read that to conceal the ills of the state is *li* 禮 or ritually proper. He seems to prefer the example of Dong Hu, from *Zuozhuan*, Xuan 2, who wrote historical judgments and censured the state with a "straight brush," concealing nothing. Ge Hong also refers to Jia Yi's 賈誼 (201–169 BCE) essay "Guo Qin lun" 過秦論, which is translated by Burton Watson as "The Faults of Qin."[106] Jia Yi writes, "Former affairs, not forgotten, may guide later events" 前事之不忘, 後事之師也,[107] a sentiment echoed in both "The Faults of Han" and

"The Failings of Wu." Although Jia Yi's essay may have provided a precedent or model for Ge Hong, Jia Yi devoted considerably more space to historical details such as people, geography, and political events, things that Ge Hong carefully omitted. While Jia Yi may have intended his historical narrative of the Qin era as a warning or admonition to his contemporaries in the early Han, with Ge Hong we see a much more naked attack on the contemporary political and social order.

We can conclude that Ge Hong may have seen his own criticism in terms of the broader model of the scholar-official exemplified by figures such as Dong Hu and Jia Yi, who operated within the Confucian tradition of historiography to use the past to criticize the present. However, in his essays on Han and Wu, Ge Hong eschews historical narrative and sidesteps issues of historical accuracy while embracing the sensibility and purpose of early Chinese historiography to admonish and censure. The prerogatives of the historian provided independent scholars such as Ge Hong with avenues for political and social criticism. Laying claim to the tradition of historiography gave such criticism at least a nominal legitimacy, although, as we have seen, such writing still required considerable justification on the part of most authors. At the same time, the potential for an unfair historical judgment prompted concern on the part of Ge Hong, who chose to craft his own historical identity through his *Waipian zixu*. Lacking Cao Pi's lofty status, Ge Hong seems to have been aware of the audacity of his act of writing himself. His defensive posture regarding his autobiographical postface indicates that the prerogatives of the independent scholar to praise and blame did not yet extend to self-narrative.

Root, Branch, and Historical Judgment

Sima Qian's official biography by the historian Ban Gu in *Han shu* 62 provided Ge Hong with an example of the perils of traditional historiography and the potential of autobiography to overcome them. Ban Gu used both Sima Qian's *Taishigong zixu* and his "Letter to Ren Shaoqing" to create a dynamic portrait of his subject. For the most part he did little more than paraphrase or directly quote information originally presented by Sima Qian himself, even quoting from Sima Qian's dialogue with his hostile interlocutor, Hu Sui 壺遂. The biggest deviation from the *Taishigong zixu* is the inclusion of Sima Qian's famous letter, presumably reproduced in its entirety, which Ban Gu used to elaborate the circumstances of Sima Qian's castration. Intentionally or not, Sima Qian's autobiographical writing had a tremendous impact on the shape and content of Ban Gu's biography. Ban Gu departed from these sources during his lukewarm assessment of Sima Qian in the appraisal, or *zan*, at the close of the biography. He evaluated Sima Qian based not on the record of his life but rather on his life work, *Shi ji*.

> Moreover Sima Qian's praise and blame [historical evaluation] is very deficient with regard to the sages: in discussing the great Way he emphasized Huang-Lao at the expense of the Six Classics; in his accounts of knights-errant he rejects knights of high quality and praises scoundrels; in his narration of merchants he admires those who are skilled at making money and is ashamed of those who are poor; these are his deficiencies.[108]

又其是非頗繆於聖人, 論大道則先黃老而後六經, 序遊俠則退處士而進姦雄, 述貨殖則崇勢利而羞賤貧, 此其所蔽也.

Ban Gu's criticism speaks to two different standards of memory discussed in this chapter. If Wang Chong's view of the meaning and importance of literature was the norm during Ban Gu's era, then it was reasonable for Ban Gu to reserve judgment of Sima Qian's life and instead evaluate specific points of his comprehensive history. In Ge Hong's view, Sima Qian's postface was only a partial success. Although Ban Gu was compelled to convey the biographical details established by Sima Qian, he was still free to evaluate Sima Qian negatively on the basis of his writing. Sima Qian's autobiographical writing established the details of a life story, but it did not go far enough to create a strong basis for an enduring interpretation of the author's virtue.

Ge Hong's defense of Sima Qian in the *Neipian* "Clarifying the Root" (Ming Ben 明本) chapter suggests he was troubled by Ban Gu's negative evaluation and the possibility that poor historical judgment could warp the legacy of the individual. The chapter reveals that Ge Hong was troubled by the possibility that poor historical judgment and erroneous interpretations could warp the legacy of the individual. Thus, for Ge Hong, the conflict between Zhao Dun and Dong Hu in *Zuozhuan*, *Xuan* 2, over the interpretation of historical events raised the important question of what happens if we are misremembered or misinterpreted.

Ge Hong ostensibly intends the chapter to clarify the relationship between *Dao* and *Ru*. The text begins on a broad philosophical note by illustrating the superiority of Daoism over Confucianism, describing Daoism as the basis of Confucian thought, which in turn deals with the superficial aspects or "ends" of Daoism. "Someone asked how Confucianism and Daoism were ordered. Baopuzi replied, saying, 'Daoism is the root of Confucianism; Confucianism is the extension of Daoism'" 或問儒道之先後. 抱朴子答曰: 道者, 儒之本也; 儒者, 道之末.[109] Ge Hong defines Daoism and Confucianism in terms of one another as the root and branch of the same system; the superiority of Daoism is evident not because it exists to the exclusion of Confucianism but because it acts as the root from which Confucianism arises.[110] Ge Hong then clarifies this initial statement by quoting a section of Sima Tan's "Liujia zhi yaozhi," 六家之要旨 or "Outline of the Six Schools," found in the *Taishigong zixu* of Sima Qian. [111]

> Now,[112] on account of the many proscriptions of Yin-Yang theory, people were constrained and frightened; the scope of Confucianism was broad but lacking in essentials, with little reward for the effort; Moism was stingy and hard to follow and was not applicable in all cases; legalism was strict and had little kindness, harming and wearing down benevolence and righteousness. Only the teachings of Daoism caused people's vitality to be undivided and to take action in accordance to the formless, encompassing the good points of Confucianism and Moism, summarizing the key points of the logicians and the legalists, moving with the needs of the times, adapting to the transformation of things, its objectives clear and easy to grasp, attending to few matters but accomplishing much, its important function lies in preserving the simplicity of the ancestor of existence and defending that which is the genuine source [of creation].[113]

> 先以爲陰陽之術, 眾於忌諱, 使人拘畏; 而儒者博而寡要, 勞而少功; 墨者儉而難遵, 不可遍循; 法者嚴而少恩, 傷破仁義. 唯道家之教, 使人精神專一, 動合無形, 包儒　墨之善, 總名法之要, 與時遷移, 應物變化, 指約而易明, 事少而功多, 務在全大宗 之朴, 守真正之源者也.

Sima Tan's essay seems to arrogate the positive features of the Six Schools as functions of Daoism and is viewed as an example of early Han eclecticism or syncretism that contrasted strongly with the intensely polemical texts of the late Warring States era such as *Mozi* 墨子 and *Mengz* 孟子. Ge Hong's comments in the postface to the *Waipian* that *Baopuzi* was intended to encompass both Confucianism and Daoism suggests that he borrowed the statement in the spirit of eclectic scholarship rather than as part of a sharp polemic. He states, "[My] *Neipian* discusses the matters of immortals, techniques of drugs, ghosts and strange phenomena, transformations, longevity, exorcism, and avoiding harm and belongs to the school of Daoism; [my] *Waipian* discusses success and failure in the world of men, discerns right and wrong in worldly affairs, and belongs to the school of Confucianism" 其內篇言神僊方藥鬼怪變化養生延年禳邪卻禍之事, 屬道家; 其外篇言人閒得失, 世事臧否屬儒家.[114] Furthermore, although he modestly claims to have never become a "true" Confucian scholar 不成純儒,[115] we have seen that statements regarding his broad education and allusions embedded within his writing indicate considerable fluency in the Confucian classics. Thus, like Sima Tan, Ge Hong indulged in an eclecticism that regarded Daoism as the fundamental basis of any philosophical syncretism rather than a rejection of Confucianism altogether.

Ge Hong then counters Ban Gu's criticism of Sima Qian by arranging the two historians within this philosophical scheme. He focuses on Ban Gu's remark that Sima Qian favored Daoism at the expense of Confucianism, writing, "However, Ban Gu, because Sima Qian emphasized Huang-Lao at the expense of the Six Classics, considered him erroneous" 而班固以史遷先黃老而後六經言遷爲謬.[116] I believe the proximity of Ge Hong's defense to his quotation of Sima Tan's essay indicates that he felt the essay's positive evaluation of Daoism lay at the heart of Ban Gu's negative evaluation. The criticism Ge Hong refers to is found at the close of Ban Gu's "Biography of Sima Qian" in the "historian's appraisal" or *zan*. The actual line from Ban Gu runs as follows.

> Moreover, Sima Qian's praise and blame [historical evaluation] is very deficient with regard to the sages: in discussing the great Way he emphasized Huang-Lao at the expense of the Six Classics; in his accounts of knights-errant he rejects knights of high quality and praises scoundrels; in his narration of merchants he admires those who are skilled at making money and is ashamed of those who are poor; these are his deficiencies.[117]

> 又其是非頗繆於聖人，論大道則先黃老而後六經，序遊俠則退處士而進姦雄，述貨殖則崇勢利 而羞賤貧，此其所蔽也.

Although it possesses a philosophical or ideological component, Ban Gu's criticism of Sima Qian's alleged biases for Huang-Lao Daoism seems to exist within a larger context of issues of historiography, specifically within a debate over what properly constitutes a matter of historical record. According to Ban Gu, among Sima Qian's deficiencies seems to be his ambiguous use of the "praise and blame" tradition of historiography that began with Confucius and the *Chunqiu*. Sima Qian's sympathy toward Huang-Lao is thus part of the larger problem of Sima Qian's standards of evaluation.

Ban Gu's statement tends to anticipate a body of criticism about Sima Qian and his work stretching roughly from Ge Hong's own era into the Tang period and down to the present day. Qiao Zhou 譙周 (ca. 200–70 CE), the scholar and historian of the Shu-Han 蜀漢 kingdom (ca. 220–63), appears to have written his *Gushi kao* 古史考 (Investigations of Ancient History) at least in part to amend perceived errors in Sima Qian's *Shi ji*. According to J. Michael Farmer, an investigation of the surviving fragments of Qiao Zhou's work does indeed indicate that Qiao Zhou was interested in correcting aspects of Sima Qian's work while writing his own comprehensive history. Some of these amendments were limited to proposing variant graphs or correcting scribal errors, but Qiao Zhou also rewrote some anecdotes while stopping short of changing their basic meaning.[118] Liu Zhiji 劉知幾 (661–721), the Tang historiographer, commenting on Qiao's goals, states:

> Qiao Zhou compiled the *Gushi kao* seeking to reject Sima Qian's *Shi ji* because the master [Sima Qian] had put aside the Confucian canon when writing of the matter of Li Si's removal. *Gushi kao* says, "Qin killed its grandee." [Qiao Zhou] used the title "grandee" of the feudal lords when [Li Si] was the prime minister of the Son of Heaven. By means of this, [Qiao] imitates *Chunqiu*. This is what is called "Similar appearances but different intent."[119]

Liu Zhiji's estimation of Qiao Zhou's concern with proper titles again illustrates the tension within historiography between ritualized reality and lived experience. We should note that Sima Qian "putting aside" the Confucian canon here has less to do with Ban Gu's accusation of Huang-Lao sympathies than with the perceptions of Liu and Qiao that Sima Qian's history failed to accord with the good example of historiography established by the *Chunqiu*. According to Sima Zhen 司馬真 (fl. 745), Qiao Zhou remarked on Sima Qian's less than orthodox writings, stating, "Seeing this discourse by the Grand Scribe [Sima Qian], he certainly had a great love for the strange."[120] This statement simply echoes an earlier sentiment of Yang Xiong 揚雄 that Sima Qian "loved the strange" found in the *Fayan* 法言 (Model Sayings).

> The utility of *Huainanzi* is not equal to that of the utility of *Shi ji*. As for *Shi ji*, the sages will draw from it. As for *Huainanzi*, the lesser men draw from it. It must be so, for he is a scholar! Suddenly going and coming, this is *Huainanzi*. Beautiful language but little use, this is [Sima Xiangru] Changqing. Much love but unenduring, this is [Sima Qian] Zichang. Zhongni loved much—he loved righteousness. Zichang loved much—he loved the strange.[121]

> 淮南說之用, 不如太史公之用也. 太史公, 聖人將有取焉; 淮南, 鮮取焉爾. 必也, 儒 乎! 乍出乍入, 淮南也; 文麗用寡; 長卿也; 多愛不忍, 子長也. 仲尼多愛, 愛義也. 子長多愛, 愛奇也.

Falling short of commenting on Sima Qian's philosophical or political sympathies, Yang Xiong and Qiao Zhou, like Ban Gu, are concerned with the ambiguities in Sima Qian's history that mark its deviation from the standard and tradition established by Confucius and the *Chunqiu*.

Almost five centuries later, Liu Zhiji's criticism of Sima Qian largely follows that of Qiao Zhou and Ban Gu, faulting *Shi ji* as a work of historiography while stopping short of evaluating the author in ideological or philosophical terms. Liu condemns the superficial resemblance of *Shi ji* "Basic Annals" to Confucius's *Chunqiu*, stating that Sima Qian borrowed the form but not the function of Confucius's historical classic.

> But in writing about events, Sima Qian rarely praises or censures and the events are not evaluated. Therefore, Sima Qian speaks only of putting ancient affairs in order. How could his work be compared to *Chunqiu*?[122]

Thus, while Confucius inaugurates the tradition of historiography with "carefully masked profundity," Sima Qian's work lacks the subtle evaluations of his predecessor, creating a moral universe "where standards of evaluation are, at best, unclear and, at worst, ambiguous."[123] Liu also criticizes the organization of *Shi ji* and the way in which historical figures are arranged within the structure of the text. The ancestors of the Zhou and the Qin emperors, for example, do not belong in the "Basic Annals" but rather in the "Hereditary Households."[124] As Durrant indicates, although Liu Zhiji's comments on Sima Qian might have suggested several interesting potential avenues of investigation, he remained in the end chiefly concerned with issues of formal inconsistency.[125]

Ge Hong's defense of Sima Qian at first glance seems designed to refute the kind of criticism offered by Ban Gu, Qiao Zhou, and, later Liu Zhiji. Although free of specific examples linking Sima Qian to the historiographic tradition, Ge Hong defends Sima Qian's standards of evaluation in more general terms.

> Now [Sima] Qian has seen and heard much, he is able to synthesize all manner of subtle affairs, can sift like sand the positives and negatives of affairs, and can authenticate the perverse and orthodox of the ancients. His critique is based on nature; his pronouncements are based on the strictest criteria of reason. [*Shi ji* is] free of empty praise and does not coyly conceal the unorthodox; it does not accord with the fads and opinions of the moment.[126]

夫遷之洽聞, 旁綜幽陰, 沙汰事物之臧否, 覈實古人邪. 其評論也實原本於自然 其褒貶也, 皆準的乎至理. 不虛美, 不陰惡, 不雷同以偶俗.

Curiously, Ge Hong continues to quote from the "Biography of Sima Qian" in order to refute Ban Gu's evaluation of the Western Han historian. In this case, Ge Hong adapts Ban Gu's record of Liu Xiang's 劉向 (ca. 79-76 BCE) evaluation of Sima Qian found in the same passage in *Han shu*: "Liu Xiang, a universally acknowledged genius, recognized Sima Qian's account as totally reliable; Ban Gu's discussion [of Sima Qian] is thus groundless" 劉向命世通人, 謂爲實錄; 班固之所論, 未可據也.[127] Ge Hong then ties his defense of Sima Qian to a defense of Daoism in general. "Ban was a true Confucian and never fully penetrated the meaning of 'Dao.' Accustomed to the opinions of which he had intimate knowledge, it was impossible for him to offer a balanced opinion" 固誠純儒, 不究道意. 翫其所習, 難以折中.[128] Ge Hong thus leaves his brief sojourn into historiography behind and enters into a stronger philosophical polemic. It was not Sima Qian but Ban Gu who lacked proper standards of evaluation, not because of his adherence to or deviance from the tradition of historiography but rather because of his strict Confucian orthodoxy. For Ge Hong, whether or not either historian accorded to the spirit or model of *Chunqiu* is largely irrelevant; the standard of historical judgment is at heart a question of what informs the tradition. Thus his defense of Sima Qian—at Ban Gu's expense—turns on his notion of the relationship between Daoism and Confucianism as the root and branch. By associating each historian with a philosophical school, Ge Hong hopes to demonstrate the superiority of Sima Qian by illustrating in turn the superiority of Daoism. Furthermore, as we have seen, Ban Gu as a "true Confucian" is the inverse of Ge Hong's self-description, indicating Ge Hong's own discursive position. His defense of Daoism and Sima Qian is equivalent to a defense of his own religious and philosophical stance.

But what does the "superiority" of Daoism mean in this instance? By the late Han, the political philosophy of the Huang-Lao school had become associated with the previously distinct practitioners of longevity and the search for techniques of immortality.[129] During the Wei-Jin period, Daoism was an increasingly well-organized but diverse religious movement with political overtones. Indeed, Tang Yijie states that it is impossible to consider Daoism as an organized religion without due consideration of its political position.[130] The content of the *Neipian* and the *Shenxian zhuan* illustrates that Ge Hong viewed Daoism as a religion rooted in the goal of physical immortality, reflecting the general beliefs of Daoist communities such as the "Celestial Masters" or Tianshi Dao 天師道.[131] However, in his discussion of Ban Gu and Sima Qian, Ge Hong appears to have been at pains to demonstrate that Daoism possessed a broad social and political application beyond the practice of immortality techniques.

That which [we] call "Dao," how can it be limited to techniques of longevity? The *Zhouyi* [Zhou Changes] says, "The Dao of establishing Heaven, this is called Yin and Yang together; the Dao of establishing Earth, this is called the hard and soft together; the Dao of establishing Man, this is benevolence (*ren*) and righteousness (*yi*) together."[132] It also states, "The Dao used by the sages is of four types";[133] if there are no such men, the Dao does not proceed. Moreover, when the world is governed and peace descends, this is called "possessing Dao"; when the state is in danger and is ruled by corruption, then we call this "without Dao." Furthermore, "Sitting and expounding the Dao, this is the task of the Three Ministers";[134] when the empire has the Dao, the lowly are ashamed there. All that can be said to be the Dao moves from Heaven and Earth above down to the ten thousand things; in no case is there one who proceeds except from the Dao. Thus Huangdi and Laozi encompass the root, and Confucianism and Moism govern the branch.[135]

夫所謂道, 豈唯養生之事而已乎? 易曰: 立天之道, 曰陰與陽; 立地之道, 曰柔與剛; 立人之道, 曰仁與義. 又曰: 易有聖人之道四焉, 苟非其人, 道不虛行. 又於治世隆平, 則謂之有道, 危國亂主, 則謂之無道. 又坐而論道, 謂之三公, 國之有道, 貧賤者恥焉. 凡言道者, 上自二儀, 下逮萬物, 莫不由之. 但黃老執其本, 儒墨治其末耳.

According to the ontology presented here, all natural and social phenomena proceed from the Dao, which established Heaven, Earth, and humanity by blending together the qualities of yin and yang, benevolence and righteousness, and hardness and softness. Furthermore, Ge Hong emphasizes the social and political function of the Dao to govern and order the world. Indeed, the definition of a well-ordered state is one that possesses the Dao, which presumably proceeds through the sages and is utilized by ministers to order the empire. Within such a sweeping, monistic cosmology, Daoism naturally "encompasses the root" as all things must by definition proceed from it as their basis. But rather than negate the value of Confucianism (or Moism), Ge Hong redefines their value as based, like all things, in the Dao, stating that they also have their subordinate position to "govern the branch."

As Ge Hong then makes clear, the issue is one of starting from the proper perspective, realizing that Confucianism depends on Daoism and in turn proceeds from it. Ban Gu's criticism of Sima Qian is reducible to an error of narrow vision. It is a judgment based, according to Ge Hong, on Ban's foolish reliance on the mere "branches" of what constitutes true knowledge as his standard for judgment.

The adepts of the current generation who are promoted because they know the Dao, probably all of them are erudite and informed and can observe the patterns of Heaven and the principles of the Earth;[136] understand the rules that govern the changes of nature, and browse the profound and minute principles; grasp the fate [of states that] rise and fall and illuminate the models of governance and chaos. Their hearts are without anxiety, and even though there is no question they cannot answer why do they still pursue the arts of immortality? Is it perhaps because they admire [immortals such as] Chi Songzi and Wan Ziqiao?[137] Those literati of truncated vision and shallow knowledge who jump to conclusions and speak blindly,[138] when they hear about one who dwells hidden from the world in the forest, studying the vocations of Laozi, slander and ridicule them, saying, "That is only the 'small Dao' and is fundamentally not enough to be discussed." Indeed! Those who cherish the illumination of a firefly in a small room[139] naturally cannot see the brightness of the heavens; those who also associate with the tiny *chou* fish and shrimp in turbid pools have no knowledge of the vast expanse of the four seas;[140] those who see only the depths of the Yangzi and Huang He do not know of the Kunlun peaks from whence they issue forth; those who value receiving grain do not understand that luxurious growth needs rich soil.[141] Such as these carelessly know to extol the arts of Confucianism but do not realize that they are perfected through Daoism.[142]

今世之舉有道者，蓋博通乎古今，能仰觀俯察，歷變涉微，達興亡之運，明治亂之體，心無所惑，問無不對者，何必修長生之法，慕松喬之武者哉？而管窺諸生，臆斷瞽說，聞有居山林之間，宗伯陽之業者，則毀而笑之曰，"彼小道耳，不足算也."嗟乎! 所謂抱螢燭于環堵之內者，不見天光之焜爛；侶鮒[143]蝦[144]于跡水之中者，不識四海之浩汗；重江河之深，而不知吐之者崑崙；珍黍稷之收，而不覺秀之者豐壤也. 今苟知推崇儒術，而不知成之者由道.

Ge Hong attempts to justify an interest in techniques of longevity with a description and a defense of contemporary Daoism. Even adepts who grasp the Dao and possess knowledge without limit are drawn to techniques of longevity, which are a fundamental feature of the sweeping cosmology of Daoism. The dichotomous pairs of narrow and broad perspectives suggest a difference between simply governing the state and understanding the cosmological basis of it. The sense of his argument is borrowed from the tale of the giant bird known as the *peng* and the quail in *Zhuangzi*, with the perspective of the giant *peng* associated with Daoism and the perspective of the small quail associated with Confucianism. Here Ge Hong implies that the smaller perspective by itself is insufficient, hoping to further demonstrate that the "arts of Confucianism," presumably governing and ordering the state, take Daoism as their basis.

> What we call the Dao is that which forges the hundred families,[145] rears [Heaven and Earth], gives birth to every type of thing, and formulates the customary social relationships.[146] In these times, those who are shortsighted are many, while those who are farsighted are few, and the few do not triumph over the many, which has long been true. For this reason, although the historian Sima Qian was talented [he] never saw praise, and although Ban Gu was deficient he never saw censure. If what is rare is taken as valuable, and what is commonplace is dismissed, why is this only not so with regard to human affairs? Thus weeds grow to fill the fields, and numinous mushrooms have no place to grow; thickets of thorns grow wild, and tall trees are rare;[147] sand and gravel are everywhere, while pearls and jade disks are rare, swans and hawks flock together, and the phoenix and *huan* seldom emerge; venomous snakes fill the shallows, while young dragons are rarely glimpsed. That Ban Gu created a large following is thus very appropriate.[148]

> 道也者, 所以陶冶百氏, 範鑄二儀, 胞胎萬類, 醞釀彝倫者也. 世間淺近者衆, 而深遠者少, 少不勝衆, 由來久矣. 是以史遷雖長而不見譽, 班固雖短而不見彈. 然物以少者爲貴, 多者爲賤, 至於人事, 豈獨不然? 故藜藿彌原, 而芝英不世; 枳棘被野, 而尋木間秀; 沙礫無量, 而珠璧甚; 鴻隼屯飛, 而鸞鳳罕出; 虺蝎盈藪, 而虯龍希覿; 班生多黨, 固其宜也.

Here Ban Gu's worldly success is a victory for all that is commonplace, the result of meager vision and confused standards of value. Thus talented officials never receive the rewards due to them while the commonplace rises to prominence. The image of weeds choking or crowding out precious plants such as the *zhi* 芝 is drawn from any variety of earlier sources such as "Li sao" as political metaphors for the court's unjust rejection of talented retainers.[149]

Ge Hong appears to use Sima Qian's association with the poet Chu Yuan in the *Taishigong zixu* and the "Letter to Ren An" as the basis for his discussion. In both instances, Sima Qian's self-description plays out the theme of rejection, unfair censure, and unrecognized talent: "If [my work] may be handed down to men who will appreciate it and penetrate to the villages and great capitals, though I should suffer a thousand mutilations, what regret should I have? Such matters as these may be discussed with a wise man, but they are difficult to explain to ordinary people" 傳之其人通邑大都, 則

僕償前辱之責, 雖萬被戮, 豈有悔哉? 然此可爲聖者　道, 難爲俗人言也.[150] In Ge Hong's view, Sima Qian thus suffers on two counts: as a talented official, he cannot find honor and praise because in human affairs men value mediocrity; and as a Daoist he suffers censure from people, such as Ban Gu, who possess meager vision and a truncated perspective.

The criticism of Ban Gu as a historian or biographer seems to rest ultimately on Ban's unfair evaluation of Sima Qian rather than on questions about the reliability of *Han shu*. Both Ban Gu and Sima Qian are seen as reliable sources for anecdotes, evidence, and details supporting Ge Hong's construction of Daoism. Ge Hong's criticism of Ban Gu's standards of evaluation in the "Ming Ben" chapter seems to coexist alongside a steady use of *Han shu* for historical data to support claims about Daoist historical figures. In the *Neipian*'s "On Immortals" (Lun Xian 論仙) chapter, Ge Hong states:

> Both *Han shu* and *Shi ji* recount how Han Emperor Wu gave the title of *Wen cheng jiangjun* to Shao Weng [the *fangshi*] of Qi. When Emperor Wu's favorite concubine died, Shao Weng was able to cause Emperor Wu to see her as if she were still alive. He also caused Emperor Wu to see [the Kitchen God] Zao Shen. This is clearly recorded in the histories.[151]

> 按漢書及太史公記皆云齊人少翁, 武帝以爲文成將軍. 武帝所幸李夫人死, 少翁能令武帝見之如生人狀. 又令武帝見灶神, 此史籍之明文也.

Ge Hong's emphasis on the issue of Sima Qian's "Daoism" in the "Clarifying the Root" chapter not only appears to have been fairly unique during his era, but it also appears to have been unique to *Baopuzi* itself. Although Sima Qian and *Shi ji* are used to verify Ge Hong's statements about the existence of a wide variety of fantastic events, as with the statement above, the issue is one of historical reliability, not an evaluation of Sima Qian or his philosophical leanings. For example, in the *Neipian*'s "Rebutting Popular Conceptions" (Dui Su 對俗) chapter, Ge Hong states:

> This evidence is sufficient to know for certain that tortoises have a method for not dying, and if those who cultivate techniques of immortality imitate them, they can also achieve the same result as the tortoise. [These anecdotes of] Sima Qian and Zhong Gong are not merely empty talk. There are many things that crawl and fly over the earth, but the ancients mention only these two animals, so it is clear that they differ from the whole group; merely from this one corner this can be realized.[152]

此又足以知龜有不死之法，及爲道者效之，可與龜同年之驗也.
史遷與仲弓，皆非妄說者也. 天下之蟲鳥多矣，而古人獨舉斯二
物者，明其獨有異於衆故也，睹一隅則可以悟之矣.

Ge Hong cites both historians on the basis of his need for historical evidence, not because of their alleged Confucian or Daoist proclivities.

Ge Hong employs Sima Qian's themes of rejection, unfair censure, and unrecognized talent as the basis for his rebuttal of Ban Gu. Furthermore, by identifying with Sima Qian on an intellectual level as a "Daoist," Ge Hong is speaking to the possibility that he also might face unjust historical criticism on the basis of his unorthodox religious and intellectual interests. His defense of Sima Qian helps explain his desire for a detailed account of his life, particularly as it might defend his interests in immortality and Daoism. As a talented individual, honor and praise might elude him because in human affairs men value mediocrity. More important, as a Daoist, he might suffer censure from the strict Confucian tradition of historical writing. Based on Ge Hong's defense of Sima Qian, the logic of Ge Hong's self-narrative lay in carving out a space for himself as a Daoist within traditional Confucian historiography.

His criticism of Ban Gu's judgment of Sima Qian reveals that Ge Hong's use of the function of historiography in other sections of *Baopuzi*—a few of which we have surveyed—did not constitute the wholesale acceptance of the authority of the historian. Although it is not an attempt to overthrow historiography as such, the discussion in the chapter "Clarifying the Root" raises the issue of which perspective provides the clearest basis for judgment. In Ge Hong's view, if the standards of evaluation are in doubt the historical judgment is erroneous and cannot stand. However, this issue does not seem to influence Ge Hong's use of historical material in other parts of *Baopuzi* but seems to be located exclusively within his discussion of these two historians, suggesting that his emphasis on Ban Gu's criticism of Sima Qian's "Daoism" speaks to a more fundamental question. In my own view, Ban Gu's unfair— in the eyes of Ge Hong—judgment of Sima Qian illustrates the potential treachery of historical memory, perverting the meaning of an individual life. Ge Hong's emphasis on Sima Qian's lack of fame, suffering, and political isolation, tracks both the *Taishigong zixu* and the "Letter to Ren An." He even points to Ban Gu's success in an effort to exaggerate further Sima Qian's plight. He thus imbues Sima Qian with beliefs, attitudes, and a sense of failure that he intends as a mirror of his own and closely echoes this sentiment in the autobiographical postface to the *Waipian*.

Ge Hong's discussion of Sima Qian and Ban Gu shows, among other things, that historiography was not monolithic despite its strong tradition.

However, it was precisely the arbitrary nature of historical writing that troubled him. As Ban Gu demonstrates, history is never a precise record of the past but is inspired, like all literature, by the character and concerns of the author. In this way the ideological or political agenda of the historian could easily distort the legacy of the best people. Furthermore, the tradition of historiography itself was deeply imbued with Confucian sensibilities that were hostile to the unorthodox. By Ge Hong's time, the proliferation of historical writing coupled with political chaos and factionalism may have increased the odds that someone in the future would get it all wrong. This anxiety over the historical record may help explain the departure of Ge Hong's autobiography from the works of his predecessors as a text meant to reveal something more than the author's impulse to write literature. Thus, while Ge Hong seems to have embraced the role of the historian to censure the unrighteous, his distrust of the historical record led to a provocative new view of the limits and meaning of autobiography.

Conclusion

Autobiography and Transcendence
in Ge Hong's *Baopuzi*

We have seen that autobiographical prose in Europe and China emerged from fundamentally different assumptions about the self and its expression. The self-narrative of Augustine of Hippo was rooted in an early Christian discourse of penitence and salvation that regarded accurate, historical self-disclosure as a theological requirement and basic guiding principle. The result was a narrative that claimed the epithet of accuracy, a summary record of the interior journey of the soul toward God paralleled with the material, historical journey of the body. Over time, the confessional aspect of the narrative was discarded, but the concept of verisimilitude—or at least its conceit—remained, even when in the service of modernism or nationalism.

Recent studies of Western autobiography, influenced by poststructuralism, have called into question the verisimilitude of the autobiographical, narrative self by describing it in terms of metaphor and performance: the self rendered as signs in language. Some critics have gone farther by ultimately questioning the notions of autonomy and individuality that underlie the Augustinian model of self-narrative. An ontologically unstable self implies that verisimilitude is essentially impossible and, furthermore, that autobiography becomes meaningful in its intelligibility to others, not because of assumed historical accuracy. However, this analysis has had little impact on the study of early Chinese autobiography, which is typically regarded in modern terms. Poetry is generally discarded in this scheme, while prose is considered to be the premodern antecedent of the modern genre and generally limited to a group of authorial postfaces.

Ge Hong's sense of the postface as a legitimate vehicle for self-expression was unique in terms of theories of self-narrative from his period. He eschewed reticence in favor of extensive self-description and saw his work in the context of earlier precedents such as the work of Cao Pi and Wang Chong. Nevertheless we must be cautious when reading such texts as naked autobiography, for, as we have seen, their autobiographical impact was constrained by their use of the form as a defense of other literary endeavors or as professional self-promotion. The arresting detail and colorful self-description of authors such as Ge Hong must be read within this context and do not represent a trend toward individualistic self-narrative. Indeed, the tropes of self-description in many ways concealed the individual behind literary and historical precedent, negating the value of verisimilitude by merging the self with historical tradition to create a more durable, lasting image of the author. However, because this authorial image is conflated with myth and history, it represents more than an account of an autonomous, isolated individual and is a matrix for the transmission of an archetypal or ideal character from the past.[1] Thus Ge Hong's autobiographical postface simultaneously obliterates the historical individual within literary and historical tropes yet reaffirms the value of the summary self-expression. The success of the autobiography lay in its accuracy as an expression of character, which was unhinged from the Augustinian reliance on historical detail.

Ge Hong's notion of self-narrative largely stemmed from his understanding of the growing power of historiography rather than an emergent individualism during his era. He wrote knowing that historians may prove to be the most unforgiving readers. History shared serious literature's high esteem but had long since acquired the authority to sit in judgment on those who fell under its gaze. Unlike those of his predecessors, the content of Ge Hong's fictitious debate with a nameless interlocutor at the close of his "Authorial Postface" is almost entirely concerned with defending his autobiographical narrative rather than justifying the writing of *Baopuzi*. This short dialogue shifts the focus of the autobiographical narrative from literature to the self as a viable subject. Moreover, it demonstrates the potential of autobiography to act as a counterweight to a potentially unfair—or nonexistent—historical judgment. For Ge Hong, what is at stake is the privilege to record his own life and thereby gain control over his historical legacy.

In this regard, subjectivity becomes a point of resistance to the mandala of official history. As William H. Nienhauser states, "Traditional Chinese biographies were generally short, stereotyped narrative intended to emphasize the social role of the subject rather than the subject's individuality."[2] In other words, the biography is a fragment of the larger historical work and must fit into the broader context of didactic historiography. Early Chinese historians presented historical subjects in relationship to each other; basic annals (*ben ji* 本紀) and biographies (*zhuan* 傳) were not about those individual subjects per se but their position within the larger mosaic of the period. We might think of official histories as a kind of large, group biography, with characters bleeding into one another and no necessary delineation beyond social roles. For this reason, early historians such as Ban Gu inaugurated the so-called nine-part biography, which emphasized such details as ancestry, significant childhood events, official positions, official documents or other writing, and the date of death, but neglected many other unique or individual details of the subject's life. The result, as Pei-yi Wu has argued, is a reticent and impersonal discourse that would appear to conceal more than it reveals.

Liu Zhiji's genealogy of the *zixu* clearly borrows the model of official biography as it had developed by the Tang period but reveals a large gulf between literary theory and the practice of authors. Liu demands a very contextualized and economical self-presentation, but according to his dim appraisal of the genre during the Wei-Jin era, people were doing quite the opposite. Liu praises only those authorial accounts that impart a sense of cultural or familial identity such as those of Qu Yuan, Sima Qian, Ban Gu, and Yang Xiong. However, Ge Hong writes against the qualities associated with historical writing, and his isolation represents an escape from classical biography. Ge Hong breaks free of the genre of biography by rejecting reticence and claiming a subjective experience that is bounded, unique, and resists the discursive demands of historiography. His self-presentation may have been influenced by "pure critique" (*qing yi* 清議), "pure conversation" (*qing tan* 清談), and the intellectual fad of character evaluation that became the basis of selection for office after the Han. Regardless, the resulting impression of the subject is akin to the kind of self-presentation that is typically reserved for verse. Verse is the most developed genre of the early period as well as the most overdetermined mode of self-disclosure; it was the most acceptable and widely used mode of confessional self-narrative. While the author of verse frequently commented on the contemporary political and social scene, self-definition was achieved through recourse to the past and literary tradition.

Ge Hong defines himself through reference to literary and historical tradition, invoking canonical figures such as Confucius alongside specific authors of self-narrative and significant cultural archetypes. For Ge Hong, writing the authorial postface becomes a question of which archetypes, and which pasts, to follow in his self-creation. The confessional model of autobiography, in which the author attempts to become a model for future readers, is offset by our example of Ge Hong, whose motivations are far more defensive. Indeed, as we have seen, the narrative was also meant for contemporary readers as a kind of extended resume.

Insofar as Ge Hong is focused on the future, he is more concerned with the nominally religious ambition of transcendence. Ge Hong is attempting to create a space for himself as a Daoist within a tradition strongly influenced by canonical Confucian texts. The defense of his character through recourse to eremitism and other tropes provide him with the ingredients for his own alchemy of self-presentation. As with Ge Hong's own alchemical practice, the success of the adept rested on a solid foundation of the most important Confucian virtues; only then could an esoteric recipe succeed. Ge Hong blends as many socially significant virtues as he can, hoping in this way to be a transcendent being in text as well as deed. He may thus escape the tyranny of state-sanctioned history and create a durable self-presentation.

This notion of transcending history parallels Ge Hong's pursuit of religious transcendence in several fundamental ways, suggesting that he might have viewed literary longevity and techniques of immortality as complimentary rather than mutually exclusive categories. Indeed, as Yu Ying-shih has commented, "It goes without saying that the two kinds [of immortality] are not always easy to distinguish because of their mutual influence or cross-fertilization. Moreover, it is also true that later in Han times . . . the two streams tended to merge into one."[3] Just as a natural tension existed between historiography and autobiography, so, too, do techniques of immortality imply a direct challenge to the authority of the historian. After all, the life of a living person can hardly be recorded as historical narrative, while hagiography, which records the transcendence of virtuous individuals, carries an implicit, positive appraisal. We see the tension between historiography and immortality fully developed in Sima Qian's *Shi ji*. Sima Qian is highly critical of the efforts of the First Emperor of Qin 秦始皇帝 (r. 221–210 BCE) to pursue techniques of immortality. The first Qin emperor, according to Sima Qian, spent a lot of time traveling and offering various sacrifices to curry divine favor, indulged practitioners of the magical arts, and even sent fleets to search in vain for the island of Penglai, the haven of the immortals. His narrative treats the emperor and his entourage of *fangshi,* or "occultists," with ridicule and contempt, recording the emperor's somewhat ridiculous death while traveling to perform still more sacrifices in pursuit of longevity. It has been argued elsewhere that Sima Qian's rather scathing portrayal of the first Qin emperor is meant to resonate with his portrayal of his own sovereign, Emperor Wu, who also engages in sacrifices meant to promote longevity and sends fleets to find the mythical island of Penglai. On the other hand, Sima Qian extols the virtues of Han Wendi 漢文帝 (r. 180–157 BCE), who refused to participate in such sacrifices and accepted the fact that "Death is the order of Heaven and Earth, the natural principle of things."[4] Perhaps to the scribe immortality meant the possibility of escape from the rigors and control of the ritualized and moral paradigm represented in the praise and blame strategy of classical historiography.

There are, of course, enormous gulfs between the two concepts of transcendence, notably in the adept's relationship with society. The kind of immortality sought by the author is more akin to fame, as one seeks to be recognized on the strength of one's work. In contrast, the ritual requirements of elixir fabrication required considerable isolation, especially from non-believers, and when a transcendent walked among mortals he or she was rarely recognized as such.

> Suppose there was a person of exceptional knowledge and great ability, living in reclusion without office, concealing his circumstances and literary talent, expelling contrivance and eliminating desire, clinging to his own nature in the midst of utmost purity, forgetting the engagements and trifles of the common world. The average person already is unable to distinguish between such a man and the ordinary, unable in his words and actions to see his outstanding conduct and will, and in his crude form investigate sufficiently the true expression of his spirit. How much more so the transcendent, whose inclinations follow a different path, who takes wealth as misfortune, who sees glory as obscene, who takes pleasure to be dust and sees renown as the morning dew. He treads on fire but is not scorched, walks on the waves but with a lighter step than on land, beats his wings through the void, rides the clouds in a celestial chariot, looking up he traverses the polestar, looking down he perches on Kun Lun. How could walking corpses [ordinary people] see such things?[5]

> 設有哲人大才，嘉遯勿用，翳景掩藻，廢僞去欲，執太璞於至醇之中，遺末務於流俗之外，世人猶尟能甄別，或莫造志行於無名之表，得精神於陋形之裏，豈況仙人殊趣異路，以富貴爲不幸，以榮華爲穢汙，以厚玩爲塵壤，以聲譽爲朝露，蹈炎飆而不灼，躡玄波而輕步，鼓翮清塵，風駟雲軒，仰淩紫極，俯棲崑崙，行尸之人，安得見之？

It is also clear that the reclusion of the transcendent was very similar to the reclusion of the hermit in that society is viewed as defilement. The lofty of spirit—and those possessed of high moral character in either case—shunned social recognition in favor of identification with higher planes of conduct, morality, and spiritual development.

Ge Hong's account of his own reclusion early in his adult life bears the hallmarks of this kind of ethical transcendence, but he also used the occasion to generate a large body of writing through which he hoped to become known. He states that, cut off from the north, he returned south and gained a position under Ji Han, styled Jundao 君道 (d. 306), a descendent of Ji Kang. Holding a minor official position in the south certainly would have helped Ge Hong avoid often deadly political entanglements, but the period during which he served Ji Han also had the benefit of providing him an arena in which to pursue esoteric techniques of longevity. After Ji Han's untimely death, Ge Hong appears to have avoided office for some time.[6] In his view, the complications of a political career are detrimental to the pursuit of longevity and so are best avoided: "The Dao does not reside in the mountains and forests, but those in antiquity who cultivated the Dao felt it necessary to enter mountains and forests out of a true desire to place themselves far from the noise and clamor and put their minds at ease."[7] Moreover, Ge Hong vowed to travel to Mount Song to follow in the footsteps of those who abandoned the world and pursued transcendence; he need only first put in order his inner and outer chapters to "set them forth as an example for those who will come after."[8] His interest in esoteric pursuits such as techniques of longevity may have fulfilled certain stereotypical expectations of retirement during the late Han and early medieval period. Even Wang Chong, who argued against Daoist notions of longevity, wrote a book on nourishing life after his retirement. However, Ge Hong's belief in the possibility of immortality adds a new dimension to his justification for his literary accomplishments by casting the *Neipian* as a pedagogical tool meant to transmit esoteric knowledge to posterity but also as a way to make himself known and allay the doubts of future seekers of longevity.[9] While the text may act to transmit esoteric knowledge to future readers, as a work of literature it will also perpetuate Ge Hong's name, and he would seem to have spent several years in reclusion engaged with the concept of immortality on several levels, using longevity studies as one justification for writing *Baopuzi*.

It seems evident that Ge Hong either wished to reconcile literary and religious immortality or simply did not see them as contradictory, something that should not surprise us given his interest in fusing diverse textual traditions into "one school" of thought. In chapter 4, I described how Ge Hong regarded *ru* and *dao* as complimentary aspects of one another and believed one must first fulfill the ethical precepts of Confucianism prior to aspiring to the ultimate value system of Daoism. In this regard secular immortality in the form of literary fame had merit as a signifier of good conduct, which prior to Ge Hong's era had already been fused. In one sense, it is logical to assume that both may operate at the same time and, indeed, support one another. We might say that his autobiography imitates the stages of perfection necessary for immortality, for all modes of immortality in early China, whether literary or religious, made claims of self-perfection and moral cultivation.

Both the immortality conveyed by autobiography and the immortality gained through esoteric religious practice involve the annihilation of the self, albeit to different degrees. The *Neipian* conveys an almost technocratic approach to the process of transcendence, and at times the details of Ge Hong's notion of immortality and its techniques suggest that mystical union with the Dao was not at the forefront of his theory. Indeed, Ge Hong's notion of immortality emphasized the mixing and ingesting of elixirs to achieve desired results: "If a transcendent man by use of medicines nurtures his body and uses the arts to multiply his fated lifespan, he will cause the inside of his body to be free of disease and the outside of his body to be impervious to harm; in this way he may not die and his former body does not change 若夫仙人, 以藥物養身, 以術數延命, 使內疾不生, 外患不入, 雖久視不死, 而舊身不改."[10] Yet even this mechanical approach to religious transcendence is ultimately based in a mystical understanding of the Dao. Ge Hong defines the notion of *xuan dao* 玄道 not only as the basis of the universe but also as the basis of longevity of any kind, stating, "It is only the Mysterious Dao that may impart longevity" 其唯玄道, 可與爲永.[11] This is because the presence of the Dao brings life itself: "Therefore, that in which the Mysterious is present knows inexhaustible happiness; that from which the Mysterious leaves finds its body broken and spirit departed" 故玄之所在, 其樂不窮. 玄之所去, 器弊神逝.[12] In this regard, we may say that a transcendent being has made moot the context held dear by the autobiography, which is the social and ethical context, by identifying with the single, ultimate source of all existence.

In early China, autobiography also annihilated the individual to a significant degree by demanding a reticence so strong that it bordered on self-negation in Augustinian terms. In contrast to modern self and self-narrative, much of the author's "individual" identity vanishes into a web of familial or professional bonds, archetypes, and publicly agreed-upon tropes. The summary expression may be unique in some regard, but the text does not posit a unique self or express individuality in the modern sense of the term. It is, rather, an expression of character made legible through recourse to literary tradition. In the case of both autobiography and religious transcendence, the author/adept dissolves his or her uniqueness into an impossibly wide context.

Ge Hong appears to have sought religious transcendence with great conviction and often at the expense of his official career, but he frequently lamented his inability to achieve the Daoist immortality that eluded him. I believe that, faced with the possibility of failure, he ultimately turned to the immortality of the literary tradition and wrote *Baopuzi* as an attempt to establish "one school of discourse," in essence hedging his bets. However, as we saw in the example of Sima Qian and Ban Gu, literary fame did not guarantee a fair judgment or honest appraisal. Thus he was left with a further problem: how to overcome the praise and blame strategy of classical historiography. The answer to this question was to create his own legacy through self-narrative, a text that would define and constrain how he would be "read" by future generations. In this pursuit, Ge Hong was extremely successful. Many historical and religious sites in modern Zhejiang with only a tenuous connection to Ge Hong draw on his legacy and claim that there, too, the famous author mixed elixirs of immortality. Moreover, his official biography in *Jin shu* repeats almost verbatim many of the details of Ge Hong's life found in his autobiographical account, recording his Daoist convictions alongside his distinguished military career and limited success as a local official. On one detail his biographer differs with Ge Hong's own account. His biography states that at the auspicious age of eighty-one, Ge Hong wrote to his associate, Deng Yue 鄧嶽 (fl. ca. 330), and informed him of his imminent death. Deng rushed to Ge Hong's residence but arrived too late. Upon his death, the coloring of Ge Hong's body remained the same as when he was alive. His body was soft and very light, "as if his clothing were empty." His biographer in *Jin shu* can only conclude that Ge Hong's contemporaries "believed that he had achieved immortality."[13]

Appendix A

Autobiographical Postface of Cao Pi's
Authoritative Discourses 典論自序

I n the first year of the Chuping era [190–94], Dong Zhuo [d. 192][1] killed the emperor and poisoned the empress,[2] toppling the royal house. At that time, the empire had suffered under the government of the Zhongping era [184–89], and [the people] uniformly detested Dong Zhuo's brutality and disloyalty. Every clan was troubled by the chaos, and everyone's life was in jeopardy. The regional[3] governors all made use of the *Chunqiu* principle, [which says] "the people of Wei punished Zhou Xu at Pu,"[4] saying that all people should punish the rebels. Thereupon there rose in great numbers troops loyal [to the emperor], and famous heroes and great knights, wealthy families and powerful clans, all came together from thousands of miles away to assist the royal family like a gathering of clouds; troops from Yan and Yu fought [the rebels] at Xingyang; soldiers from Henei encamped at Mengjin. Zhuo therefore forced the emperor to move to Chang'an and made it the capital. But in the rest of the empire the most powerful individuals joined together prefectures and kingdoms; those below them [of more modest rank] encircled cities and towns while the smallest occupied farms and fields, and each devoured the other. At that time the Yellow Turbans[5] flourished on the eastern coast near Mount Tai.[6] These "mountain bandits" pillaged the prefectures of Bing and Ji, and, availing themselves of their victories, they turned and swept south. Villagers and townspeople, seeing the smoke rise in the distance, all fled, while those living in walled cities, seeing the dust rise [from the approaching bandits] scattered. The people were slain and killed; their bleached bones like a tangled thicket [were left unburied in the open].

初平之元, 董卓殺主鴆后, 蕩覆王室. 是時四海既困中平之政, 兼惡卓之凶逆, 家家思亂, 人人自危. 山東牧守, 咸以春秋之義, "衛人討州吁于濮," 言人人皆得討賊. 於是大興義兵, 名豪大俠, 富室強族, 飄揚雲會, 萬里相赴; 兗, 豫之師戰于榮陽, 河內之甲軍于孟津. 卓遂遷大駕, 西都長安. 而山東大者連郡國, 中者嬰城邑, 小者聚阡陌, 以還相吞滅. 會黃巾盛於海, 岱, 山寇暴於并, 冀, 乘勝轉攻, 席卷而南, 鄉邑望煙而奔, 城郭睹塵而潰, 百姓死亡, 暴骨如莽.

At that time I was five years old, and the emperor [Cao Cao],[7] because the kingdom was in chaos, taught me archery; by the age of six I had mastered archery. [He] also taught me horsemanship; by the age of eight I was capable of mounted archery. On account of the troublesome period [of warfare and chaos], every time [my father] went to battle I always followed along. At the beginning of the Jian'an era [196–220], the emperor went south and attacked Jingzhou, and when [his army] arrived at Wan, Zhang Xiu [d. 207][8] capitulated but rebelled again after ten days; thus I lost my older brother Zixiu [d. 197],[9] who was a worthy candidate for office [to Zhang Xiu's deception], as well as my cousin An Min [d. 197].[10] At that time I was ten years old and only managed to escape on horseback.

余時年五歲, 上以世方擾亂, 教余學射, 六歲而知射, 又教余騎馬, 八歲而能騎射矣. 以時之多故, 每征, 余常從. 建安初, 上南征荊州, 至宛, 張繡降. 旬日而反, 亡兄孝廉子修, 從兄安民遇害. 時余年十歲, 乘馬得脫.

Now, as for the ways of *wen* [culture] and *wu* [warfare], each is used according to the appropriate time. I was born in the Zhongping era and grew up in the midst of warfare and soldiers; for this reason I was fond of archery and horsemanship when I was young and still am to this day. When hunting fowl I always [give chase] for ten miles,[11] shooting from horseback often from one hundred paces; over time my body grew strong, and my heart never grew tired [of this]. In the tenth year of the Jian'an era [ca. 206], Jizhou[12] had just been pacified, [the tribe of] Huimo[13] paid tribute [to the emperor] with exceptional bows, and [the people of] Yan[14] and Dai[15] presented [the emperor] with fine horses. At that time it was late spring, Gou Mang[16] presided over the season, a peaceful wind fanned the world, the bow was dry and the hand was supple, the grass grazed low and the game was fat; with my cousin Zidan [d. 231],[17] we hunted west of Ye all day, killing nine deer and thirty pheasants and rabbits.

夫文武之道, 各隨時而用, 生于中平之季, 長于戎旅之間, 是以少好弓馬, 于今不衰; 逐禽輒十里, 馳射常百步, 日多體健, 心每不厭. 建安十年, 始定冀州, 濊, 貊貢良弓, 燕, 代獻名馬. 時歲之暮春, 勾芒司節, 和風扇物, 弓燥手柔, 草淺獸肥, 與族兄子丹獵于鄴西, 終日手獲獐鹿九, 雉兔三十.

Sometime afterward, the army went south on a campaign, encamping at Quli; Commander Secretary Xun Yu [163–212][18] was acting under orders to reward the troops. He saw me, and at the end of our discussion Yu said, "I have heard that you are able to shoot a bow either left- or right-handed, this is truly a rare talent." I said, "Has your honor heard of [a mounted archer in such harmony with his horse that horse and rider look up and down at the targets in perfect accord]?"[19] Yu laughed merrily and said, "Is that so!" I said, "The field [for archery practice] has a fixed track and the target has a fixed position; even if one were to hit the target every time, this is not the utmost in skill. Now, as for riding across the plains, plunging into thick grass, chasing crafty beasts, leading[20] swift birds, not wasting a single shot, and hitting the mark each time, this can be called skillful." At that time the army libationer, Zhang Jing,[21] was sitting in attendance, and looking back at Yu he clapped his hands, saying, "Excellent!"

後軍南征次曲蠡, 尚書令荀彧奉使犒軍, 見余談論之末, 彧言: "聞君善左右射, 此實難能." 余言: "執事未睹夫項發口縱, 俯馬蹄而仰月支也." 彧喜笑曰: "乃爾!" 余曰: "埒有常徑, 的有常所, 雖每發輒中, 非至妙也. 若馳平原, 赴豐草, 要狡獸, 截輕禽, 使弓不虛彎, 所中必洞, 斯則妙矣." 時軍祭酒張京在坐, 顧彧拊手曰 "善."

I have also studied fencing under numerous masters. Techniques are different from place to place, but [I have found] the technique in the capital to be the best. During the time of [Han emperors] Huan [r. 147–67] and Ling [r. 168–89], there was a courageous warrior, Wang Yue,[22] who was good at this art and acclaimed at the capital. Shi A[23] from Henan said that formerly he had traveled with Yue and had mastered his technique. I, in turn, learned this technique from A and mastered it as well. Once I was drinking with Arbiter General[24] Liu Xun,[25] General Advancing Glory,[26] Deng Zhan,[27] and a few others. I had long heard that Zhan had powerful arms and had mastered the Five Weapons. It was also said that he could defeat an armed opponent with his empty hands. He and I discussed swordsmanship for quite a while, and I told him, "Your technique is wrong. I used to be fond of your technique, and then I learned a better art." Then he asked to spar with me. At the time we were all very drunk and eating sugarcane, so we used the sugarcane as swords and descending from the hall we sparred for several rounds. Three times I hit him on his arm and everybody laughed. Zhan would not concede and asked to spar again. I told him, "My technique emphasizes speed, and it would have been improper to strike your face; therefore I have simply struck your arms." Zhan said, "I still want to have another round." I knew he wanted to dash forward and strike my chest, and therefore I feigned an advance. As I predicted, he attempted to rush forward and I stepped back and hit him squarely on the forehead.[28] Everyone there was startled to see this. I returned to my seat, laughing, and said, "Formerly Yang Qing [fl. 180 BCE][29] instructed Chunyu Yi [fl. 180 BCE][30] to abandon his old method and taught him an esoteric technique. Now I also wish General Deng to disregard his old skill and accept the essential Way." The assembled guests made merry and were all pleased.

余又學擊劍, 閱師多矣, 四方之法各異, 唯京師爲善. 桓, 靈之間, 有虎賁王越善斯術, 稱於京師. 河南史阿言昔與越遊, 具得其法, 余從阿學之精熟. 嘗與平虜將軍劉勳, 奮威將軍鄧展等共飲, 宿聞展善有手臂, 曉五兵, 又稱其能空手入白刃. 余與論劍良久, 謂言 "將軍法非也, 余顧嘗好之, 又得善術." 因求與余對. 時酒酣耳熱, 方食芋蔗, 便以爲杖, 下殿數交, 三中其臂, 左右大笑. 展意不平, 求更爲之. 余言 "吾法急屬, 難相中面, 故齊臂耳." 展言 "願復一交." 余知其欲突以取交中也, 因僞深進, 展果尋前, 余卻腳鄛, 正截其顙, 坐中驚視. 余還坐, 笑曰: "昔陽慶使淳于意去其故方, 更授以祕術, 今余亦願鄧將軍捐棄故伎, 更受要道也." 一坐盡歡.

Now, in any matter, one should not boast of one's own strengths. When I was young I learned how to fight with two blades at once, and I thought I had no equal. The common name [for this technique] is "with twin halberds sitting in an iron room" and "with *xiang* and shield concealed behind the wooden door." Later I studied under Yuan Min[31] of the state of Chen, who could counter two blades with only one sword, and whom everyone considered wondrous; his opponents could not understand from where this skill had come. In an earlier day, if one had encountered Min on a narrow path, a person would have had no chance against him.

夫事不可自謂己長, 余少曉持複, 自謂無對; 俗名雙戟爲坐鐵室, 鑲楯爲蔽木戶; 後從陳國袁敏學, 以單攻複, 每爲若神, 對家不知所出, 先日若逢敏於狹路, 直決耳!

Among the other hobbies I have enjoyed since childhood, only with chess have I mastered a few of the finer points [of the game], and I wrote a *fu* about it when I was young.[32] Formerly among the [chess] masters at the capital there were Marquis Ma of Hexiang[33] and Ducal Son Zhang Anshi [d. 60 BCE][34] from Dongfang; I always regretted never having the opportunity to play against them.

余於他戲弄之事少所喜, 唯彈棋略盡其巧, 少爲之賦. 昔京師先工有馬合鄉侯, 東方安世, 張公子, 常恨不得與彼數子者對.

His Majesty [Cao Cao] had a refined appreciation for *Shi jing, Shang shu, Documents,* and literary works in general, so that even among his troops he always had a book in hand. After every battle he would calmly intone, "When people are young and fond of studying their thought is very focused, but as they age the joy [of study] is forgotten. Among those who are older but are able to study industriously, there is only myself and Yuan Boye."[35] Because of this I learned poetry and commentaries at an early age, and when I was older I thoroughly explored the Five Classics, the Four Categories [of writing], the *Shi ji,* the *Hou Han shu,* and the words of the various philosophers and the "hundred schools," all of which I comprehensively read. Of the works I have written, including essays, monographs, poetry, and *fu,* there are altogether sixty chapters. As for whether I have been wise but able to appear foolish, brave but able to retreat when need be, benevolent with others, or compassionate with my inferiors, this I leave for a good historian of a later time [to decide].

上雅好詩書文籍, 雖在軍旅, 手不釋卷, 每每定省從容, 常言 "人少好學則思專, 長則善忘, 長大而能勤學者, 唯吾與袁伯業耳." 余是以少誦詩, 論, 及長而備歷五經, 四部, 史, 漢, 諸子百家之言, 靡不畢覽. 所著書論詩賦, 凡六十篇. 至若智而能愚, 勇而能怯, 仁以接物, 恕以及下, 以付後之良史.

Appendix B

"The Authorial Postface" 序傳

by Liu Zhiji 劉知幾

In all probability, the authorial postface derives from middle antiquity.[1] The precedent is Qu Yuan's classic "Li sao"; its first section narrates his clan [origins], and then enumerates his grandfather and father. First [he] narrates his birth and then provides his name and appellative. The emerging traces of the authorial preface in truth take this as the foundation. Later was Sima Xiangru, the first to use the authorial postface as a biography, so that which he narrated was a record of his youth up to his maturity, establishing [a record of] his conduct and service and nothing more. With regard to the origins of his ancestors, this is omitted and we hear nothing. Coming to Sima Qian, in addition to recalling the story of [Qu Yuan], he imitated the recent works of [Sima Xiangru], and, taking as a model these two writers, he rolled them into one [i.e., he embodied them both].

蓋作者自敘，其流出於中古乎．案屈原離騷經，其首章上陳氏族，下列祖考．先述厥生，次顯名字．自敘發跡，實基於此．降及司馬相如，始以自敘爲傳，然其所敘者，但記自少及長，立身行事而已．逮於祖先所出，則蔑爾無聞．至馬遷又徵三閭之故事，放文園之近作，模楷二家，勒成一卷．

Thereupon Yang Xiong followed [Sima Qian's] wagon ruts, and Ban Gu ladled from his abundant wave. Indeed, [authorial postfaces] proliferated during this time. Although there were changes of style and language, the essential features remained unchanged. [When we] examine Sima Qian's *Shi ji* [it begins in] high antiquity from Xuan Yuan [the Yellow Emperor] down to the point of Emperor Wu of Han. The empire is very vast, and the roads are infinitely long. Therefore his authorial postface begins with the claim that his family descended from Chong and Li and concludes with his appointment as grand scribe.[2] Thus, [although his postface] ranges from the past to the present, ultimately it does not eclipse the time covered by the *Shi ji*.

於是揚雄遵其舊轍．班固酌其餘波．自敘之篇實煩於代．雖屬辭有異而茲體無易．尋馬遷史記，上自軒轅下窮漢武．疆宇修闊，道

路線長. 故其自敘始於氏出重黎, 終于身爲太史. 雖上下馳騁, 終
不越史記之年.

[As for] Ban Gu's *Han shu*, it is limited merely to the two hundred years of the Western Han; however, his authorial postface establishes evidence for [his ancestor Ziwen, who held the position of prime minister], beginning in the era of King Wen of Chu (r. 688–75), and records his recent rhapsody "Joking with a Guest" from the time of Emperor Ming of Han. What is conveyed by the content greatly exceeds [that of the] the text itself. But later authorial postfaces, of which there were many, raced to imitate (*xue*) Meng Jian [Ban Gu's appellative], following his style and elaborating on it. If [this style] is carried over to family genealogy, still it is probably feasible, [but if] it is applied to the dynastic history, its many faults can be observed.

班固漢書, 止於西京二百年事耳. 其自敘也則遠徵令尹, 起楚文
王之世, 近錄賓戲當漢明帝之朝. 包括所聞, 逾於本書遠矣. 而後
來敘傳, 非止一家, 競學孟堅, 從風而靡. 施於家諜, 猶或可通, 列
於國史, 多見其失者矣.

Nevertheless, as for the principle of the authorial postface, only if it is able to conceal one's faults, and praise one's strengths, then the words are not in error and it constitutes a true record. But Xiangru's authorial postface records his wandering as a guest in Ling Chong and his seduction of a woman from the Zhuo family, and so he took that which is taboo in the *Chunqiu* and advances it as lovely chit-chat. Although in affairs there may be some that are not false, a principle cannot be extracted [from them]. How could it not be shameful to record them in a biography?

然自敘之爲義也, 苟能隱己之短, 稱其所長, 斯言不謬, 即爲實
錄. 而相如自敘, 乃記其客游臨邛, 竊妻卓氏, 以春秋所諱, 持爲
美談. 雖事或非虛, 而理無可取. 載之於傳, 不其愧乎!

Moreover, the "Authorial Record" to Wang Chong's *Lunheng* is not filial in the narration of his father and grandfather, who were looked down on by their neighbors, and he responds with [the example of] Gu being obstinate and Shun divine[3] and Kun being evil and Yu sage.[4] Now, if one discusses one's family within an authorial postface, certainly [one] must take as central acclaiming one's name and glorifying one's parents, and if there is no one [deserving of praise] then this part may be omitted. Going so far as to greatly extol oneself, but widely disparage one's ancestors, how is this different from bearing witness against one's father for stealing a sheep[5] or imitating the son who called out the name of his mother?[6] [Wang Chong] must be censured according to Confucian moral teaching, and is truly a criminal deserving [death].[7]

又王充論衡之自記也, 述其父祖不肖, 爲州閭所鄙, 而己答以瞽頑舜神, 鯀惡禹聖. 夫自敍而言家世, 固當以揚名顯親爲主, 苟無其人, 闕之可也. 至若盛矜於己, 而厚辱其先, 此何異證父攘羊, 學子名母? 必責以名教, 實三千之罪人也.

Now, to act as one's own matchmaker or glorify oneself is a disgraceful action for a scholar or a lady. However, if other people do not know him, the gentleman feels no shame.[8] Accordingly, in the Kong *Analects* it is said, "In a hamlet of ten families, there is surely one who is [as] faithful and trustworthy [as me], but not one who is [as] fond of studying [as I am]."[9] It is also said, "I daily examine myself if in my conduct toward others I have not acted in good faith or in intercourse with friends I have not been sincere."[10] [Confucius] also said, "Since the death of King Wen of Zhou, has not culture been bequeathed to me?"[11] [Confucius] also said, "My old friend [Yan Hui] attempted to devote himself as such."[12] Now, when the sages set forth their words, at times they also demonstrate their talents. Sometimes [they do this] by relying on indirection to show their feelings or [they] select artful words and reveal their tracks. But they never pose and brag about themselves or stir up public talk. Moreover, when he commanded his disciples [by saying] "Each [of you] speak to your own ambition," Zi Lu was not modest and was criticized by Confucius for impropriety.[13]

夫自媒自衒, 士女之醜行. 然則人莫我知, 君子不恥. 案孔氏論語有云: "十室之邑, 必有忠信不如某之好學也" 又曰: "吾每自省吾身, 爲人謀而不忠乎? 與朋友交而不信?" 又曰: "文王既沒, 文不茲乎?" 又曰: "吾之先友嘗從事於斯矣." 則聖達之立言也, 時亦揚露己才, 或托諷以見其情, 或選辭以顯其跡, 終不盱衡自伐, 攘袂公言. 且命諸門人"各言爾志," 由也不讓, 見哂無禮.

Looking successively at Yang Xiong and those [who came] after him, their authorial postfaces began to take boasting and self-promotion as a main emphasis. When we come to the likes of Emperor Wen of Wei [Cao Pi], Fu Xuan [217–78],[14] Tao Mei,[15] and Ge Hong,[16] then they go even farther than those [who came before such as Yang Xiong]. How is that? If they possessed the slightest goodness or in their actions had some minute talent, in all cases [these things] will be analyzed and comprehensively discussed, and they were sure to record a few such things. How can this be taken as one who models the previous sages or humbly governs himself?

歷觀揚雄已降，其自敘也，始以誇尙爲宗. 至魏文帝，傅玄，陶梅，
葛洪之徒，則又逾於此者矣. 何則? 身兼片善，行有微能，皆剖析
具言，一二必載. 豈所爲憲前聖，謙以自牧者歟?

Moreover, according to the ethics of the recent past, people are fond of
claiming an eminent clan [for their ancestry]. Their ramshackle gate and
freezing family is not heard of for a hundred generations, and then a "normal
ox" stands out,[17] and in a single morning they burst into prominence; none
[of these people] will not trace back and narrate his own genealogies and
falsely claim [a sage among his ancestors]. When we come to Yi Fu and Zhen
Duo,[18] both are made the origins of the Cao clan; Chun Wei and Li Ling are
both proclaimed the beginning of the To Ba clan.[19] [As for the] ancestor of
the Ma clan in Henei, Sima Qian and Sima Biao (ca. 240–ca. 306) explain it
differently; the ancestor of the Shens of Wuxing is not the same in the words
of Shen Yue and Zhou Jiong.[20]

又近古人倫，喜稱閥閱. 其華門寒族，百代無聞，而駢角挺生，一
朝暴貴，無不追述本系，妄承先哲. 至若儀父，振鐸，并爲曹氏之
初; 淳維，李陵，俱稱拓拔之始. 河內馬祖，遷，彪之說不同; 吳興
沈先，約，炯之言有異.

In all these cases, they do not make use of true records and make no use of
their lives of leisure and wealth but only rely on classics and histories and themselves
produce contradictions. Thus we know the Yang clan resided in Xi Shu (Sichuan
province) and the Ban family dominated the northern frontier; those who
falsely claim to be descendents of Bo Qiao are the Yangs,[21] and those who
falsely claim Xiong Yi as their ancestor are the Bans.[22] I fear they are the
ones who made it ancient and pushed it farther and farther into the past!
Probably if one flatteringly sacrifices to those who are not his ghosts,[23] the
spirits will not accept the sacrifice; if one offers respect to another's relatives,
then the people will be immoral. When one composes an authorial postface,
one should thoroughly consider this [these] principle[s]. If one does not know
[who one's ancestor is], then it should be left blank. What harm is there in
this?

斯皆不因真律，無假寧楹，真據經史，自成矛盾. 則知揚姓之寓西
蜀，班門之雄朔野，或青簒伯僑，或家傳熊繹，恐自我作古，先之
彌遠者矣. 蓋諂祭非鬼，神所不歆; 致敬他親，人斯悖德. 凡爲敘
傳，宜詳此理. 不知則闕，亦何傷乎?

Notes

List of Abbreviations Used in Notes

Baopuzi Waipian	BPZWP
Baopuzi Neipian	BPZNP
Chunqiu Zuozhuan zhu	Zuozhuan
Fayan	FY
Huainanzi	HNZ
Han shu	HS
Hou Han shu	HHS
Jin shu	JS
Laozi Daode jing	Laozi
Lunheng jiaoshi	LH
Lunyu yizhu	LY
Sanguo zhi	SGZ
Shishuo xinyu	SSXY
Zhanguo ce	ZGC
Zhuangzi jinzhu jinyi	Zhuangzi
Zhouyi yizhu	Zhouyi

Introduction

[1] The title *Baopuzi* refers to the *Daode jing* 道德經 19, which states "Manifest plainness and embrace simplicity, lessen self interest and desire little" 見素抱朴, 少私寡欲. See Wang Ka 王卡, ed., *Laozi Daode jing heshang gong zhang ju* 老子道德經河上公章句 (Beijing: Zhonghua shuju, 1997), 76 (hereafter *Laozi*).

[2] See Tang Yijie 湯一介, *Wei Jin nanbeichao shiqi de daojiao* 魏晉南北朝時期的道教 (Taibei: Dongda tushu gongsi yinhang, 1991), 170.

[3] Dating his death to 363 granted Ge Hong the auspicious age of eighty-one upon his death.

[4] James Olney, ed., *Autobiography: Essays Theoretical and Critical* (Princeton: Princeton University Press, 1980), 22.

[5] Janet Ng, *The Experience of Modernity: Chinese Autobiography of the Early Twentieth Century* (Ann Arbor: University of Michigan Press, 2003), 4.

[6] Pei-yi Wu, *The Confucian's Progress: Autobiographical Writings in Traditional China* (Princeton: Princeton University Press, 1990), 15.

[7] Ng, *The Experience of Modernity*, 7.

[8] See Wendy Larson's discussion of Tao Qian in *Literary Authority and the Modern Chinese Writer: Ambivalence and Autobiography* (Durham: Duke University Press, 1991), 19–26.

[9] Ng, *The Experience of Modernity*, 6.

[10] See, for example, Robert Sayre's discussion of early American autobiographies in "Autobiography and the Making of America," in *Autobiography: Essays Theoretical and Critical*, edited by James Olney, 146–68 (Princeton: Princeton University Press, 1977). Peter Brown's entire, masterful *Augustine of Hippo: A Biography* (Berkeley: University of California Press, 2000) raises doubts about the influence of confession as a genre on biographical detail.

[11] As I shall argue in chapter 1, Guo Dengfeng's 郭登峰 *Lidai zixu zhuan wenchao* 歷代自敘傳文鈔 (Taibei: Taiwan shangwu, 1965) is perhaps the best example of how modern notions of subjectivity worked to limit the genre of self-narrative in early China.

[12] See Martin J. Powers, *Pattern and Person: Ornament, Society, and Self in Classical China* (Cambridge: Harvard University Asia Center, 2006), 210–13.

[13] James Ware, *Alchemy, Medicine, and Religion in the China of A.D. 320: The Nei P'ien of Ko Hung* (New York: Dover, 1966). Earlier, incomplete

translations of selected chapters include T. L. Davis and Wu Lu-Ch'iang, "Ko Hung on the Gold Medicine and on the Yellow and the White," *Proceedings of the American Academy of Arts and Sciences* 70 (1935–36): 221–64, which translates *Baopuzi Neipian* chapters 4 and 16; and Eugene Feifel, "Pao-P'u Tzu Nei-P'ien, Chapter I–III," *Monumenta Serica* 6 (1941): 113–211.

[14] See Robert Ford Campany, *To Live as Long as Heaven and Earth: Ge Hong's Traditions of Divine Transcendents* (Berkeley: University of California Press, 2002); and Frabrizio Pregadio, *Great Clarity: Daoism and Alchemy in Early Medieval China* (Stanford: Stanford University Press, 2006).

[15] See, for example, Mu-chou Poo, "A Taste of Happiness: Contextualizing Elixirs in *Baopuzi*," in *Of Tripod and Palate: Food, Politics, and Religion in Traditional China,* edited by Roel Sterckx, 123–139 (New York: Palgrave Macmillan, 2005); and Tang Yijie's masterful *Wei Jin nanbeichao shiqi de daojiao.*

[16] See Ren Jiyu 任繼愈, ed., *Zhongguo daojiao shi* 中國道教史 (Shanghai: Shanghai renmin chubanshe, 1997), especially chapter 3.

[17] Jay Sailey, *The Master Who Embraces Simplicity: A Study of the Philosopher Ko Hung, A.D. 283–343* (San Francisco: Chinese Materials Center, 1978).

[18] Mou Zhongjian 牟鐘鑒 has an excellent essay on Confucian-Daoist synthesis through the Song period in his *Zoujin Zhongguo jingshen* 走進中國精神 (Beijing: Huawen chubanshe, 1999), 192.

[19] Keith Knapp points out that Ge Hong required the perfection of worldly, *ru*ist virtues before the adept could hope to achieve divine transcendence. See Knapp's "Ge Hong's Reconciliation of Taoism and Confucianism," in *The Proceedings of the First International Conference on Ge Hong and Chinese Culture,* 123–27 (Hangzhou: Institute on Chinese Thought and Culture, Zhejiang University, 2003).

[20] Lin Lixue 林麗雪, *Baopuzi nei wai pian sixiang xi lun* 抱朴子內外篇思想析論 (Taibei: Xuesheng, 1980).

[21] See Suzanne R. Kirschner, *The Religious and Romantic Origins of Psychoanalysis: Individuation and Integration in Post-Freudian Theory* (Cambridge: Cambridge University Press, 1996), 66–67.

[22] George Gusdorf, "Conditions and Limits of Autobiography," in *Autobiography: Essays Theoretical and Critical,* edited by James Olney, 28–48 (Princeton: Princeton University Press, 1980).

[23] Knapp, "Ge Hong's Reconciliation of Taoism and Confucianism," 123–27. Lacking the appropriate Greek word to describe the goal of transcendence in Daoist practice, I have adopted the term *soteriology* from Christian theology, though I use it here to describe any practice of salvation through which the individual religious practitioner surpasses or is liberated from the confines of the corporeal world.

Chapter One

[1] See Georg Misch, *A History of Autobiography in Antiquity*, 2 vols. (Cambridge: Harvard University Press, 1951), 13.

[2] See James Olney, "Some Versions of Memory/Some Versions of Bios: The Ontology of Autobiography," in *Autobiography: Essays Theoretical and Critical*, edited by James Olney (Princeton: Princeton University Press, 1980), 236–67, 240. Studies that take these early works as precedents of modern or twentieth-century Chinese autobiography are Janet Ng's *The Experience of Modernity: Chinese Autobiography of the Early Twentieth Century* (Ann Arbor: University of Michigan Press, 2003); and Wendy Larson's *Literary Authority and the Modern Chinese Writer: Ambivalence and Autobiography* (Durham: Duke University Press, 1991). Pei-yi Wu's *The Confucian's Progress: Autobiographical Writings in Traditional China* (Princeton: Princeton University Press, 1990) discusses late imperial autobiography and links Ming (1368–1644) and Qing (1644–1911) autobiography to these earlier texts.

[3] This literary grouping is found in Kawai Kouzō's *Chūgoku no jiden bunngaku* (Tokyo: Soubunsha, 1996) and, with some variation, in Guo Dengfeng's *Lidai zixu zhuan wenchao* 歷代自敘傳文鈔 (Taibei: Taiwan shangwu, 1965).

[4] Significantly, this genealogy neglects poetry, the most popular mode of self-expression in early China, which probably reflects the tendency of modern scholars to focus on prose works as precedents for modern autobiography. However, Tao Qian's "Gui yuan tian ju" 歸園田居 (On Returning to Live in My Garden and Field) is far more transparently autobiographical than his "Wuliu xiansheng zhuan." For Tao Qian's poem, see A. R. Davis, *Tao Yuan-ming, AD 365–427: His Works and Their Meaning*, 2 vols. (New York: Cambridge University Press, 1983), 1:45, 2:36. For Tao Qian's poetry as a form of autobiography, see Pei-yi Wu, *The Confucian's Progress*, 6.

[5] William L. Howarth, "Some Principles of Autobiography," in *Autobiography: Essays Theoretical and Critical*, edited by James Olney, 84–114 (Princeton: Princeton University Press, 1980), 88.

[6] Roy Pascal, *Truth and Design in Autobiography* (Cambridge: Harvard University Press, 1960), 9. See also Olney, "Some Versions of Memory," 240.

[7] Augustine, *Confessions*, translated by R. S. Pine-Coffin (New York: Penguin, 1961), IV.6/77. Here Augustine quotes Psalms 24:15.

[8] Augustine, *Confessions*, IV.1/71.

[9] In Western literature, one may detect the transformation of self-narrative into the genre of autobiography in the title of Benjamin Franklin's memoir, originally published as *A Life*. It was later retitled *The Autobiography* to accommodate the shift in literary criticism that occurred in the nineteenth century.

[10] This summary is drawn from James Goodwin, *Autobiography: The Self Made Text* (New York: Twayne, 1993), 3–8.

[11] Augustine, *Confessions*, II.3/45.

[12] Ibid., IV.16/ 88.

[13] Ibid., X.6/213.

[14] Charles Taylor, *Sources of the Self: The Making of Modern Identity* (Cambridge: Harvard University Press, 1989), 131.

[15] Augustine, *Confessions*, IV.2/81.

[16] Ibid., II.1/43.

[17] Taylor, *Sources of the Self*, 134.

[18] Augustine, *Confessions*, X.11/ 219.

[19] Ibid., V.6/98.

[20] Ibid., X.8/216.

[21] Ibid., X.8/214.

[22] Ibid.

[23] Ibid., X.24–26/230–231.

[24] Ibid., X.1/207.

[25] James Olney, "Autobiography and the Cultural Moment," in *Autobiography: Essays Theoretical and Critical*, edited by James Olney, 3–27 (Princeton: Princeton University Press, 1977), 20.

[26] Philippe Lejeune, *On Autobiography* (Minneapolis: University of Minnesota Press, 1989), 124.

[27] James Olney, *Metaphors of Self: The Meaning of Autobiography* (Princeton: Princeton University Press, 1972), 3.

[28] Philippe Lejeune, *On Autobiography*, 12. This is probably the broadest, most concise, and most flexible definition of autobiography as a genre offered by a contemporary critic.

[29] Taylor, *Sources of the Self*, 51.

[30] Olney, "Some Versions of Memory," 240. George Gusdorf, "Conditions and Limits of Autobiography," in *Autobiography: Essays Theoretical and Critical*, edited by James Olney, 28–48 (Princeton: Princeton University Press, 1977), 39.

[31] Pascal, *Truth and Design in Autobiography*, 2–9.

[32] Gusdorf, "Conditions and Limits," 39.

[33] Goodwin, *Autobiography*, 11.

[34] Taylor, *Sources of the Self*, 48.

[35] Augustine, *Confessions*, III.12/69.

[36] Olney, *Metaphors of Self*, 35.

[37] Stanley Cavell, *In Quest of the Ordinary: Lines of Skepticism and Romanticism* (Chicago: University of Chicago Press, 1988), 115.

[38] Jürgen Habermas, "Individuation through Socialization: On George Herbert Mead's Theory of Subjectivity," in *Postmetaphysical Thinking: Philosophical Essays*, translated by William Mark Hohengarten (Cambridge: MIT Press, 1992), 167

[39] Cavell, *In Quest of the Ordinary*, 106, 114. In James Olney's words, the "self that was not really in existence in the beginning is in the end merely a matter of the text" ("Autobiography and the Cultural Moment," 22).

[40] Habermas, "Individuation through Socialization," 168.

[41] Lydia H. Liu, *Translingual Practice: Literature, National Culture, and Translated Modernity—China, 1900–1937* (Stanford: Stanford University Press, 1995), 95.

[42] Ibid.

[43] Guo Dengfeng, *Lidai zixu zhuan*, 1.

[44] Ibid., 2.

[45] Ibid., 3.

[46] See chapter 2.

[47] This discussion is based on Stephen Owen's translation in his *Readings in Chinese Literary Thought* (Cambridge: Harvard-Yenching Institute, 1992), 40.

[48] Ibid., 38.

[49] Michael Fishlen, "Wine, Poetry, and History: Du Mu's 'Pouring Alone in the Prefectural Residence,'" *T'oung Pao* 80, 4–5 (1994) 260–97.

[50] Ronald Miao, *Early Medieval Poetry: The Life and Verse of Wang Ts'an (A.D. 177–217)* (Wiesbaden: Franz Steiner, 1982), 13; Pei-yi Wu, *The Confucian's Progress*, 16. It should be noted that challenges to historical and biographical readings existed during every period. The metaphysical poetry 玄詩 popular during Ge Hong's era came to be reviled by later critics as dull and uninspired and a general departure from traditional verse. See Xu Gongchi 徐公持, *Wei-Jin wenxue shi* 魏晉文學史 (Beijing: Renmin wenxue chubanshe, 1999), 460. Wu Fusheng, in *The Poetics of Decadence: Chinese Poetry of the Southern Dynasties and Late Tang Periods* (Albany: State University of New York Press, 1998), argues that so-called palace poetry during the Southern dynasties and late Tang was largely concerned with aesthetics rather than alluding to the biographical circumstances of the author. And Stephen Owen notes that the most serious attack on the reading strategy outlined in the "Great Preface" occurred during and after the Song period (*Chinese Literary Thought*, 37).

[51] Stephen Owen, "The Self's Perfect Mirror: Poetry as Autobiography," in *The Vitality of the Lyric Voice: Shih Poetry from the Late Han to the T'ang*, edited by Shuen-fu Lin and Stephen Owen, 71–102 (Princeton: Princeton University Press, 1986).

[52] Pei-yi Wu, *The Confucian's Progress*, 15.

[53] Rather than retranslating or reprinting a work that has been translated elsewhere, I simply refer readers to either Pei-yi Wu's excellent translation (*The Confucian's Progress,* 15) or that of A. R. Davis (*Tao Yuan-ming*, 1:208).

[54] Larson, *Literary Authority*, 23. Wu (*The Confucian's Progress*, 16) attributes the style of the autobiography to such precedents as Huang Fumi's 皇甫謐 (215–82) *Shengxian gaoshi zhuan* 聲線高士傳 (Accounts of Sage Lofty Gentlemen), although, as will be discussed in chapter 3, reclusion and eremitism have a long history in Chinese literature and many archetypes were available for imitation.

[55] Larson, *Literary Authority*, 22.

[56] Stephen Durrant, "Self as the Intersection of Traditions," *Journal of the American Oriental Society* 106.1 (1986): 33–40, 36; Ng, *Experience of Modernity*, 5.

[57] Durrant, "Self as Intersection of Tradition," 36; Wendy Larson, *Literary Authority and the Modern Chinese Writer: Ambivalence and Autobiography* (Durham: Duke University, 1991). 16.

[58] Janet Ng, *The Experience of Modernity: Chinese Autobiography of the Early Twentieth Century* (Ann Arbor: University of Michigan Press, 2003), 6.

[59] Larson, *Literary Authority*, 22.

[60] Ibid., 12.

[61] Pei-yi Wu uses each of these subgenres in *The Confucian's Progress*.

[62] Pei-yi Wu, for example, generally omits poetry and letters but includes *nianpu* 年譜 or annalistic biographies.

[63] Pei-yi Wu, *The Confucian's Progress*, 269.

[64] Larson, *Literary Authority*, 13–15.

[65] Zhao Guoxi, "Sima Qian xie '*Shi ji* Taishigong zixu' wei ziji shubei lizhuan" 司馬遷寫"史記太史公自序" 為自己樹碑立傳, *Jilin shifan xueyuan xuebao* 9 (1996): 6–9, quoted at 6.

[66] Sima Qian's biography demonstrates the way in which a wide range of autobiographical material was used as the primary sources for historical writing, but its juxtaposition with supporting documents does not necessarily support the notion that the authorial postface represents early autobiography as such as much as it was considered another source of personal information about the historical subject. Some authorial postfaces may have been entirely absorbed into the later biographies of their subjects, explaining their disappearance from the textual record. Ban Gu's biography of Yang Xiong 揚雄 (53 BCE–18 CE) in *Han shu* 87 is almost certainly composed at least in part of Yang's authorial postface to his *Model Sayings,* or *Fayan* 法言, an argument made by David Knechtges with which I wholeheartedly agree. See Ban Gu, *Han shu* (Beijing: Zhonghua shuju chubanshe, 1997), 11:87A/B (hereafter *HS*); and David Knechtges, *The Han shu Biography of Yang Xiong (53 B.C.–A.D. 18)* (Tempe: Center for Asian Studies, Arizona State University, 1982).

Chapter Two

[1] Liu Zhiji, quoted in Hong Xingzu's 洪興祖 (1090–1155) *Chuci buzhu* 楚辭補注 (Beijing: Zhonghua shuju, 2002), 3. The original text is from Liu Zhiji's *Shitong*, "neipian" (Taibei: Wenhai chubanshe, 1953), 256–59 (trad. 9/3b–4b) (hereafter *Shitong*).

[2] Mark Edward Lewis, *Writing and Authority in Early China* (New York: State University of New York Press, 1999), 186.

[3] Stephen Durrant, *The Cloudy Mirror: Tension and Conflict in the Writings of Sima Qian* (Albany: State University of New York Press, 1995), 16.

[4] Liu Zhiji, *Shitong*, 256.

[5] One can see this in later criticism of Sima Qian, which ultimately stems from the critic's acknowledgment that Sima Qian was interested in a more complex narrative structure that attached a life or official career to a theme, usually the subject's character. See William H. Nienhauser Jr., "Early Biography," in *The Columbia History of Chinese Literature*, edited by Victor H. Mair, 511–26 (New York: Columbia University Press, 2001), 514.

[6] See ibid.

[7] Liu's claim that the origins of the postface may be traced to the opening lines of "Li sao" anticipates the way in which modern critics cite diverse texts as precedents to create genealogies for later genres.

[8] Liu Zhiji, *Shitong*, 256.

[9] It is this final itemization of the content of Yang Xiong's *Fayan,* that leads me to believe that his official biography in *HS* 11:87A/B was at one point the authorial postface to this work. See David Knechtges, *The Han shu Biography of Yang Xiong (53 B.C.–A.D. 18)* (Tempe: Center for Asian Studies, Arizona State University, 1982).

[10] *HS,* 10:100/4225.

[11] For the influence of the figure of Confucius on the work of Ban Gu, see Anthony Clark, "Historian of the Orchid Terrace: Partisan Polemics in Ban Gu's Han shu," PhD diss., University of Oregon, 2005. For Yang Xiong's use of Confucius as a model for his own work, I have relied on Matthew Cochran's conference paper "Yang Xiong as Newer-World Confucius," delivered at the Pacific Regional Conference of the Association for Asian Studies (ASPAC), University of Oregon, Eugene, June 10, 2004. It has been observed that by including the "Letter to Ren An" at the end of Sima Qian's *Han shu* biography Ban Gu may have sought to intensify the subjectivity of Sima Qian's narrative, thereby rendering his own authorial postface all the more reserved by comparison.

[12] Stephen Durrant, "Self as the Intersection of Traditions," *Journal of the American Oriental Society,* 106.1 (1986): 33–40.

[13] Dennis Twitchett, *The Writing of Official History under the Tang* (New York: Cambridge University Press, 1992), 67.

[14] Ibid., 74.

[15] Pei-yi Wu, *The Confucian's Progress: Autobiographical Writings in Traditional China* (Princeton: Princeton University Press, 1990), 19.

[16] Ibid., 6.

[17] Ibid., 12. It may have been the subjectivity of verse that prompted Yang Xiong to write in *Fayan* 2.1, "Someone asked, 'May the *Fu* be used for subtle rebuke?' I replied, 'Subtle rebuke indeed! It should stop at subtle rebuke. If it does not stop, then I fear it will not avoid encouraging excess.' He said, 'The finest silk weave is beautiful.' And I replied, 'The ruination of women's work!' [He said,] 'The "Essay on Swordsmanship" says, "Swordsmanship can be pursued to protect oneself."' But I say, 'Does swordsmanship's highest skill cause one to increase in ritual behavior?'" 或曰: "賦可以諷乎?" 曰: "諷乎! 諷則已, 不已, 吾恐不免於勸也." 或曰: "霧縠之組麗." 曰: "女工之蠹矣." 劍客論曰: "劍可以愛身." 曰: "狴犴使人多禮乎?" Wang Rongbao 汪榮寶, ed., *Fayan yishu* 法言義疏 (Beijing: Zhonghua, 1987), 45 (hereafter *FY*).

[18] Twitchett, *Writing Official History*, 78.

[19] Wu, *The Confucian's Progress*, 8.

[20] Ibid., 13.

[21] Liu Zhiji, *Shitong*, 9/257.

[22] Ibid.

[23] See Alfred Forke, *Lun-Heng: Philosophical Essays of Wang Chung*, 2 vols. (New York: Paragon, 1962), 1:64; and Wang Chong, *Lunheng jiaoshi* 論衡校釋, 4 vols. (Beijing: Zhonghua shuju, 1996), 4:30/1187 (hereafter *LH*).

[24] Yang Bojun 楊伯峻, ed., *Lunyu yizhu* 論語譯注 (Beijing: Zhonghua shuju, 2002), 13.18 (hereafter *LY*).

[25] Gao You 高誘 (fl. 210), ed., *Zhangguo ce Gao You jiao zhu* 戰國策高誘校註 (Taibei: Taiwan shang wu yin shu guan, 1956), Wei 魏 3/11 (hereafter *ZGC*).

[26] Liu Zhiji, *Shitong*, 9/257. The final line alludes to the *Shang shu* 尚書 (Book of Documents. See James Legge, *The Shoo King or Book of Historical Documents* (Hong Kong: Hong Kong University Press, 1960), 605–6.

[27] Liu Zhiji, *Shitong*, 9/258. Here Liu refers to *LY,* 11.26.

[28] Owen, "The Self's Perfect Mirror," 74.

[29] Donald Munro, *The Concept of Man in Early China* (Ann Arbor: Center for Chinese Studies, University of Michigan, 1969), 153.

[30] Chen Shou 陳壽, *Sanguo zhi* 三國志, 5 vols. (Beijing: Zhonghua shuju, 1982), 1:1/44 (hereafter *SGZ*). Fu Xuan's postface is no longer extant.

[31] Dates unknown. A contemporary of Ge Hong, Tao Mei also served on Wang Dao's staff. His postface is no longer extant.

[32] Fang Xuanling 房玄齡 et al., *Jin shu* 晉書, 10 vols. (Beijing: Zhonghua shuju, 1998), 6:72/1910 (hereafter *JS*).

[33] Liu Zhiji, *Shitong*, 9/258.

[34] *LY,* 3.7 .

[35] Of aristocratic upbringing, Xun Yu opposed Cao Cao's bid for power and ultimately committed suicide by drinking poison. *SGZ,* 2:10/307; Fan Ye 范曄, *Hou Han shu* 後漢書, 12 vols. (Beijing: Zhonghua shuju, 1997), 6:49/1646 (hereafter *HHS*).

[36] Leading birds means shooting them by anticipating the path of their flight.

[37] Zhang Jing (no certain dates) was a military official of the Later Han period for whom this text marks the earliest reference.

[38] *SGZ,* 1:2/89–90.

[39] For example, in *LY,* 3.16, Confucius states that in archery competition one should not pierce the target completely lest the strength of the competitors be unfavorably compared. The implication of Cao Pi's comments is quite the opposite, that true skill is impossible to conceal.

[40] Arbiter General is a position of the third grade 三品. Liu Xun (no certain dates) was a general and official under Cao Cao. *HHS,* 8:69/2243; *SGZ,* 2:12/387. General advancing glory is a position of the fourth grade 四品. This text marks the earliest reference to Deng Zhan (no certain dates).

[41] The sense of this sentence is that Cao Pi used the momentum of Zhan's advance to allow his opponent to strike his forehead on the piece of sugarcane.

[42] Yang Qing was a physician of the early Han 漢 dynasty and the teacher of Chunyu Yi. Cao Pi is probably referring to *Shi ji,* 105. See Sima Qian, *Shi ji,* 10 vols. (Beijing: Zhonghua shuju, 1999), 9:105/2794 (hereafter *SJ*). Chunyu Yi was a physician of the Former Han dynasty and a student of Yang Qing. During the time of Han Wendi 文帝 (r. 180–157 BCE) he

served as Director of the Imperial Granaries 太倉令 of Qi 齊. Slandered and imprisoned, he is famous for having been saved from corporal punishment by his daughter's appeal to the emperor (*SJ,* 9:105/2809).

⁴³ *SGZ,* 1:2/90.

⁴⁴ Yuan Min was possibly the younger brother of Yuan Hui 袁徽 (*SGZ* 2:11/336). The quote is from *SGZ,* 1:2/90.

⁴⁵ Wei Wendi 魏文帝 was the reign title of Cao Pi.

⁴⁶ Here I am reading 數 as 敷 (fū), according to Yang Mingzhao's 楊明照 suggestion in *Baopuzi Waipian jiaojian* 抱朴子外篇校箋, 2 vols. (Beijing: Zhonghua shuju, 1997), 2:50/107–8 (hereafter *BPZWP*).

⁴⁷ Here Gettang quotes *Lunyu* 5.10, "Tsai Yü was asleep in the daytime. The Master said, 'A piece of rotten wood cannot be carved, nor can a wall of dried dung be troweled. As far as Yü is concerned, what is the use of condemning him?'" 宰予晝寢. 子曰: " 朽木不可雕也, 糞土之牆不可杇也, 於予與何誅. The translation is from D. C. Lau, *Confucius: The Analects* (New York: Penguin Group, 1979), 77. See also *LY,* 5.10.

⁴⁸ *BPZWP,* 2:50/703. See also Jay Sailey, *The Master Who Embraces Simplicity: A Study of the Philosopher Ko Hung* (San Francisco: Chinese Materials Center, 1978), 267. *Shupu* is the name of an ancient gambling game.

⁴⁹ Guo Dengfeng, *Lidai zixu zhuan,* 396. See also Cyril Birch, *Anthology of Chinese Literature,* 2 vols. (New York: Grove, 1965), 1:162–68.

⁵⁰ The use of alleged deficiencies to allude to the author's good character reached its full flower in the poetry of Tao Qian, whose pose as a simple farmer became the template for poetic apology for future generations of Tang and Song poets. See Owen, "The Self's Perfect Mirror," 81.

⁵¹ *Fayan* 2.1 says, "Someone said, 'When you were young, sir, were you fond of writing *fu*?' I said, 'Yes. A child carves bug-script seal characters.' After a while, I added, 'This is what a grown man does not do.' 或問 "吾子少而好賦". 曰: "然. 童子雕蟲篆刻." 俄而, 曰: "壯夫不爲也. (*FY,* 2.1/45). For a discussion of Jin dynasty metaphysical poetry and its criticism, see Xu Gongchi, *Wei-Jin wenxue shi,* 460.

⁵² *BPZWP,* 2:50/705; Sailey, *The Master Who Embraces Simplicity,* 175–76.

⁵³ Particularly see *BPZWP,* 2:44/444, "The Hundred Schools" 百家; and Sailey, *The Master Who Embraces Simplicity,* 222–23. For a full discussion of Ge Hong's attitude toward verse and rhyme prose, see Luo Zongqiang 羅

宗強, *Wei-Jin Nan Bei chao wenxue sixiang shi.* 魏晉南北朝文學思想史 (Beijing: Zhonghua shuju, 1996), 160–62.

[54] *BPZWP,* 2:50/709; Sailey, *The Master Who Embraces Simplicity,* 267.

[55] Cao Pi, "Postface," in *SGZ,* 1:2/90.

[56] Liu Dajie 劉大杰, *Wei-Jin sixiang lun* 魏晉思想論 (Shanghai: Shanghai guji chubanshe, 2000), 145.

[57] Ying-shih Yü, "Individualism and the Neo-Taoist Movement in Wei-Chin China," in *Individualism and Holism: Studies in Confucian and Taoist Values,* edited by Donald Munro, 121–56 (Ann Arbor: Center for Chinese Studies, University of Michigan, 1985), 121.

[58] *Mingjiao* 名教 was a broad philosophical stance during the early medieval period generally infused with Confucian terms, but it should not be regarded as a "school" or *jia* 家.

[59] Mou Zhongjian 牟鐘鑒, *Zoujin Zhongguo jingshen* 走進中國精神 (Beijing: Huawen chubanshe, 1999), 198. Tang Changru 唐長孺 points out that this debate was not simply an abstract discussion but carried important political implications by drawing on established traditions such as Confucianism and Daoism. Tang Changru, *Wei-Jin Nan Bei chao shi lun cong* 魏晉南北朝史論叢 (Shijiazhuang: Hebei jiaoyu chubanshe, 2000), 298.

[60] For example, the distance between Wang Bi's view of nonbeing and that of Guo Xiang was considerable, although scholars retrospectively designate each as *xuan xue jia* 玄學家 or "metaphysician."

[61] See Tang Yongtong 湯用彤, *Wei-Jin Xuan xue lun gao* 魏晉玄學論稿 (Shanghai: Shanghai guji chubanshe, 2001), 24. For an excellent summary of abstruse learning and this entire, sometimes confusing debate, see Nanxiu Qian, *Spirit and Self in Medieval China: The Shih-shuo hsin-yü and Its Legacy* (Honolulu: University of Hawai'i Press, 2001), 68–70.

[62] This notion is remarkable for its resemblance to Emerson's concept of "involuntary perception" and the "aboriginal self," as intuition for Emerson was "the last fact behind which analysis cannot go" but was expressed through recourse to the rational self. Ralph Waldo Emerson, "Self-Reliance," in *Selected Essays of Ralph Waldo Emerson* (New York: Penguin, 1984), 187.

[63] According to Nanxiu Qian, *shen* does not represent a single personality trait but means the totality of one's personality as a manifestation of one's unique nature. See Qian, *Spirit and Self in Medieval China,* 153. In this usage,

the term *shen* bears more than a superficial resemblance to Dewey's notion of *character* as the interpenetration of habits. John Dewey, *Human Nature and Conduct* (New York: Random House, 1922), 38.

[64] Richard Mather, trans. *A New Account of Tales of the World* (Ann Arbor: Center for Chinese Studies, University of Michigan, 2002).

[65] Liu Yiqing, *Shishuo xinyu*, 2 vols. (Beijing: Zhonghua shuju, 1999), 2:23.11 (hereafter *SSXY*). Note that citations for *SSXY*, like those for *LY* and *FY,* are provided according to volume, chapter, and entry number rather than page number. For Mather's translation, see his *A New Account of Tales of the World,* 403.

[66] Richard Mather, "Individualist Expressions of the Outsiders during the Six Dynasties," in *Individualism and Holism: Studies in Confucian and Taoist Values*, edited by Donald Munro, 199–214 (Ann Arbor: Center for Chinese Studies, University of Michigan, 1985), 200.

[67] As Qian points out, the phrase *ren lun* 人倫 simultaneously meant both character appraisal and social relationships, the latter being a more traditional reading from *Mengzi* 孟子, V.4. Qian, *Spirit and Self in Medieval China*, 22.

[68] *HHS,* 8:67/2185. This citation is used by Nanxiu Qian in *Spirit and Self in Medieval China*, 30.

[69] *SSXY,* 6.15. The translation is based on Mather, *A New Account of Tales of the World*, 195.

[70] Qian, *Spirit and Self in Medieval China*, 47.

[71] Ying-shih Yü, "Individualism and the Neo-Taoist Movement," 126.

[72] Mather, "Individualist Expressions," 204.

[73] Qian, *Spirit and Self in Medieval China*, 44.

[74] It cannot be denied that the notion of the individual as expressed in these sources entailed an appeal to an assumed inviolable nature. However, although each individual was attempting to express a natural or "self-so" (zi ran 自然) state of being, this state was understood to proceed from nonbeing, thereby conforming to a broader cosmological context. In this way, a being in a "natural" state was still not regarded as having independently arisen but only existed as a result of a prior relationship with the Dao.

[75] *SSXY* does treat female models of virtue, though whether these were intended for male or female readers is up for debate.

Chapter Three

[1] Charles Taylor, *Sources of the Self: The Making of Modern Identity* (Cambridge: Harvard University Press, 1989), 36.

[2] Stephen Durrant, "Self as the Intersection of Traditions," *Journal of the American Oriental Society* 106.1 (1986): 33–40, 36.

[3] Jay Sailey, *The Master Who Embraces Simplicity: A Study of the Philosopher Ko Hung* (San Francisco: Chinese Materials Center, 1978), 277.

[4] *BPZWP*, 2:50/644; John Knoblock and Jeffrey Riegel, trans., *The Annals of Lu Buwei: Lushi Chunqiu* 呂氏春秋 (Stanford: Stanford University Press, 2000), 146 (5/5.3).

[5] Liu Zhiji, *Shitong,* 9/258.

[6] Ibid.

[7] Ibid.

[8] Yang Mingzhao offers extensive notes demonstrating that the identity of this ancestor is nearly impossible to determine. See *BPZWP*, 2:50/645.

[9] The position of junior mentor was potentially very powerful as the holder of this office had direct access to the emperor.

[10] Du Yu would return to the north and write his commentary to *Zuozhuan* (Zuo Commentary to the Spring and Autumn Annals) after the conquest of Wu in 280.

[11] Sailey, *The Master Who Embraces Simplicity*, 278.

[12] *BPZWP*, 2:50/649; Sailey, *The Master Who Embraces Simplicity*, 246.

[13] *BPZWP*, 2:50/649; Yang Bojun, *Chunqiu Zuozhuan zhu* 春秋左傳注, 4 vols. (Beijing: Zhonghua shuju, 2000), 4:Duke Ding 定公, 1.1/1524 (hereafter *Zuozhuan*).

[14] *BPZWP*, 2:50/650.

[15] Luo Zhiye 羅志野, ed., *Shang shu* 尙書 (Changsha: Hunan chubanshe, 1997), Yao 2/3 (hereafter *Shang shu*).

[16] David R. Knechtges, "Sweet-Peel Orange or Southern Gold? Regional Identity in Western Jin Literature," in *Studies in Early Medieval Chinese Literature and Cultural History*, edited by Paul Kroll and David Knechtges, 27–80 (Boulder: T'ang Studies Society, 2003). Lin Lixue 林麗雪 supports Knechtges's assertion, arguing that the Ru tradition in the south was much more conservative than it became in the north under the influence of

metaphysical intellectual currents or *xuan xue* 玄學. See Lin Lixue , *Baopuzi nei wai pian sixiang xi lun* (Taibei: Xuesheng, 1980), 19.

[17] J. Michael Farmer, "Zhang Hua," in *Dictionary of Literary Biography*: *Classical Chinese Writers, Pre-Tang Era (–598)*, edited by Curtis Dean Smith (Columbia, SC: Bruccoli Clark Layman, 2010).

[18] Knechtges, "Sweet-Peel Orange," 42.

[19] *SJ*, 7:67/2201; Knechtges, "Sweet-Peel Orange," 47.

[20] Sailey, *The Master Who Embraces Simplicity*, 408.

[21] *SSXY* 5.18; Richard Mather, trans., *A New Account of Tales of the World* (Ann Arbor: Center for Chinese Studies, University of Michigan, 2002), 167.

[22] Knechtges, "Sweet-Peel Orange," 63.

[23] Ibid., 64. Knechtges here draws on Tang Changru's more extensive study of differences between Jin and Wu culture in his *Wei Jin Nan Beichao shi lun cong* (Shi Jia Zhuang: Hebei jiaoyu chubanshe, 2000); see especially pages 338–46.

[24] Knechtges, "Sweet-Peel Orange," 48. The passage to which Knechtges refers is in *BPZWP*, 1:15/411. See also Sailey, *The Master Who Embraces Simplicity*, 99–100.

[25] For Ge Hong's similarities with Lu Ji and admiration of his work, see Sailey, *The Master Who Embraces Simplicity*, 498–506.

[26] Tang Changru, *Wei Jin Nan Beichao shi lun cong*, 346. Ge Hong does decry the use of five-minerals powder by those in mourning, as proper mourning rites prohibited taking drugs of any kind. See *BPZWP*, 2:26/16; and Sailey, *The Master Who Embraces Simplicity*, 159. Sailey has a decent discussion of five-minerals powder that draws on a variety of primary sources and secondary studies by Chinese scholars on the subject (427–32).

[27] *SSXY*, 23.35; Mather, *A New Account of Tales of the World*, 413.

[28] *BPZWP*, 2:26/17. See also Sailey, *The Master Who Embraces Simplicity*, 160.

[29] *BPZWP*, 1:24/570. See also Sailey, *The Master Who Embraces Simplicity*, 118.

[30] *BPZWP*, 1:24/594. See also Sailey, *The Master Who Embraces Simplicity*, 129.

[31] *JS*, 6:72/1911.

[32] *BPZWP*, 2:50/703; Sailey, *The Master Who Embraces Simplicity*, 265.

[33] The text says thirteen years old, following the Chinese system for calculating ages from conception. Yang Mingzhao believes Ge Hong's statement that he lost the tutelage of his father to be an oblique reference to a passage from *LY*, 16/13, in which Po Yu 伯魚 describes to Chen Kang 陳亢 his father's exemplary conduct (*BPZWP*, 2:50/653).

[34] *BPZWP*, 2:50/653.

[35] Sailey, *The Master Who Embraces Simplicity*, 279.

[36] Much of this argument is summarized quite well in ibid.

[37] *JS*, 6:72/1911; *BPZWP*, 2:50/ 655.

[38] *BPZWP*, 2:50/695.

[39] Ibid., 1:1/1; Sailey, *The Master Who Embrace Simplicity*, 3–4.

[40] *BPZWP*, 1:1/1.

[41] Ibid., 1:1/23.

[42] Ibid., 2:50/664.

[43] Ibid., 2:50/665.

[44] See Chen Guying 陳鼓應, ed., *Zhuangzi jinzhu jinyi* 莊子今注譯 (Beijing: Zhonghua shuju, 1994), 28.8/757 (hereafter *Zhuangzi*). The translation is from Burton Watson, *The Complete Works of Chuang Tzu* (New York: Columbia University Press, 1968), 315–16.

[45] *LY,* 1:1.

[46] *BPZWP*, 2:50/677–8; Sailey, *The Master Who Embraces Simplicty*, 256–57.

[47] *BPZWP*, 2:50/682; Sailey, *The Master Who Embraces Simplicity*, 258.

[48] Stylistically, the end of this section marks a definitive end to the first portion of the text. The disjuncture in themes, as well as the gap in narrative flow, suggests that Ge Hong might have intended this half of the "Waipian Zixu" to stand alone as an account of the author but subsequently added the remainder of the text as we have it today.

[49] See Durrant, "Self as the Intersection of Traditions," 34, 39. See also Stephen Durrant, *The Cloudy Mirror: Tension and Conflict in the Writings of Sima Qian* (Albany: State University of New York Press, 1995), 16; and Larson, *Literary Authority*, 13.

[50] *SJ,* 10:130/ 3300.

[51] *LH,* 4:30/1204.

[52] *BPZWP,* 2:50/667. This loosely follows Sailey's translation in *The Master Who Embraces Simplicity*, 251.

[53] Wolfgang Bauer, "The Hidden Hero: Creation and Disintegration of the Ideal of Eremitism," in *Individualism and Holism: Studies In Confucian and Taoist Values*, edited by Donald Munro, 157–91 (Ann Arbor: Center for Chinese Studies, University of Michigan, 1985), 169–71.

[54] *LY,* 16.12. The translation is from Edward Slingerland's *Confucius: Analects* (Indianapolis: Hackett, 2003), 196.

[55] *LY,* 8.13. The translation is from D. C. Lau's *Confucius: The Analects* (New York: Penguin Group, 1979), 94.

[56] Elsewhere in *Lunyu* (e.g., 16.11 and 18.7) reclusion is treated with more ambiguity. Nevertheless, Aat Vervoorn considers pronouncements attributed to Confucius to play a pivotal role in defining reclusion prior to and during the Han. See Alan Berkowitz, "Reclusion and 'The Chinese Eremitic Tradition,'" *Journal of the American Oriental Society* 113.4 (1993): 579; and Aat Vervoom, *Men of Cliffs and Caves: The Development of the Chinese Eremitic Tradition to the End of the Han Dynasty* (Hong Kong: Chinese University Press, 1990), 28.

[57] *JS,* 7:79/2072. Lin An is modern Hangzhou.

[58] Quoted in Mou Zhongjian, *Zoujin Zhongguo jingshen* (Beijing: Huawen chubanshe, 1999), 198.

[59] Commentary to *SSXY,* 4.91, translated in Mather, *A New Account of Tales of the World*, 147.

[60] Ralph Waldo Emerson, *Selected Essays of Ralph Waldo Emerson* (New York: Penguin, 1984), 181.

[61] See Bauer, "The Hidden Hero," 157–91.

[62] Alan Berkowitz, *Patterns of Disengagement: The Practice and Portrayal of Reclusion In Early Medieval China* (Stanford: Stanford University Press, 2000), 134.

[63] Mather, "Individualist Expressions," 204.

[64] Luo Zongqiang 羅宗強, *Wei-Jin Nan Bei chao wenxue sixiang shi* 魏晉南北朝文學思想史 (Beijing: Zhonghua shuju, 1996), 77.

[65] See Berkowitz, *Patterns of Disengagement*; Bauer, "The Hidden Hero"; and Vervoom, *Men of Cliffs and Caves* among others. Berkowitz in particular has a very thorough bibliography of sources in many languages.

⁶⁶ *Zhouyi*, "Xi ci xia" 繫辭下. See also Zhou Zhenfu 周振甫, ed., *Zhouyi yizhu* 周易譯注 (Beijing: Zhonghua shuju, 1999), 260 (hereafter *Zhouyi*).

⁶⁷ *BPZWP*, 1:19/474.

⁶⁸ Here Ge Hong quotes *Shi ji*, 5:33/1518.

⁶⁹ *BPZWP*, 1:2/71.

⁷⁰ Ibid., 1:2/72.

⁷¹ Berkowitz, *Patterns of Disengagement*, 136.

⁷² Chi Chao was an official who served under Huan Wen 桓文 (*JS*, 6:67/1802).

⁷³ Dai Kui's biography is found in the collective biography of recluses in ibid., 8:94/2457.

⁷⁴ *SSXY*, 18.5; Mather, *A New Account of Tales of the World*, 361.

⁷⁵ *JS*, 6:72/1911.

⁷⁶ Ibid., 1:6/145.

⁷⁷ Ibid., 6:72/1911. Ge Hong also records the event in his *Waipian zixu* (*BPZWP*, 2:50/721).

⁷⁸ *JS*, 7:82/ 2150.

⁷⁹ Wei Zheng 魏徵, *Sui shu*, 3 vols. (Beijing: Zhonghua shuju, 1973), 2:34/961 (hereafter *SSh*).

⁸⁰ William H. Nienhauser Jr., "An Interpretation of the Literary and Historical Aspects of the *Hsi-ching Tsa-chi* (Miscellanies of the Western Capital)," PhD diss., Indiana University, 1972, 28–30.

⁸¹ Here I follow Chen Feilong 陳飛龍 in his assessment that Ge Hong first met Bao Jing on Mount Luofu and not after returning home to Jurong as some contend. *Baopuzi neipian jin zhu jin yi* 抱朴子內篇今註今譯 (Taibei: Taiwan Commercial Press Publishing House, 2001), 841–43 (hereafter *BPZNP*). For the alternate view, see Robert Ford Campany, *To Live as Long as Heaven and Earth: Ge Hong's Traditions of Divine Transcendents* (Berkeley: University of California Press, 2002), 16, although Campany does not explain his timing of the event.

⁸² *JS*, 6:72/1911, 8:95/2482.

⁸³ *BPZNP*, 842.

⁸⁴ *SSXY*, 18.4; Mather, *A New Account of Tales of the World*, 357.

⁸⁵ *JS* 8:94/2440

[86] Ibid.

[87] James Ware, *Alchemy, Medicine, and Religion in the China of A.D. 320* (Boston: MIT Press, 1966).

[88] *BPZWP*, 2:50/715.

[89] Ibid., 2:50/660.

[90] *Laozi,* 48/186.

[91] The translation is based on Yang Bojun's notes. See *LY,* 2.4.

[92] 先生以始立之盛. *BPZWP,* 2:50/715. I examine more fully Ge Hong's use of Confucius's brief narrative in chapter 4.

[93] *JS,* 7:76/2015.

[94] *BPZWP,* 2:50/685.

[95] Ibid., 2:50/709; Sailey, *The Master Who Embraces Simplicity,* 267.

[96] *Zuozhuan,* 3:Xiang 24.1/1088.

[97] *Zhuangzi,* 13.8/357.

[98] Pu Youjun, *Zhongguo wenxue piping shi lun* 中國文學批評史論 (Chengdu: Ba-Shu shu she, 2001), 249–50.

[99] Wang Yunxi 王運熙, *Wei-Jin Nan Bei chao wenxue piping shi* 魏晉南北朝文學批評史 (Shanghai: Shanghai guji chubanshe, 1989), 133.

[100] Pu Youjun, *Zhongguo wenxue,* 251.

[101] *BPZWP,* 2:32/107; Sailey, *The Master Who Embraces Simplicity,* 177.

[102] *BPZWP,* 2:32/109; Sailey, *The Master Who Embraces Simplicity,* 177.

[103] *BPZWP,* 2:32/98; Sailey, *The Master Who Embraces Simplicity,* 173.

[104] *BPZWP,* 2:32/103; Sailey, *The Master Who Embraces Simplicity,* 175.

[105] *BPZWP,* 2:32/99; Sailey, *The Master Who Embraces Simplicity,* 174.

[106] *BPZWP,* 2:43/435.

[107] Wang Yunxi, *Wei-Jin Nan Bei chao wenxue piping shi,* 140.

[108] *BPZWP,* 2:32/101; Sailey, *The Master Who Embraces Simplicity,* 174.

[109] *BPZWP,* 2:50/698.

[110] *BPZWP,* 2:50/695.

[111] Wang Yunxi, *Wei-Jin Nan Bei chao wenxue piping shi,* 137. For Ge Hong's view of the poetry of his era, see chapter 2 of this volume.

[112] *BPZWP*, 2:50/697.

[113] See, for example, ibid., 2:37/220, in which the Master's disciples 門人 are sitting together discussing benevolence 仁.

[114] Pu Youjun, *Zhongguo wenxue*, 255.

[115] Jürgen Habermas, "Individuation through Socialization: On George Herbert Mead's Theory of Subjectivity," in *Postmetaphysical Thinking: Philosophical Essays*, translated by William Mark Hohengarten (Cambridge: MIT Press, 1992), 164.

Chapter Four

[1] William Least Heat Moon. *Blue Highways: A Journey into America* (New York: Little, Brown, 1999), 418.

[2] Here I refer to both of Ge Hong's authorial accounts together, one from the "inner" *Neipian* 內篇 chapters and the other, more lengthy text found in the "outer" *Waipian* 外篇 chapters.

[3] *Shang shu*, "Jin teng," 1/127.

[4] *Shang shu*, "Jin teng," 3/131.

[5] Xu Fuguan, "You zongjiao tongxiang renwen de shixue de chengli" 由宗教通向人文的史學的成立, in *Zhongguo shixue shilun wen xuan ji* 中國史學史論文選集, edited by Du Weiyun 杜推運 and Huang Jinxing 黃進興 (Taibei: Huashi chubanshe, 1976) , 7–9.

[6] Ibid., 8.

[7] Ibid., 14.

[8] *Zuozhuan*: Xiang 24.1/1087–88.

[9] Steven Shankman and Stephen Durrant, *The Siren and the Sage: Knowledge and Wisdom in Ancient Greece and China* (New York: Cassell, 2000), 84.

[10] Xu Fuguan, "You zongjiao tongxiang renwen de shixue de chengli," 25.

[11] Ibid., 32.

[12] Ibid., 31.

[13] Yang Bojun 楊伯峻, ed., *Mengzi* 孟子, 2 vols. (Beijing: Zhonghua shuju, 2000), 1:6.9/155 (hereafter *Mengzi*).

[14] David Schaberg, *A Patterned Past: Form and Thought in Early Chinese Historiography* (Cambridge: Harvard University Press, 2001), 267.

[15] *SJ*, 2:40/509.

[16] Because of the influence of *Lunyu* 論語 we perhaps erroneously regard Confucius as a philosopher rather than a historiographer. Confucius himself reportedly stated, "Those who know me will do so because of the *Spring and Autumn Annals!* Those who condemn me will do so because of the *Spring and Autumn Annals!*" 知我者其惟春秋乎 罪我者其惟春秋乎. See *Mengzi*, 1:6.9/155.

[17] Schaberg, *A Patterned Past*, 258.

[18] Schaberg believes that accounts of historians in *Zuozhuan* represent a self-reflective impulse by the author/historians to portray their own occupation according to an idealized notion of the historiographic tradition of Confucius (ibid., 256).

[19] *Zuozhuan* 3:Xiang 25.2/ 1099.

[20] Schaberg, *A Patterned Past*, 266.

[21] Ibid., 262.

[22] Ibid., 273.

[23] *Zuozhuan* 2:Wen 16.3 /662–63.

[24] Guo Dengfeng, *Lidai zixu zhuan wenchao* (Taibei: Taiwan shangwu, 1965), 1–12.

[25] *SJ*, 10:130/3299. See also Stephen Durrant, "Self as the Intersection of Traditions," *Journal of the American Oriental Society* 106.1 (1986): 33–40, quoted at 38.

[26] *SJ*, 10:130/3300.

[27] Durrant discusses this point in "Self as the Intersections of Traditions," 34. See also Stephen Durrant, *The Cloudy Mirror: Tension and Conflict in the Writings of Sima Qian* (Albany: State University of New York Press, 1995), 16; and Wendy Larson, *Literary Authority and the Modern Chinese Writer: Ambivalence and Autobiography* (Durham: Duke University, 1991), 13.

[28] *SJ*, 10:130/3300.

[29] James Olney, "Autobiography and the Cultural Moment," in *Autobiography: Essays Theoretical and Critical*, edited by James Olney, 3–27 (Princeton: Princeton University Press, 1977), 22.

[30] *SJ*, 10:130/3295.

[31] Larson, *Literary Authority*, 15.

[32] Mark Edward Lewis, *Writing and Authority in Early China* (New York: State University of New York Press, 1999), 155.

[33] *HS,* 9:62/2735.

[34] *LH,* 4:30/1206.

[35] Ibid., 4:30/1204.

[36] Ibid.

[37] Ibid.

[38] Ibid., 4:30/1205.

[39] Lin Lixue , *Baopuzi nei wai pian sixiang xi lun* (Taibei: Xuesheng, 1980), 8.

[40] *SGZ,* 1:2/89.

[41] Yuan Boye was an official who held various positions, including prefect of Yangzhou 揚州 (*SGZ,* 1:1/6–7, n. 6).

[42] The last half of this pronouncement regarding the breadth of Cao Pi's learning does not appear in *SGZ* but does appear in *Quan shanggu sandai qinhan sanguo liuchao wen* 全上古三代秦漢三國六朝文, 2:8.7–9 and is reprinted in Guo Dengfeng, *Lidai zi xuzhuan,* 156.

[43] Guo Dengfeng, *Lidai zi xuzhuan,* 157.

[44] Translation is from Stephen Owen, *Readings in Chinese Literary Thought* (Cambridge: Harvard-Yenching Institute, 1992), 69. According to Owen (57), the "Lun wen" was originally one chapter of the *Dian lun.*

[45] *BPZWP,* 2:30/65. For this section of *Baopuzi,* I use Jay Sailey's translation of the title in his *The Master Who Embraces Simplicity: A Study of the Philosopher Ko Hung* (San Francisco: Chinese Materials Center, 1978), 162.

[46] The phrase "soar like dragons" alludes to the *Zhouyi,* hexagram 1 (Qian 乾 卦), which states, "Nine at the fourth line, whether the dragon soars high or remains in the deep, he will be free from harm" (*Zhouyi,* 1/5).

[47] During the Zhou, the *meng fu* 盟府 was a place where records of oaths were kept. See *Zuozhuan* 1: Xi 僖 26.3/440.

[48] *BPZWP,* 2:50/719. The phrase refers to a song composed for Zhong Shanfu 仲山甫. See *Shi jing* 詩經, no. 260, "Zheng min" 烝民, in James Legge, *The She King or Book of Poetry* (Taibei: SMC Publishing, 2000), 545 (hereafter *Shi jing*).

[49] *BPZWP,* 2:50.682.

⁵⁰ Hu Fuchen, *Baopuzi neipian yanjiu* 抱朴子內篇研究 (Beijing: Xinhua chubanshe, 1991), 83–85.

⁵¹ Interestingly, Ge Hong's style of self-presentation is highly reminiscent of Ji Kang's famous letter "Breaking Off Relations with Shan Tao" 與山巨源絕交書, in which the author describes his privileged childhood and lofty virtues with ironic self-deprecation. Kawai Kouzō, *Chūgoku no jiden bunngaku* (Tokyo: Soubunsha, 1996), 49. For the text of Ji Kang's letter, see *Ji Kang ji jiao zhu* 嵇康集校注 (Beijing: Renmin wenxue chubanshe, 1962), 113–29.

⁵² *LY,* 2.4/12.

⁵³ Ibid.

⁵⁴ The phrase used here, literally "beautiful fragrance," is a metaphor for virtue taken from the *Chu ci* 楚辭, "Jiu zhang" 九章, "Xi wang ri" 惜往日. See Jin Kaicheng 金開誠, ed., *Qu Yuan ji jiao zhu* 屈原集校注, 2 vols. (Beijing: Zhonghua shuju, 1999), 2:600 (hereafter *Qu Yuan*).

⁵⁵ *BPZWP,* 2:50/715.

⁵⁶ *SJ,* 10:130/3299.

⁵⁷ Whether Ge Hong saw Confucius's statement as a real model for self-narrative is hard to say. Confucius's brief "autobiography" does not sanction any space for a moment of summary self-expression but is instead a narrative of moral development. As a protagonist in his own story, Ge Hong displays little if any of the "character development" suggested by Confucius but tends to be a very static character, like a stock type in a drama.

⁵⁸ Here Ge Hong alludes to *Qu Yuan*, "Xi song" 惜誦/446. The poem is a *sao* 騷 style complaint of a rejected courtier.

⁵⁹ *HS,* 9:59/2637, 9:68/2959. These were famous wealthy men from the Han period.

⁶⁰ Ibid., 10:72/3058.

⁶¹ The *qi lin* (a mythical animal often translated as "unicorn") typically signifies a sage or a peaceful world. Perhaps Ge Hong is suggesting that neither exists during his time or that he will not be remembered as a sage.

⁶² The term *liu xu* 六虛 originally referred to the positions of the six lines in the *Yi* (see *Zhouyi*, "Fan ci xia" 繫辭下, 269), but by Ge Hong's time it had come to connote six directions, the four cardinal directions plus up and down (or above and below).

[63] This is obviously an allusion to *Zhuangzi,* "Xiao yao" 逍遙.

[64] Bells and tripods are traditional mediums for recording the actions of one's ancestors.

[65] *BPZWP,* 2:50/721.

[66] Lin Lixue, *Baopuzi nei wai pian sixiang xi lun,* 9.

[67] Clearly, if Ge Hong managed to achieve immortality his virtue would not be in doubt, as the perfection of what we might call "Confucian" morality was fundamental to the pursuit of "Daoist" immortality. See Keith Knapp, "Ge Hong's Reconciliation of Taoism and Confucianism," in *The Proceedings of the First International Conference on Ge Hong and Chinese Culture,* 123–27 (Hangzhou: Institute on Chinese Thought and Culture, Zhejiang University, 2003), 125.

[68] Cao Pi wrote the text less than a century before *Baopuzi,* and Ge Hong briefly mentions it in his postface as influential for his own narrative (*BPZWP,* 2:50/702).

[69] Ibid., 2:50/698.

[70] The existing text appears to have older layers that may date to the Wei-Jin period that are probably genuine, attested to in a variety of contemporary sources. See Robert Ford Campany, *To Live as Long as Heaven and Earth: Ge Hong's Traditions of Divine Transcendents* (Berkeley: University of California Press, 2002), 108.

[71] *JS* 6:72/1913. Considering that Ban Gu and Sima Qian were the two towering figures of Han historiography, it stands to reason that Ge Hong was very familiar with both.

[72] The *Baopuzi neipian zixu* chapter's count of 116 chapters differs from almost every other source. Obviously, the *Neipian zixu* differs radically from the *Waipian* text, which states that by around 304 CE Ge Hong had completed 70 total chapters. The *Jin shu* biography itself is no help in this regard as it lists *Baopuzi* among Ge Hong's writings without providing any description of the text. The *Waipian zixu* lists a variety of other writings, and perhaps other texts are conflated into the total chapter count, though this seems unlikely as the description of the text in both *zixu* seems to clearly indicate *Baopuzi* independent of any other texts. Sun Xingyan 孫星衍 does not explicitly comment on the discrepancy, but he does note it without explanation in his edition of *Baopuzi* (Sun's edition, with his notes on his textual reconstruction of *Baopuzi,* is in the *Zhuzi jicheng* 諸子集成, 8 vols. (Beijing: Zhonghua shuju, 1996), 8:3. Sailey translates an extensive

note from Wu Shijian, a contemporary of Sun, who takes very seriously the suggestion that we may only have 30 to 40 percent of the original text in our possession. Wu Shijian relates the story of copyists who sold *Baopuzi* to government officials and received twelve bolts of silk for each chapter and subsequently increased the number of chapters to 166 to increase their profits (Wu Shijian in Sailey, *The Master Who Embraces Simplicity*, 529–30). The story demonstrates that the text faced severe corruption over time, with different bibliographies and dynastic histories gaining or losing 10 or 20 chapters.

[73] Zhang Xincheng 張心澂, *Wei shu tong kao, v. 1* 僞書通考 (Hong Kong: Youlian chubanshe, 1939), 655–56.

[74] *BPZWP,* 2:50/700.

[75] Lü Zongli 呂宗力, in William H. Nienhauser Jr. *The Indiana Companion to Traditional Chinese Literature,* (Bloomington: Indiana University Press, 1998), 2:39–40.

[76] Sailey, *The Master Who Embraces Simplicity*, 264.

[77] Ibid., 388–92.

[78] *BPZWP,* 2:33/121.

[79] I refer to this strand of Ge Hong's thought as "Legalist" simply because Legalism has supported a counterdiscourse on history, either questioning its value of or viewing historical writing with extreme cynicism and suspicion.

[80] *BPZWP,* 2:30/78.

[81] Sima Qian's construction of the Qin 秦 and Tacitus's account of the Germans are perhaps the two best examples of this kind of historical narrative.

[82] Zang Wenzhong 臧文仲 appears in *Lunyu* (15.14) as a minister who refuses to promote men of talent out of jealousy. Liezi appears in the *Zhuangzi* (28.6/753) as impoverished and unemployed because "the ruler does not care for scholars" 君无乃爲不 好士乎.

[83] This line appears in *Shang shu,* "Hongfan 洪范" (2.6/118) as the catastrophic result of ministers acquiring too much power. The larger issue here is the proper use of officials by the ruler.

[84] Here Ge Hong refers to Lüshi Chiunqui. See John Knoblock and Jeffrey Riegel, trans., *The Annals of Lu Buwei: Lüshi Chunqiu* (Stanford: Stanford University Press, 2000), 579–80.

[85] *BPXWP,* 2:33/135.

[86] For the status of southern literati under the Jin, see Sailey, *The Master Who Embraces Simplicity*, 278; and Charles Holcombe, *In the Shadow of the Han: Literati Thought and Society at the Beginning of the Six Dynasties* (Honolulu: University of Hawai'i Press, 1994), 28.

[87] *Lunyu,* 15.8.

[88] The translation is from Knoblock and Riegel, *The Annals of Lu Buwei*, 580.

[89] For a complete discussion of the complexities of Ge Hong's intellectual lineage, see Ren Jiyu 任繼愈, ed., *Zhongguo daojiao shi* 中國道教史 (Shanghai: Shanghai renmin chubanshe, 1997), 74–78.

[90] *BPZWP*, 2:34/156. Zuo Ci predicts the fall of the Han and the glory of the Wu, signified by the movement of specific celestial bodies.

[91] See *Laozi* 70, "Because of this the sage wears coarse clothing but holds a jade to his bosom" 是以聖人被褐懷玉. The Heshanggong commentary states, "One who wears coarse clothing disdains the external, one who clasps a jade takes as substantial the internal, concealing his value and hiding his virtue, not displaying them to others" 被褐者薄外, 懷玉者厚內, 匿寶藏德, 不以示人也.

[92] See *Laozi* 16, "Keep profound tranquility" 守靜篤. The Heshanggong commentary states, "Preserve pure tranquility, enact profound sincerity" 守清靜, 行篤厚.

[93] *Zhouyi* 周易, Xici xia 繫辭下 /262, "The gentleman conceals the [bow] on his person and acts at the proper time, [thus] all is advantageous" 君子藏器于身, 待時而動, 何不利之有.

[94] See the *Zhongyong* 中庸 (The Doctrine of the Mean) section of the *Liji* 禮記 (Book of Rites), 20.14, which states, "Not acting contrary to propriety, in this way cultivating the person" 非禮不動, 所以修身. See James Legge, *Confucius: Confucian Analects, The Great Learning, and The Doctrine of the Mean* (New York: Dover, 1971), 410. Also, in *Lunyu,,* 12.1, Confucius instructs Yan Yuan 顏淵 in propriety with the imperative, "Do not act contrary to propriety" 非禮勿動.

[95] Wang Wenjin 王文錦, ed., *Liji yi jie* 禮記議解 (Beijing: Zhonghua shu ju, 2001), "Ruxing" 儒行 41/887.

[96] See the *Zhouyi*, 1/5, "Wen Yan" 文言 exegesis for the bottom line, which reads, "The dragon [in this line], [is a metaphor for] the virtuous man who remains hidden. Not known in his generation, without a [lofty] name, living concealed but having no remorse, the people of his era do not see his real virtues, but he has no remorse."

[97] See *Zhongyong* 中庸, 11.3, in Legge, *Confucius*, 391.

[98] *Zhouyi*, "Xici shang" 繫辭上/233, "Wide ranging action without excess, delighting in heaven and knowing fate, for this reason [the gentleman] does not worry" 旁行而不流樂天知命故不憂.

[99] *BPZWP*, 2:34/16 4.

[100] Tang Yijie, *Wei Jin nanbeichao shiqi de daojiao* 魏晉南北朝時期的道教 (Taibei: Dongda tushu gongsi yinhang, 1991), 198–99.

[101] Both earlier and later times had been/will be better than the present age. The statement alludes to *Shi jing,* Mao 192/314–315 and Mao 264/563, in which the speaker is respectively full of suffering or a sorrowful heart and wonders why terrible events did not come before and would not come after him 不自我前不 自我後.

[102] *BPZWP*, 2:34/166. The vanquished opponent presents a cart with his own coffin, placing his life in the hands of the conqueror. See *Zuozhuan*, Duke Xi 僖, 6.3/314.

[103] The statement alludes to *Shi jing,* Mao 264/559, in which the speaker laments the ills visited on him by an unkind Heaven.

[104] From *Zuozhuan*, xi 1.1/277, it is "ritual" to conceal the ills of the state 諱 過惡,禮也.

[105] *BPZWP*, 2:34/170.

[106] See Burton Watson, *Records of the Grand Historian, Qin Dynasty* (New York: Columbia University Press, 1993), 74–83. This title could also be rendered as "Faulting Qin."

[107] *SJ*, 1:6/278.

[108] *HS*, 9:62/2737–38.

[109] The pair or complements *ben* 本 and *mo* 末 recall *Laozi,* 28, in which the author presents a logical sequence illustrating the relationship between the properties or characteristics of *dao* 道, *de* 德, *ren* 仁, *yi* 義, and *li* 禮: "Therefore after *dao* is lost there is *de*, after *de* is lost there is *ren*, after *ren* is lost there is *yi*, and after *yi* is lost there is *li*" 故失道而後得, 失得而後仁, 失仁而後義, 失義而後禮. The *Heshanggong* commentary to the *Daode jing* tracks the literal meaning fairly closely, stating, "This refers to when *dao* is in decline, and *de* subsequently arises" 言道衰而德化生也. The *Laozi* then continues, "Now that which is *li*, it is the thin [veneer] of loyalty and trust" 夫禮者, 忠信之薄. The *Heshanggong* glosses this line as "This refers to when *li* discards the root and governs the branch, and loyalty and trust day

by day thus decline and grow thin" 言裡廢本治末忠信日以衰薄. Implicit (or explicit) in this declining sequence is that *dao* is equivalent to the "basic" or "root" 本 while *li* is a mark of decline and inevitable decay. Because *li* came to be associated with Confucianism, it seems reasonable to speculate that Ge Hong may have read the *Laozi* passage as an anti-Confucian polemic.

[110] Tang Yijie believes this discourse of root and branch illustrates the influence of Wei-Jin "abstruse learning," or *xuan xue* 玄學, in *Baopuzi*, although Ge Hong himself seemed to reject *xuan xue*. See Tang Yijie, *Guoxiang yu Wei-Jin xuanxue* 郭象與魏晉玄學 (Beijing: Beijing University Press, 2000), 25, 104.

[111] *SJ,* 10:130/3289.

[112] This follows Wang Ming's 王明 commentary and translation of *xian* 先 as *fu* 夫. See Wang Ming 王明, ed., *Baopuzi neipian jiaoshi* 抱朴子內篇校釋 (Beijing: Zhonghua shuju, 1996), 10/189–90.

[113] *BPZNP,* 10/371.

[114] *BPZWP,* 2:50/698.

[115] Ibid., 2:50/655.

[116] *BPZNP,* 10/374.

[117] *HS,* 9:62/2737–38.

[118] J. Michael Farmer, "The World of the Mind in Early Medieval China: The Life and Works of Qiao Zhou," PhD diss., University of Wisconsin–Madison, 2001, 240–48.

[119] Ibid., 222.

[120] Ibid., 255.

[121] The translation is from Ibid., 255. See also *FY,* 12.9/507.

[122] Translation from Stephen Durrant, "Liu Chih-chi on Ssu-ma Ch'ien," *Diyijie guoji Tangdai xueshu huiyi lunwenji* 第一屆國際唐代學術會議論文集 (Taipei: Xuesheng shuju, 1989), 40.

[123] Ibid.,40–41.

[124] Ibid., 45.

[125] Ibid., 48.

[126] *BPZNP,* 10/374.

[127] Ibid., 10/375; *HS,* 9:62/2738.

[128] *BPZNP,* 10/375.

[129] Tang Yijie, *Wei Jin nanbeichao shiqi de daojiao* (Taibei: Dongda tushu gongsi yinhang, 1991).78–79.

[130] Tang Yijie, *Guoxiang yu Wei-Jin xuanxue*, 100–103.

[131] For an excellent and concise study of the religion expressed in Ge Hong's writing, see ibid.,103.

[132] *Zhouyi*, "Shuo Gua" 說卦/280.

[133] *Zhouyi*, "Xici shang"/244.

[134] *Shang shu*, "Zhou guan" 周管2/422.

[135] *BPZNP*, 10/376.

[136] *Zhouyi*, "Xici shang,"/232.

[137] These are two legendary immortals that seem to have no basis in historical or semihistorical figures.

[138] See Ban Biao's 班彪 essay "Discussion of the Mandate of Kings" 王命論 in *HS*, 100/4212.

[139] See *Zhuangzi*, 28.8/757.

[140] See Sima Xiangru's 四馬相如 "Shanglin fu" 上林賦, in Fei Zhengang 費振剛 et al., *Quan Han fu* 全漢賦 (Beijing: Beijing University Press, 1993), 62.

[141] This is probably a reference to *Shang shu*, "Jun chen" 君陳/431 or "Jiu gao" 酒告/159. Both chapters associate harvesting grain with a well-structured, ordered state.

[142] *BPZNP*, 10/376.

[143] This character, read "chou," a small kind of small fish, is constructed from the radicals above. It is not found in the Chinese input system.

[144] In the original text, the character "xia1" is written using the 魚 instead of the 虫 radical.

[145] Ping Yi 憑逸, ed., *Huainan honglie jijie* 淮南鴻烈集解, 2 vols. (Beijing: Zhonghua shuju, 1997), 1:2/45 (hereafter *HNZ*). The Dao forges the ten thousand things, discerns the fine details, and gives birth to the root.

[146] Here Ge Hong alludes to *Shang shu*, "Hong fan," 1.1/109. The chapter outlines the principles of political management.

[147] In Zuo Si's 左思 "Yong shi shi" 詠史詩, thorns are a metaphor for

obstacles on the path to success. The narrator's description of his ramshackle dwelling at the end of a lonely lane is very similar to Ge Hong's. See Lu Qinli 逯欽立, *Xian Qin Han Wei-Jin Nan Bei chao shi* 先秦漢魏晉南北朝詩, 3 vols. (Beijing: Zhonghua shuju, 1999), 1:734.

[148] *BPZNP*, 10/378.

[149] *Qu Yuan*, 1:31.

[150] Translation based on Burton Watson, *Ssu-Ma Ch'ien: Grand Historian of China* (New York: Columbia University Press, 1958), 65; and *HS* 9:67/2735.

[151] *BPZNP*, 2/66.

[152] *BPZNP*, 3/91. "One corner" is an obvious reference to *Lunyu*, 7.8.

Conclusion

[1] Stephen Durrant, "Self as the Intersection of Traditions," *Journal of the American Oriental Society* 106.1 (1986): 33–40, 39.

[2] William H. Nienhauser Jr., "Early Biography," in *The Columbia History of Chinese Literature*, edited by Victor H. Mair, 511–26 (New York: Columbia University Press, 2001), 520.

[3] Ying-shih Yü, "Life and Immortality in Han China," *Harvard Journal of Asiatic Studies* 25 (1964–65): 80–112.

[4] Steven Shankman and Stephen Durrant, *The Siren and the Sage: Knowledge and Wisdom in Ancient Greece and China* (New York: Cassell, 2000), 128–30.

[5] *BPZNP*, 34–35.

[6] Echoing Wang Chong before him, Ge Hong wrote, "Honor, position, influence, and wealth are like guests, since they are not eternal things, and once they go they cannot be retained. . . .[A]cquiring them is not a pleasure, and what sadness is there in their departure?" *BPZWP*, 2:50.690. See also Jay Sailey, *The Master Who Embraces Simplicity: A Study of the Philosopher Ko Hung* (San Francisco: Chinese Materials Center, 1978), 261. Here Ge Hong refers to *Zhuangzi* ,16.3/409.

[7] *BPZWP*, 2:50.694; Sailey, *The Master Who Embraces Simplicity*, 262.

[8] *BPZWP*, 2:50.694; Sailey, *The Master Who Embraces Simplicity*, 263.

[9] Wang Ming 王明, ed., *Baopuzi neipian jiaoshi* 抱朴子內篇校釋 (Beijing: Zhonghua shuju, 1996), 368.

[10] *BPZNP,* 32.

[11] Ibid., 6.

[12] Ibid., 5.

[13] *JS,* 6:72/1913.

Appendix A

[1] Dong Zhuo's official biography is in *HHS,* 8:72/2319.

[2] This is a reference to Liu Bian 劉辯, posthumously known as the prince of Hongnong 弘農懷王 (176–90), and his mother, Empress Dowager He 何皇后 (d. 189).

[3] Here "Shandong" refers to the eastern part of the empire.

[4] This is a reference to *Zuozhuan,* Yin 隱 4.6/38.

[5] The Yellow Turbans, peasants who organized an uprising in 184, were known for tying yellow scarves around their heads in battle.

[6] *Quan shanggu sandai qinhan sanguo liuchao wen* 全上古三代秦漢三國六朝文, 2:8.7b, reads 海岱 as "seas and mountains."

[7] Cao Cao never became emperor, but he was posthumously referred to as Emperor Wu of Wei 魏武帝.

[8] *HHS,* 8:70/2285. See also *SGZ,* 1:8/262.

[9] Zixiu was also known as Cao Ang 曹昂 (*SGZ,* 2:20/579).

[10] An Min was the son of Cao Cao's younger brother (ibid., 1:1/14).

[11] A *li* 里 is about one-third of a mile.

[12] An area in northern China, roughly coterminous with modern Shanxi 山西 and Hebei 河北.

[13] The name refers to a large tribal nation in what is now the Korean Peninsula.

[14] The name refers to people from the area around what is now Beijing 北京.

[15] An area about one hundred miles northwest of modern Beijing, which during the Wei-Jin era was home to various foreign tribes such as the Xiongnu 匈奴.

[16] The name of a spirit of late spring (early June) possessing various fantastic features such as a bird's body, grassy horns, a human face, and so forth.

[17] Cao Zhen 曹真 (*SGZ*, 1:9/280).

[18] Of aristocratic upbringing, Xun Yu opposed Cao Cao's bid for power and ultimately committed suicide by drinking poison (ibid., 2:10/30/; *HHS*, 6:49/1646).

[19] 執事未睹夫項發口從,俯馬蹄而仰月支也.

[20] Shooting birds by anticipating the path of flight.

[21] No certain dates, a military official of the Later Han period. This text marks the earliest reference to him.

[22] No certain dates. This text marks the earliest reference to him.

[23] No certain dates. This text marks the earliest reference to him.

[24] A position of the third grade 三品.

[25] No certain dates, a general and official under Cao Cao (*HHS*, 8:69/2243; *SGZ*, 2:12/387).

[26] A position of the fourth grade 四品.

[27] No certain dates. This text marks the earliest reference to him.

[28] The sense of this sentence is that Cao Pi used the momentum of Zhan's advance to allow his opponent to strike his own forehead on the sugarcane.

[29] A physician of the early Han 漢 dynasty and the teacher of Chunyu Yi. Cao Pi is probably referring to *Shi ji* 史記 105. See *SJ*, 9:105/2794.

[30] A physician of the early Han dynasty and student of Yang Qing. During the time of Han Wendi 文帝 (r. 180–157 BCE) he served as director of the imperial granaries 太倉令 of Qi 齊. Slandered and imprisoned, he is famous for having been saved from corporal punishment by his daughter's appeal to the emperor (*SJ*, 9:105/2809)

[31] Possibly the younger brother of Yuan Hui 袁徽 (*SGZ*, 2:11/336).

[32] This *fu* no longer exists.

[33] No certain dates. This text marks the earliest reference.

[34] *HS*, 9:59.2647.

[35] An official who held various positions, including that of prefect of Yangzhou 揚州 (see *SGZ*, 1:1/6–7, n. 6).

Appendix B

[1] This essay is chapter 9 of Liu Zhiji's *Shitong* 史通.

[2] Liu Zhiji seems to suggest that Sima Qian's record of his ancestry, which begins in deep antiquity, seems appropriate given the scope of *Shi ji* (*SJ*, 10:130/3285).

[3] Ibid., 1:1/32.

[4] Ibid., 1:1/20.

[5] *LY*, 13.18.

[6] *ZGC*, Wei 魏, 3/11.

[7] James Legge, *The Shoo King or Book of Historical Documents* (Hong Kong: Hong Kong University Press, 1960), 605–6.

[8] *LY*, 1.1.

[9] Ibid., 5.27.

[10] Ibid., 1.4.

[11] Ibid., 9.5.

[12] Ibid., 8.5.

[13] Ibid., 11.26.

[14] *SGZ*, 1:1/44.

[15] Dates unknown. Tao Mei was a contemporary of Ge Hong. He also served on Wang Dao's staff.

[16] *JS*, 6:72/1910.

[17] *LY*, 6.6.

[18] *SJ*, 10:130/3286. According to Pu Qilong's 浦起龍 (1679–?) Qing dynasty commentary to *Shitong* (9/262), Liu Zhiji here refers to Sima Biao's *Jiuzhou Chunqiu* 九州春秋, which is no longer extant.

[19] Liu Zhiji is pointing out that Chun Wei was supposedly the ancestor of the Xiong Nu and so logically should not also be considered a progenitor of the To Ba. See *SJ*, 9:110/2879.

[20] Pu Qilong appears to have been bemused by Liu's assertion, for both Shen Yue's authorial postface to the *Song shu* 宋書自序 and the biography of Zhou Jiong in the *Nan shi* 南史 give the same account of the Shen family ancestry (*Shitong*, 9/262).

[21] See Yang Xiong's biography/autobiography in *HS*, 11:87A/3513.

[22] Ban Gu states that his ancestors shared the same surname as the founders of the state of Chu, whose progenitor was Xiong Yi according to Pu Qilong. See *HS*, 12:100/4197; and *Shitong*, 9/263.

[23] *LY*, 2.24.

Bibliography

Augustine, *Confessions*. Translated by R. S. Pine-Coffin. New York: Penguin, 1961.

Ban Gu 班固. *Han Shu* 漢書. Beijing: Zhonghua shuju chubanshe, 1997.

Bauer, Wolfgang. "The Hidden Hero: Creation and Disintegration of the Ideal of Eremitism." In *Individualism and Holism: Studies in Confucian and Taoist Values*, edited by Donald Munro, 157–91. Ann Arbor: Center for Chinese Studies, University of Michigan, 1985.

Beasley, W. G., and, E. G. Pulleyblank, eds. *Historians of China and Japan*. London: Oxford University Press, 1961.

Berkowitz, Alan. *Patterns of Disengagement: The Practice and Portrayal of Reclusion in Early Medieval China*. Stanford: Stanford University Press, 2000.

———. "Reclusion and 'The Chinese Eremitic Tradition.'" *Journal of the American Oriental Society* 113.4 (1993): 575–84.

Birch, Cyril. *Anthology of Chinese Literature*. 2 vols. New York: Grove, 1965

Brown, Peter. *Augustine of Hippo: A Biography*. Berkeley: University of California Press, 2000.

Cai, Zong-qi, ed. *Chinese Aesthetics: The Ordering of Literature, the Arts, and the Universe in the Six Dynasties*. Honolulu: University of Hawai'i Press, 2004.

Campany, Robert Ford. *To Live as Long as Heaven and Earth: Ge Hong's Traditions of Divine Transcendents*. Berkeley: University of California Press, 2002.

Cavell, Stanley. *In Quest of the Ordinary: Lines of Skepticism and Romanticism*. Chicago: University of Chicago Press, 1988.

Chen Feilong 陳飛龍, ed. *Baopuzi Neipian jin zhu jin yi* 抱朴子內篇今註今譯. Taibei: Taiwan Commercial Press Publishing House, 2001.

Chen Guying 陳鼓應, ed. *Zhuangzi jinzhu jinyi* 莊子今注今譯. Beijing: Zhonghua shuju, 1994.

Chen Shou 陳壽. *Sanguo zhi* 三國志. 5 vols. Beijing: Zhonghua shuju, 1982.

Clark, Anthony. "Historian of the Orchid Terrace: Partisan Polemics in Ban Gu's Han shu." PhD diss., University of Oregon, 2005.

Couvreur, Séraphin, S. J. *Li Ki ou Mémoires sur les Beinséances et les Cérémonies.* 2 vols. Ho Kien Fou. Imprimerie de la Mission Catholique, 1913.

Davis, A. R. *Tao Yuan-ming, A.D. 365–427: His Works and Their Meaning.* 2 vols. New York: Cambridge University Press, 1983.

Davis, T. L., and Wu Lu-Ch'iang. "Ko Hung on the Gold Medicine and on the Yellow and the White." *Proceedings of the American Academy of Arts and Sciences* 70 (1935–36): 221–64.

Dewey, John. *Human Nature and Conduct.* New York: Random House, 1922.

Durrant, Stephen. *The Cloudy Mirror: Tension and Conflict in the Writings of Sima Qian.* Albany: State University of New York Press, 1995.

———. "Liu Chih-chi on Ssu-ma Ch'ien." *Diyijie guoji Tangdai xueshu huiyi lunwenji* 第一屆國際唐代學術會議論文集. Taipei: Xuesheng shuju, 1989.

———. "Self as the Intersection of Traditions: The Autobiographical Writings of Ssu-ma Ch'ien." *Journal of the American Oriental Society* 106.1 (1986): 33–40.

Durrant, Stephen, with Steven Shankman. *The Siren and the Sage: Knowledge and Wisdom in Ancient Greece and China.* New York: Cassell, 2000.

Emerson, Ralph Waldo. *Selected Essays of Ralph Waldo Emerson.* New York: Penguin, 1984.

Fan Ye 范曄. *Hou Han shu* 後漢書. 12 vols. Beijing: Zhonghua shuju, 1997.

Fang Xuanling 房玄齡 et al. *Jin shu* 晉書. 10 vols. Beijing: Zhonghua shuju, 1998.

Farmer, J. Michael. "The World of the Mind in Early Medieval China: The Life and Works of Qiao Zhou." PhD diss., University of Wisconsin–Madison, 2001.

———. "Zhang Hua." In *Dictionary of Literary Biography: Classical Chinese Writers, Pre-Tang Era (–598),* edited by Curtis Dean Smith. Columbia, SC: Bruccoli Clark Layman, 2010.

Fei Zhengang 費振剛. *Quan Han fu* 全漢賦. Beijing: Beijing University Press, 1993.

Feifel, Eugene. "Pao-P'u Tzu Nei-P'ien, Chapter I–III." *Monumenta Serica* 6 (1941): 113–211.

Fishlen, Michael. "Wine, Poetry, and History: Du Mu's 'Pouring Alone in the Prefectural Residence.'" *T'oung Pao* 80, 4–5 (1994) 260–97.

Forke, Alfred. *Lun-Heng: Philosophical Essays of Wang Chung.* 2 vols. New York: Paragon, 1962.

Gao You 高誘, ed. *Zhangguo ce Gao You jiao zhu* 戰國策高誘校註. Taibei: Taiwan shang wu yin shu guan, 1956.

Goodwin, James. *Autobiography: The Self Made Text.* New York: Twayne, 1993.

Guo Dengfeng 郭登峰. *Lidai zixu zhuan wenchao* 歷代自敘傳文鈔. Taibei: Taiwan shang wu yin shu guan, 1965.

Guo Shaoyu 郭紹虞. *Zhongguo wenxue piping shi* 中國文學批評史. Beijing: Zhonghua shuju chubanshe, 1961.

Gusdorf, George. "Conditions and Limits of Autobiography." In *Autobiography: Essays Theoretical and Critical*, edited by James Olney, 28–48. Princeton: Princeton University Press, 1980.

Habermas, Jürgen. "Individuation through Socialization: On George Herbert Mead's Theory of Subjectivity." In *Postmetaphysical Thinking: Philosophical Essays*, translated by William Mark Hohengarten. Cambridge: MIT Press, 1992.

Holcombe, Charles. *In the Shadow of the Han: Literati Thought and Society at the Beginning of the Six Dynasties.* Honolulu: University of Hawai'i Press, 1994.

Holzman, Donald. *Chinese Literature in Transition from Antiquity to the Middle Ages.* Brookfield: Ashgate, 1998.

———. *Poetry and Politics: The Life and Works of Juan Chi, A.D. 210–263.* New York: Cambridge University Press, 1976.

Hong Xingzu 洪興祖, ed. *Chuci bu zhu* 楚辭補注. Beijing: Zhonghua shuju, 2002.

Howarth, William L. "Some Principles of Autobiography." In *Autobiography: Essays Theoretical and Critical*, edited by James Olney, 84–114. Princeton: Princeton University Press, 1980.

Hu Fuchen 胡孚琛. *Baopuzi neipian yanjiu* 抱朴子內篇研究. Beijing: Xinhua chubanshe, 1991.

Jin Kaicheng 金開誠 and Gao Dongjin 高董金, eds. *Chu Yuan ji jiaozhu* 屈原集校注. 2 vols. Beijing: Zhonghua shuju, 1999.

Kawai Kouzō. *Chūgoku no jiden bunngaku.* Tokyo: Soubunsha, 1996.

Kermode, Frank. "Memory and Autobiography." *Raritan* 15.1 (1995): 36–50.

Kirschner, Suzanne R. *The Religious and Romantic Origins of Psychoanalysis: Individuation and Integration in Post-Freudian Theory.* Cambridge: Cambridge. University Press, 1996.

Knapp, Keith. "Ge Hong's Reconciliation of Taoism and Confucianism." In *The Proceedings of the First International Conference on Ge Hong and Chinese Culture,* 123–27. Hangzhou: Institute on Chinese Thought and Culture, Zhejiang University, 2003.

Knechtges, David. *The Han Shu Biography of Yang Xiong (53 B.C.–A.D. 18).* Tempe: Center for Asian Studies, Arizona State University, 1982.

———. "Sweet-Peel Orange or Southern Gold? Regional Identity in Western Jin Literature." In *Studies in Early Medieval Chinese Literature and Cultural History*, edited by Paul Kroll and David Knechtges, 27–80. Boulder: T'ang Studies Society, 2003.

Knoblock, John, and Jeffrey Riegel, trans. *The Annals of Lu Buwei: Lushi Chunqiu* 呂氏春秋. Stanford: Stanford University Press, 2000.

Kroll, Paul, and David Knechtges, eds. *Studies in Early Medieval Chinese Literature and Cultural History.* Boulder: T'ang Studies Society, 2003.

Larson, Wendy. *Literary Authority and the Modern Chinese Writer: Ambivalence and Autobiography.* Durham: Duke University, 1991.

Lau, D. C. *Confucius: The Analects.* New York: Penguin Group, 1979.

Least Heat Moon, William. *Blue Highways: A Journey into America.* New York: Little, Brown, 1999.

Legge, James. *Confucius: Confucian Analects, The Great Learning, and The Doctrine of the Mean.* New York: Dover, 1971.

———. *The She King.* Taipei: SMC Publishing, 2000.

———. *The Shoo King or Book of Historical Documents.* Hong Kong: Hong Kong University Press, 1960.

———. *The Works of Mencius.* New York: Dover, 1970.

Lejeune, Philippe. *On Autobiography.* Minneapolis: University of Minnesota Press, 1989.

Lewis, Mark Edward. *Writing and Authority in Early China*. New York: State University of New York Press, 1999.

Li Wai-yee. "*Shishuo xinyu* and the Emergence of Aesthetic Self-Consciousness in the Chinese Tradition." In *Chinese Aesthetics: The Ordering of Literature, the Arts, and the Universe in the Six Dynasties,* edited by Cai Zong-qi, 237–76. Honolulu: University of Hawai'i Press, 2004.

Lin Lixue 林麗雪. *Baopuzi nei wai pian sixiang xi lun* 抱朴子內外篇思想析論. Taibei: Xuesheng, 1980.

Lin Shen-fu, and Stephen Owen, eds. *The Vitality of the Lyric Voice: Shih Poetry from the Late Han to the T'ang*. Princeton: Princeton University Press, 1 Dajie 劉大杰. *Wei-Jin sixiang lun* 魏晉思想論. Shanghai: Shanghai guji chubanshe, 2000.

Liu, Lydia H. *Translingual Practice: Literature, National Culture, and Translated Modernity—China, 1900–1937*. Stanford: Stanford University Press, 1995.

Liu Shao 劉劭. *Ren wu zhi* 人物志. Edited by Ma Junqi 馬駿騏. Guiyang: Guizhou renmin chubanshe, 1998.

Liu Yiqing 劉義慶. *Shishuo xinyu jiaojian* 世說新語校箋. Beijing: Zhonghua shuju chubanshe, 1999.

Liu Zhiji 劉知幾. *Shitong* 史通. Taibei: Wenhai chubanshe, 1953.

Lu Qinli 逯欽立. *Xian Qin Han Wei-Jin Nan Bei chao shi* 先秦漢魏晉南北朝詩. Beijing: Zhonghua shuju, 1999.

Lü Zongli 呂宗力. "Fan Ye" in *The Indiana Companion to Traditional Chinese Literature,* vol. 2, 38–42, edited by William H. Nienhauser Jr. Bloomington: Indiana University Press, 1998.

Luo Zhiye 羅志野, ed. *Shang Shu* 尚書. Changsha: Hunan chubanshe, 1997.

Luo Zongqiang 羅宗強. *Wei-Jin Nan Bei chao wenxue sixiang shi* 魏晉南北朝文學思想史. Beijing: Zhonghua shuju, 1996.

Mair, Victor H., ed. *The Columbia History of Chinese Literature*. New York: Columbia University Press, 2001.

Martin, Raymond, and John Barresi. *The Rise and Fall of the Soul and Self: An Intellectual History of Personal Identity*. New York: Columbia University Press, 2006.

Mather, Richard, trans. *A New Account of Tales of the World*. Ann Arbor: Center for Chinese Studies, University of Michigan, 2002.

Mather, Richard. "Individualist Expressions of the Outsiders during the Six Dynasties." In *Individualism and Holism: Studies in Confucian and Taoist Values*, edited by Donald Munro, 199–214. Ann Arbor: Center for Chinese Studies, University of Michigan, 1985.

Miao, Ronald. *Early Medieval Poetry: The Life and Verse of Wang Ts'an (A.D. 177–217)*. Wiesbaden: Franz Steiner, 1982.

Misch, Georg. *A History of Autobiography in Antiquity.* 2 vols. Cambridge: Harvard University Press, 1951.

Mou Zhongjian 牟鐘鑒. *Zoujin Zhongguo jingshen* 走進中國精神. Beijing: Huawen chubanshe, 1999.

Munro, Donald. *The Concept of Man in Early China.* Ann Arbor: Center for Chinese Studies, University of Michigan, 1969.

Munro, Donald, ed. *Individualism and Holism: Studies in Confucian and Taoist Values.* Ann Arbor: Center for Chinese Studies, University of Michigan, 1985.

Nienhauser, William H., Jr. "Early Biography." In *The Columbia History of Chinese Literature,* edited by Victor H. Mair, 511–26. New York: Columbia University Press, 2001.

———."An Interpretation of the Literary and Historical Aspects of the *Hsi-ching Tsa-chi* (Miscellanies of the Western Capital)." PhD diss., Indiana University, 1972.

Ng, Janet. *The Experience of Modernity: Chinese Autobiography of the Early Twentieth Century.* Ann Arbor: University of Michigan Press, 2003.

Olney, James. "Autobiography and the Cultural Moment." In *Autobiography: Essays Theoretical and Critical*, edited by James Olney, 3–27. Princeton: Princeton University Press, 1980.

———. *Metaphors of Self: The Meaning of Autobiography.* Princeton: Princeton University Press, 1972.

———. "Some Versions of Memory/Some Versions of Bios: The Ontology of Autobiography." In *Autobiography: Essays Theoretical and Critical,* edited by James Olney, 236–67. Princeton: Princeton University Press, 1980.

Owen, Stephen. *Readings in Chinese Literary Thought.* Cambridge: Harvard University Press, 1992.

———. "The Self's Perfect Mirror: Poetry as Autobiography." In *The Vitality of the Lyric Voice: Shih Poetry from the Late Han to the T'ang*, edited by Shen-fu Lin and Stephen Owen, 71–102. Princeton: Princeton University Press, 1986.

Pascal, Roy. *Truth and Design in Autobiography*. Cambridge: Harvard University Press, 1960.

Ping Yi 憑逸, ed. *Huainan honglie jijie* 淮南鴻烈集解. 2 vols. Beijing: Zhonghua shuju, 1997.

Poo, Mu-chou. "A Taste of Happiness: Contextualizing Elixirs in *Baopuzi*." In *Of Tripod and Palate: Food, Politics, and Religion in Traditional China*, edited by Roel Sterckx. New York: Palgrave Macmillan, 2005.

Powers, Martin. *Art and Political Expression in Early China*. New Haven: Yale University Press, 1991.

———. *Pattern and Person: Ornament, Society, and Self in Classical China*. Cambridge: Harvard University Asia Center, 2006.

Pregadio, Frabrizio. *Great Clarity: Daoism and Alchemy in Early Medieval China*. Stanford: Stanford University Press, 2006.

Pu Youjun. *Zhongguo wenxue piping shi lun* 中國文學批評史論. Chengdu: Ba-Shu shu she, 2001.

Qian Nanxiu. *Spirit and Self in Medieval China: The Shih-shuo hsin-yü and Its Legacy*. Honolulu: University of Hawai'i Press, 2001.

Ren Jiyu 任繼愈, ed. *Zhongguo daojiao shi* 中國道教史. Shanghai: Shanghai renmin chubanshe, 1997.

Rogers, Michael. "The Myth of the Battle of the Fei River." *T'oung Pao* 54 (1968): 50–72.

Sailey, Jay. *The Master Who Embraces Simplicity: A Study of the Philosopher Ko Hung, A.D. 283–343*. San Francisco: Chinese Materials Center, 1978.

Sayre, Robert F. "Autobiography and the Making of America." In *Autobiography: Essays Theoretical and Critical*, edited by James Olney, 146–68. Princeton University Press, 1980.

Schaberg, David. *A Patterned Past: Form and Thought in Early Chinese Historiography*. Cambridge: Harvard University Press, 2001.

Shryock, J. K. *The Study of Human Abilities: The Jen wu chih of Liu Shao*. New Haven: American Oriental Society, 1937.

Sima Qian. *Shi ji* 史記. 10 vols. Beijing: Zhonghua shuju, 1999.

Slingerland, Edward. *Confucius: Analects*. Indianapolis: Hackett, 2003.

Spiro, Audrey. *Contemplating the Ancients: Aesthetic and Social Issues in Early Chinese Portraiture*. Berkeley: University of California Press, 1990.

Tang Changru 唐長孺. *Wei-Jin Nan Bei chao shi lun cong* 魏晉南北朝史論叢. Shi Jia Zhuang: Hebei jiaoyu chubanshe, 2000.

Tang Yijie 湯一介. *Guoxiang yu Wei-Jin xuanxue* 郭象與魏晉玄學. Beijing: Beijing University Press, 2000.

———. *Wei Jin Nan Bei Chao shiqi de daojiao* 魏晉南北朝時期的道教. Taibei: Dongda tushu gongsi yinhang, 1991.

Tang Yongtong 湯用彤. *Wei-Jin xuan xue lungao* 魏晉玄學論稿. Shanghai: Shanghai guji chubanshe, 2001.

Taylor, Charles. *Sources of the Self: The Making of the Modern Identity*. Cambridge: Harvard University Press, 1989.

Twitchett, Dennis. "Chinese Biographical Writing." In *Historians of China and Japan*, edited by W. G. Beasley and, E. G. Pulleyblank, 95–114. London: Oxford University Press, 1961.

———. *The Writing of Official History under the Tang*. New York: Cambridge University Press, 1992.

Vervoom, Aat. *Men of Cliffs and Caves: The Development of the Chinese Eremitic Tradition to the End of the Han Dynasty*. Hong Kong: Chinese University Press, 1990.

Wang Chong. *Lunheng jiaoshi* 論衡校釋. 4 vols. Beijing: Zhonghua shuju, 1996.

Wang Ka 王卡, ed. *Laozi Daodejing Heshanggong zhangju* 老子道德經河上公章句. Beijing: Zhonghua shuju, 1997.

Wang Liqi 王利器. *Ge Hong lun* 葛洪論. Taibei: Wunan tushu chubanshe, 1997.

Wang Ming 王明, ed. *Baopuzi neipian jiaoshi* 抱朴子內篇校釋. Beijing: Zhonghua shuju, 1996.

Wang Rongbao 汪榮寶, ed. *Fayan yishu* 法言義疏. Beijing: Zhonghua shu ju, 1987.

Wang Wenjin 王文錦, ed. *Liji yi jie* 禮記議解. Beijing: Zhonghua shu ju, 2001.

Wang Yao 王瑤. "Zhongguo wenxue piping yu zongji" 中國文學批評與總集. In *Guanyu Zhongguo gu dian wen xue wen ti* 關於中國古典文學問題. Shanghai: Shanghai gudian wenxue chubanshe, 1956.

Wang Yunxi 王運熙. *Wei-Jin nan bei chao wenxue piping shi* 魏晉南北朝文學批評史. Shanghai: Shanghai guji chubanshe, 1989.

Wang Zhongluo 王仲犖. *Wei-Jin Nan Bei chao shi* 魏晉南北朝史. Shanghai: Shanghai renmin chubanshe, 2003.

Ware, James. *Alchemy, Medicine, and Religion in the China of A.D. 320: The Nei P'ien of Ko Hung.* Boston: MIT Press, 1966.

Watson, Burton. *The Complete Works of Chuang Tzu.* New York: Columbia University Press, 1968.

———. *Records of the Grand Historian, Qin Dynasty.* New York: Columbia University Press, 1993.

———. *Ssu-Ma Ch'ien: Grand Historian of China.* New York: Columbia University Press, 1958.

Wu Fusheng. *The Poetics of Decadence: Chinese Poetry of the Southern Dynasties and Late Tang Periods.* Albany: State University of New York Press, 1998.

Wu Pei-yi. *The Confucian's Progress: Autobiographical Writings in Traditional China.* Princeton: Princeton University Press, 1990.

Xu Fuguan 徐復觀. "You zongjiao tongxiang renwen de shixue de chengli" 由宗教通向人文的史學的成立. In *Zhongguo shixue shilun wen xuan ji* 中國史學史論文選集, edited by Du Weiyun 杜推運 and Huang Jinxing 黃進興. Taibei: Huashi chubanshe, 1976.

Xu Gongchi 徐公持. *Wei-Jin wenxue shi* 魏晉文學史. Beijing: Renmin wenxue chubanshe, 1999.

Xu Kangsheng 許抗生. *Wei-Jin sixiang shi* 魏晉思想史. Taibei: Guiguan tushu gufen youxian gongsi, 1992.

Yang Bojun 楊伯峻, ed. *Chunqiu zuozhuan zhu* 春秋左傳注. 4 vols. Beijing: Zhonghua shuju, 2000.

———. *Lunyu yizhu* 論語譯注. Beijing: Zhonghua shuju, 2002.

———. *Mengzi* 孟子. 2 vols. Beijing: Zhonghua shuju, 2000.

Yang Mingzhao 楊明照, ed. *Baopuzi waipianjiaojian* 抱朴子外篇校箋. 2 vols. Beijing: Zhonghua shuju, 1997.

Yü Ying-shih. "Individualism and the Neo-Taoist Movement in Wei-Chin China." In *Individualism and Holism: Studies in Confucian and Taoist Values*, edited by Donald Munro, 121–56. Ann Arbor: Center for Chinese Studies, University of Michigan, 1985.

————. "Life and Immortality in Han China." *Harvard Journal of Asiatic Studies* 25 (1964–65): 80–112.

Zhang Minggao 張明高, ed. *Wei-Jin Nan Bei Chao wen lun xuan* 魏晉南北朝文論選. Beijing: Renmin wenxue, 1999.

Zhang Xincheng 張心澂. *Wei shu tong kao shang* 偽書通考上. Hong Kong: Youlian chubanshe, 1939.

Zhao Guoxi 趙國熙. "Sima Qian xie 'Shi ji Taishigong zixu' wei ziji shubei lizhuan" 司馬遷寫 "史記太史公自序" 爲自己樹碑立傳. *Jilin shifan xueyuan xuebao* 9 (1996): 6–9.

Zhou Yiliang 周一良. *Wei-Jin Nan Bei chao shi lun ji* 魏晉南北朝史論. Beijing: Beijing daxue chubanshe, 1997.

Zhou Zhenfu 周振甫, ed. *Zhouyi shizhu* 周易譯注. Beijing: Zhonghua shuju, 1999.

Zhuzi jicheng 諸子集成. 8 vols. Beijing: Zhonghua shuju, 1996.

Index

Lightning Source UK Ltd.
Milton Keynes UK
UKHW011526071122
411795UK00007B/637